# BE WISE

Desiree Alcantara

ISBN 978-1-68517-710-2 (paperback)
ISBN 978-1-68517-712-6 (digital)

Christian Faith Publishing, Inc.
832 Park Avenue
Meadville, PA 16335
www.christianfaithpublishing.com

Printed in the United States of America

Maintain humanity under 500,000,000 in
perpetual balance with nature.

—The Georgia Guidestones,
(written in eight different languages)

World events do not occur by accident. They are made to happen,
whether it is to do with national issues or commerce; and most of
them are staged and managed by those who hold the purse strings.

—Denis Healey, UK Secretary of State
for Defense from 1964–1970 and Chancellor
of the Exchequer from 1974–1979

We'll know our disinformation program is complete when
everything the American public believes is false.

—CIA Director William Casey,
first staff meeting in 1981

# CHAPTER 1

‹✆›

# Illuminati Training Video Leaked

Hello, Initiates,

I would like to officially welcome you as a member of our team. You've joined our organization at perhaps the most exciting point in all our long history. Our founders shared a passion and dream to transform this country, and eventually the whole word, into one cohesive organization. When Illumicorp finishes gaining centralized control of the resources of the planet—and we will—we can then organize, distribute, and govern for the benefit of all. After competition and dissent are eliminated, we'll build a Utopia for the people of the world to share, based on need, and rejoice together in our harmonious new world.

This presentation is designed to enlighten you about our organization's goals and achievements. As your guide, I will help to answer some basic questions you might have about Illumicorp and familiarize you with the valuable role you will play in helping us reach our prime objective. So please, take a tour with me as we march together to an exciting new world.

All people are aware of class; to them, society is made up of the rich, the middle, and the poor. The one thing that all three classes don't understand is that the pyramid continues upward. There is a detached hidden capstone that is made up of an elite board of directors who mold and manage Illumicorp.

The three classes below, in essence, become the assets and resources of Illumicorp. Illumicorp is divided into various administrative branches. Each branch is the same five levels in their hierarchy. We will begin at the bottom in initiate category:

Initiate
Initiate Supervisor
Executive Manager
Supreme Council
President/CEO

As such, your role will be to make sure that your orders are carried out to the subcorporations and institutions that are controlled by Illumicorp. You'll be placed in plain sight at the head of the company or institution of the public sector, to carry out the plans delivered from above. Remember, your role is very important. You'll be the face of Illumicorp to the outside world. You are our connection to the masses below; never speak publicly about your orders or your masters.

Now let's look at Illumicorp's six administrative branches and their functions. You'll be placed in a top position of power among one of the following sectors. In this way, as you are monitored and guided from above, you will decide strategies and introduce programs that further our goals; for that is the secret to Illumicorp's success. You control the head, and you control the body.

I.   *Banking and business*
This is potentially Illumicorp's most effective instrument for global control. Through international banking, we manipulate the face of all countries. We've introduced many institutions, such as the IMF and WTO, that work in our favor to impoverish disobedient nations. Always remember, debt is a powerful weapon against countries that don't share Illumicorp's vision. Perhaps our greatest achievements in banking is the Federal Reserve System, a collection of international banks owned by Illumicorp's members and finan-

ciers. It was created to form a centralized banking system through the Federal Reserve Act of 1913. An act that was deepened by some of our most esteemed members.

Many of you might still assume that the government self-prints and issues the currency. That is not the case. When America needs money, they go to our boys and ask for it. The money is printed, but it is only representative of a loan. Interest accrues on that dollar until it is paid back to the fed through the IRS. In fact, the federal taxes paid by the American population go almost entirely in paying off this debt. So you see, Illumicorp drives a healthy amount to its operation funding directly from the debt of the public. Needless to say, this is one of our most crucial sources of funding and one of our proudest achievements here in Illumicorp. Through merges and acquisitions, we have slowly and silently bought up the majority of the US industry.

Illumicorp and its members own most of the oil, transport, banking, media, food, and communications industries in America and abroad. Through fewer and fewer conglomerates, we are able to affect, with great precision, the machinations of labor and government. Ultimately corporations will replace government as a centralized international body that can meet the needs of the public worldwide, without the chaos created by national self-interest.

When Illumicorp goes public, corporatism will lead the foundation for world government. Conglomerates will merge into one cohesive corporation that is responsible only to Illumicorp and the needs of its global employment force.

II. *Military and intelligence*
Illumicorp's control of the American military is another impressive tool in our possession. We have nurtured these institutions lavishly to serve as the prototype for our global police force. When ready, our technology and manpower

will dominate those who oppose the coming New World Order. By utilizing American patriotism, we have fostered the American soldier. The philosophy of peace through a superior force. When the time is right, we'll migrate that mentality toward the belief of a global government who must protect all people through superior force.

We have used the American military-industrial complex to build the arsenal necessary to instigate the final cleansing outlined in Illumicorp's great plan. Our primary target will be the Islamist nations who will never submit to our Western-centric domination. They also hold much of the remaining oil reserve of the planet. Illumicorp must own that precious resource, as it is crucial in maintaining our domination over the countries of the world. Through Illumicorp's enormous federal funding of the military, we can develop new forms of warfare and *population reduction*. The public can't imagine what we are in the process of developing! Soon even the weather will be a weapon under our control. We'll be able to create droughts, floods, hurricanes, and even tsunamis, with no fingerprints attached.

*III. Politics*

The political system of America has been under direct control from Illumicorp for some time. It was actually a relatively easy acquisition, and it has been even easier to manage. Politicians know of our unspoken agreement. They'll do anything to stay in power. A two-party system benefits Illumicorp in that it reduces all issues into a black-and-white debate. Through media, we can play side against side, using each when necessary to support our own goals. Due to a diminishing faith among the public, Illumicorp has designed a rogue candidate program to provide a voice for the dispossessed. This disperses the emphasis for dissent among those who do not feel represented by our candidates and builds a database of potential dissidence.

IV. *Education*

At the turn of the last century, Illumicorp took a serious interest in public education. Our Supreme Council realized that by creating a private organization to dictate curriculum on a federal level, children could be conditioned on a mass scale. In the interest of promoting Illumicorp's principles in the classrooms, hundreds of millions of dollars were invested to create the general education board in 1902; the result of doing this is evident today. The doctrines of public education have transformed recent generations into a weaker, more docile mass.

Through meticulously planned curriculum, we have control over the process of how the average child learns, thus we can mold them into obedient workers who are conditioned to accept the implementation of the great plan. In addition, Illumicorp has set up many associations, including the American Historical Association that determines and uphold the official view of history. Knowledge is power, so we must, at all cost, be the authors of the truth by writing history that suits our interests; dissenting voices cannot gain ground, and we can vast the influence cultured to achieve our primed objective.

V. *Media*

Illumicorp uses the media to shape the public's opinion about current events and conditions desired attitudes about our future agenda. Through news, entertainment, and advertising, we can program a variety of emotions and responses into the collective unconscious. In the past, we were limited entirely to print media, but now we have multiple mediums to utilize in programming and conditioning the masses. With cable news, we have directed the public to a more entertainment-based consumption of world events. Infotainment. This medium is far more effective in subliminal reinforcement of desired attitudes toward our objectives.

For instance, we are currently instilling a sense of duty toward environmental issues. With our growing control of weather through HARP and chemtrails, we will scare the public into accepting our global protection agendas. We will then phase into the great cleansing which must occur to *return the global population to a manageable size.*

We reinforce the desired norm through advertising, creating models of people to look up to that is virtually impossible. The result is an incomplete desperate individual seeking acceptance. Through reality television game shows, we repeat the pattern of individual survival versus group survival. This breaks down the idea of community and breeds individuals who seek only their self-interest. With a public that is constantly suspicious and scheming, we maintain the status quo of a divided population that never thinks to look up.

VI. *Religion*

Religion has served its purpose incredibly well. It is the oldest, and perhaps the broadest, form of social control utilized by Illumicorp. With religion, there is a written code of conduct that must be followed. The authors of the Holy Scriptures knew quite well how to lace that code with commands to maintain their dominance over the population. This system has survived through millennia, to hold the flock together and bring us to today.

Admittedly religion is losing its power for control. However, the fanatism that has arisen through this decline is particularly helpful to Illumicorp. Our invisible influence in the church has helped bring Christian fundamentalists out of the background. We control their opinion on current issues through policies designed and written right here in Illumicorp headquarters. They are sent to our ministers, who then preach the Word of God and their interpretations of the Bible to their followers.

Their blind faith is used to transform them into willing soldiers to defend our cause during the catastrophes ahead. As the final phase is enacted, we'll propagate "end-time prophecy" to convince them of their convictions. The rise of Islamic fundamentalists works to Illumicorp's advantage, as a threat that will demand violent action. In the coming years, planned terrorist's attacks will warrant full-scale retaliation and initiate the final phase of the great plan.

Christians will support our actions since they'll believe them to be proof of the end-time prophecy by Illumicorp's religious leaders.

A word from our president:

> We are in the last days of darkness. Together in secret, we wait to begin the final phase of the great plan. The sun is rising, and it will beam a glorious dawn upon our New World. As an employee of Illumicorp, you are above the limitations of nationality, class, and religion. You are a member of the Illumicorp now. Your loyalty and your devotion belong only with us. Help us finish the plan. Together we will proudly initiate the New World Order.

Now that you have the basic understanding on how we work in Illumicorp, I would like to introduce to you one of our latest projects.

## The Control Grid

Since ancient times, it is being the desired of the Illumined to wield control of the masses below, both to protect us from them and them from themselves. The tools of the ages have been effective, but now with the release of new technologies of the masses, we have the real ability to implement a control grid with finance, industry, government, and military under our strict control. We can safely shift the population into a New World, monitored and controlled by Illumicorp. Technology such as the Internet, GPS and RFID chips are pillars of the invisible prison we are erecting around the people. Within a decade, we will have real ID cards that contain criminal records and printed information all linked to federal databases. Cell phones will tell us where each individual lives, linked to the same database. Through intelligence agencies and Homeland Security, we'll monitor individuals who oppose the great plan and remove them from the grid. Quickly the population will learn that they have a choice: support the system and benefit from its luxuries, or reject it and lose access to the grid.

Well, that was quite an overview. I hope it gave you an understanding of our process and basic overall structure here at Illumicorp. The dawn of a new era is on the horizon, and it will shine gloriously over the New World Order that we have created together.

**For we wrestle not against flesh and blood, but against principalities, against powers, against the rulers of the darkness of this world, against spiritual wickedness in high places. (Ephesians 6:12)**

**Be sober, be vigilant; because your adversary the devil, as a roaring lion, walketh about, seeking whom he may devour. (1 Peter 5:8)**

We have before us the opportunity to forge for ourselves
and for the future generations, a NEW WORLD ORDER.
A world where the conduct of LAW, not the law of the
jungle, GOVERNS the conduct of nations. When we are
successful, and WE WILL BE, we have a real chance at this
NEW WORLD ORDER. An order in which a creditable
United Nations can use its "peace keeping" role to
fulfill the promise and vision of the U.N.'s founders.[1]

—George Bush on August 2,1990

---

[1] An excerpt of George Bush's speech to the American people, explaining why
the United States was going to war with Iraq and Kuwait in Operation Desert
Storm. One of the reasons is to try and establish a one-world government.

# CHAPTER 2

—— ✑ ——

# Decoding the Message

## I. *Banking and Business*

> He who owns the gold makes the rules.
> (Napoleon Bonaparte)

There is a documentary titled *The Money Masters 1996 Full Documentary*.[2] It was produced by William T. Still. In this documentary, we can clearly see how this whole world is truly ruled by this people. This is the best historical documentary concerning our economic system. It should be taught in every single high school in America, but it is not!

## II. *Military and Intelligence*

General Wesley Clark said in an interview that wars were planned. Seven countries in five years.

Originally published in March 2007, General Wesley Clark said:

> Because I had been through the Pentagon
> right after 9/11. About ten days after 9/11, I

---

[2] www.billstill.com.

went through the Pentagon and I saw Secretary Rumsfeld and Deputy Secretary Wolfowitz. I went downstairs just to say hello to some people on the Joint Staff who used to work for me, and one of the generals called me in. He said, "Sir, you've got to come in and talk to me a second." I said, "Well, you're too busy." He said, "No, no." He says, "There's nothing new that way. They just made the decision to go to war with Iraq." He said, "I guess it's like we don't know what to do about terrorists, but we've got a good military and we can take down governments." And he said, "I guess if the only tool you have is a hammer, every problem has to look like a nail."

So, I came back to see him a few weeks later, and by that time we were bombing in Afghanistan. I said, "Are we still going to war with Iraq?" And he said, "Oh, it's worse than that." He reached over his desk. He picked up a piece of paper. And he said, "I just got this down from upstairs"—meaning the Secretary of Defense's office—"today". And he said, "This is a memo that describes how we're going to take out seven countries in five years, starting with Iraq, and then Syria, Lebanon, Libya, Somalia, Sudan and finishing off, Iran." I said, "Is it classified?" He said, "Yes, sir." I said, "Well, don't show it to me." And I saw him a year or so ago, and I said, "You remember that?" He said, "Sir, I didn't show you that memo! I didn't show it to you!"

Please watch General Wesley Clark explain, in more details, the truth about the American policy in the Middle East.[3]

> **I know thy works, and tribulation, and poverty, (but thou art rich) and I know the blasphemy of them which say they are Jews, and are not, but are the synagogue of Satan. (Revelation 2:9)**

> **Behold, I will make them of the synagogue of Satan, which say they are Jews, and are not, but do lie; behold, I will make them to come and worship before thy feet, and to know that I have loved thee. (Revelation 3:9)**

## III. *Politics*

> Political language is designed to make lies sound truthful and murder respectable. (George Orwell)

> The more you can increase fear of drugs and crime, welfare mothers, immigrants and aliens, the more you control all the people. (Noam Chomsky)

> Neoliberal democracy. Instead of citizens, it produces consumers. Instead of communities, it produces shopping malls. The net result is an atomized society of disengaged individuals who feel demoralized and socially powerless. In sum, neoliberalism is the immediate and foremost enemy of genuine participatory democracy, not just in the United States but across the planet

---

[3] *THE WORLD IS THINKING*, www.FORA.tv.

and will be for the foreseeable future. (Noam Chomsky)

## IV. *Education*

Governments don't want well informed, well educated people capable of critical thinking. That is against their interests. They want obedient workers, people who are just smart enough to run machines and do the paperwork. And dumb enough to passively accept it. (George Carlin)

Don't just teach your children to read... Teach them to question what they read... Teach them to question everything. (George Carlin)

## V. *Media*

Whoever controls the media, controls the mind. (Jim Morrison)

He who controls the media controls the mind of the public. (Noam Chomsky)

The TV set, or Satanic family altar, has grown more elaborate since the early 50's, from the tiny, fuzzy screen to huge "entertainment centers) covering entire walls with several TV monitors. What started as an innocent respite from everyday life has become in itself a replacement for real life for millions, a major religion of the masses. (Anton LaVey, *The Devil's Notebook*, 86. [Founder of the Church of Satan and author of the Satanic Bible])

## VI. *Religion*

This people draweth nigh unto me with their mouth, and honoureth me with their lips; but their hearts is far from Me. But in vain they do worship Me, teaching for doctrines the commandments of men. (Matthew 15:8–9)

What doeth it profit, my brethren, though a man say he hath faith, and have not works? Can faith save him? If a brother or sister be naked, and destitute of daily food, and one of you say unto them, depart in peace, be ye warmed and filled; notwithstanding ye give them not those things which are needful to the body; what doeth it profit? Even so faith, if it hath no works, is dead, being alone. Yea, man may say, thou hast faith, and I have works: shew me thy faith without thy works, and I will shew thee my faith with my works. Thou believest that there is one God; thou doest well: the devils also believe, and tremble. But wilt thou know, O vain man, that faith without works is dead? (James 2:14–20)

In the scores of books lining the shelves of New Age bookstores, there are instructions for guided meditations, creative visualizations, out of body experiences, getting in touch with your spirit guides, fortune telling by cards, crystal ball on the stars. What if Satanists reclaimed these for their own dark purposes and integrated them into rituals dedicated to the devil, where they belong. New Agers have freely drawn upon all manner of Satanic material, adapting it to their own hypocritical purposes. But in truth, all new age labeling is again, trying to play the devil's game without taking his infernal name. (Anton LaVey, Church of Satan; Blanche Barton, 107)

Now the spirit speaketh expressly, that in the latter times some shall depart from the faith, giving heed to seducing spirits, and doctrines of devils; speaking lies in hypocrisy; having their conscience seared with a hot iron; forbidding to marry, and commanding to abstain from meats, which God hath created to be received with thanksgiving of them which believe and know the truth. (1 Timothy 4:1–3)

Pure religion and undefiled before God and the Father is this, to visit the fatherless and widows in their affliction, and to keep himself unspotted from the world. (James 2:27)

Mortify (Put to death) therefore your members (the works of the flesh) which are upon the earth; fornication, uncleanness, inordinate affection, evil concupiscence, and covetousness, which is idolatry; For which things sake the wrath of God cometh on the children of disobedience. (Colossians 3:5–6)

Then said Jesus unto His disciples, "If any man will come after Me, let him deny himself, and take up his cross, and follow Me. For whosoever will save his life shall lose it; and whosoever will lose his life for my sake shall find it. For what is a man profited, if he shall gain the whole world, and lose his own soul? Or what shall a man give in exchange for his soul? **For the Son of man shall come in the glory of his Father with his angels; and then he shall reward every man according to his works."** (Matthew 17:2427)

## The Control Grid

**HAARP: Weather Control.** Is the HAARP Project a Weather Control Weapon?

"It isn't just conspiracy theorists who are concerned about HAARP. The European Union called the project a global concern and passed a resolution calling for more information on its health and environmental risks. Despite those concerns, officials at HAARP insist the project is nothing more sinister than a radio science research facility." (From documentary on HAARP weather-control capabilities by Canada's CBC)

HAARP: What is it?

HAARP (High-Frequency Active Auroral Research Program) was a little known yet critically important US military defense project which generated quite a bit of controversy over its alleged weather-control capabilities and much more.

## Global Warming Is a Hoax!

They have also mastered the art of manipulating our emotions with these types of technologies.

*HAARP and manipulation of emotions*: The capability of influencing and even controlling human emotions has been studied by the military and intelligence services of the world for many decades. A concise information-packed description of such programs with links to declassified CIA documents for verification is available here.

One thoroughly researched book, titled *Mind Controllers*, describes an effective method of remotely influencing human emotions. Here is a key quote from this revealing book:

> With the use of powerful computers, segments of human emotions which include anger, anxiety, sadness, fear, embarrassment, jealousy, resentment, shame, and terror, have been identified and isolated within the EEG signals as "emotion signature clusters." Their relevant frequencies and amplitudes have been measured. Then the very frequency/amplitude cluster is synthesized and stored on another computer. Each one of these negative emotions is properly and separately tagged. **They are then placed on the Silent Sound carrier frequencies and could silently trigger the occurrence of the same basic emotion in another human being.**[4]

## Chemtrails

> What are chemtrails? Chemtrails are geo-engineered aerosols that are loaded with toxic chemicals, including but not limited to: barium, strontium 90, aluminum, cadmium, zinc, viruses and "chaff." Chaff looks like snow but it's actually Mylar fibers (like in fiberglass) coated with aluminum, desiccated blood cells, plastic, and paper. Polymer chemist Dr. R. Michael Castle has studied atmospheric polymers for years, and he has identified microscopic polymers comprised of genetically-engineered fungal forms

---

[4]  https://www.wanttoknow.info/war/haarp_weather_modification_electromagnetic_warfare.

mutated with viruses, which are now part of the air we breathe.

Chemtrails have nothing to do with the jet engine combustion process. They are often laid in a grid-like pattern by multiple planes (even drones) where they disperse slowly taking on the appearance of odd, at first narrow, but widening, smoky clouds until merging together to form, if sufficiently numerous, an aerosol bank that obscures the blue sky and gives the appearance of a dirty white overcast.

Still having doubts? Please download this PDF file[5] called HR 2977 "The Space and Preservation Act of 2001." **In this document the United States Government openly admits the existence of chemtrails.**[6]

## The Codex Alimentarius: The Sinister Truth Behind Operation Cure All

They use food to mind control us and to weaken our immune systems and get us sick. They stripped most of the nutrition out of our daily foods and are aggressively working on making it illegal for us to consume the foods that are truly healthy.

According to John Hammell, a legislative advocate and the founder of International Advocates for Health Freedom (IAHF), here is what we have to look forward to:

> If Codex Alimentarius has its way, then herbs, vitamins, minerals, homeopathic remedies, amino acids and other natural remedies you have taken for granted most of your life will be gone.

---

5   http://www.gpo.gov/fdsys/pkg/BILLS-107hr2977ih.pdf.
6   https://thetruthaboutcancer.com/what-are-chemtrails-doing-food-water-supply/.

The name of the game for Codex Alimentarius is to shift all remedies into the prescription category so they can be controlled exclusively by the medical monopoly and its bosses, the major pharmaceutical firms. Predictably, this scenario has been denied by both the Canadian Health Food Association and the Health Protection Branch of Canada. (HPB).

Do your own research please.[7]

## The Dangers of Drinking Water with Fluoride or Brushing Our Teeth with Fluoridated Toothpaste

Fluoride seems to fit in with lead, mercury, and other poisons that cause chemical brain drain... The effect of each toxicant may seem small, but the combined damage on a population scale can be serious, especially because the brain power of the next generation is crucial to all of us. (Dr. Mercola, Dr. Paul Connett)[8]

## The Dangers of 5G

Thousands of studies link low-level wireless radio frequency radiation exposures to a long list of adverse biological effects, including:

- DNA single and double strand breaks
- Oxidative damage
- Disruption of cell metabolism
- Increased blood brain barrier permeability

[7] http://www.natural-health-information-centre.com/codex-alimnetarius.html.
[8] https://articles.mercola.com/sites/articles/archive/2014/07/01/water-supply-fluoridation.as.

- Melatonin reduction
- Disruption to brain glucose metabolism
- Generation of stress proteins

Let us not also forget that in 2011 the World Health Organization (WHO) classified radio frequency as a possible 2B carcinogen. Frequency radiation of the type currently used by cell phones can cause cancer.[9]

Moreover if the health hazards are not bad enough, our technology apps are also spying on all of us, just as they said they would.

Edward Snowden revealed an NSA program called Optic Nerves. The operation was a bulk surveillance program under which they captured webcam images every five minutes from Yahoo users' video chats and then stored them for future use. It is estimated that between 3% and 11% of the images captured contained "undesirable nudity".

Government security agencies like the NSA can also have access to your devices through in-built backdoors. This means that these security agencies can tune in to your phone calls, read your messages, capture pictures of you, stream videos of you, read your emails, steal your files... at any moment they please.[10]

---

[9]  https://www.electricsense.com/5g-radiation-dangers/.
[10]  https://www.google.com/amp/s/amp.theguardian.com/commentisfree/2018/apr/06/phone-camera-microphone-spying.

## The RFID Chip

Even if you are not religious, Sander's knowledge about the inner workings of the global elite are amazing and quite informative. He paints a clear picture of just how dangerous our future is.

SANDERS ENCOURAGES PEOPLE NOT TO TAKE THE CHIP

In no uncertain terms, this microchip inventor discusses why we should not take the RFID chip even if it becomes mandatory. He believes there are positive alternatives. One of which is to stand up and demand that all chip implantations be stopped.

At a time when newborns and children are being chipped without parental consent and our freedoms and our families are at serious risk, we need to rise up and protest the use of RFID chips...which can cause cancer and can control the mind.

It is important to take Dr. Sanders seriously when he says this was a horrible mistake and not to be lulled into taking the chip out of concern for security or for mere convenience.

By taking the chip we not only lose our identity but our minds as well.[11]

CARL SANDERS, ELECTRONIC ENGINEER, DEVELOPER OF RFID MICROCHIP.

In a joint venture, General Electric, Motorola and the US government worked on a project to create an implantable chip that would positively locate anyone who has it. Carl Sanders headed a team of scientists to develop the RFID-

---

[11] http://www.truth-it.net/microchip_inventor.html.

chip. It took 20 years, but the team did create a chip so small that it can easily pass through a hypodermic needle.

CARL SANDERS NOW ACTIVELY CAMPAIGNS AGAINST THE RFID MICROCHIP, AND THAT WE SHOULD NOT TAKE IT EVEN IF IT BECOMES MANDATORY!

The chip is powered by a tiny **lithium battery** that is recharged by the change in body temperature. The two places in the body that vary the most in temperature are the forehead, which we feel for fever or rise in body temperature. Secondly, the top of the right hand, as most people are right-handed, this hand is a great deal exposed to outside temperature change, i.e. washing hands with hot or cold water, etc. However, if the lithium escapes into the body through atomic radiation, it gives a ugly, painful, grievous sore or boil.[12]

The book of Revelation teaches us that the first aftereffect of the nuclear war is, **"There fell a noisome and grievous sore upon the men which had the mark of the beast, and upon them which worshipped his image... And blasphemed the God of heaven because of their pains and their sores, and repented not of their deeds"** (Revelation 16:2, 11).

---

[12] https://telepathherosummary.blogspot.com/2015/07/dr-carl-sanders-microchip-inventor-rfid.

*And it came to pass when the children of men had multiplied that in those days were born unto them beautiful and comely daughters. And the angels, the children of the heaven, (the fallen angels) saw and lusted after them, and said to one another: "Come, let us choose us wives from among the children of men and beget us children." And Semjaza, who was their leader, said unto them: "I fear ye will not indeed agree to do this deed, and I alone shall have to pay the penalty of a great sin." And they all answered him and said: "Let us all swear an oath, and all bind ourselves by mutual imprecations not to abandon this plan but to do this thing." Then sware they all together and bound themselves by mutual imprecations upon it. And they were in all two-hundred; who descended in the days of Jared on the summit of Mount Hermon, and they called it Mount Hermon, because they had sworn and bound themselves by mutual imprecations upon it. And these are the names of their leaders: Semiazaz, their leader, Arakiba, Rameel, Kokabiel, Tamiel, Ramiel, Danel, Ezeqeel, Baraqijal, Asael, Armaros, Batarel, Ananel, Zaqiel, Samsapeel, Satarel, Turel, Jomjael, Sariel. These are their chiefs of tens.*

—The Book of Enoch, ch. 6, p. 4)

# CHAPTER 3

⸎

# The Pharmaceutical Industry

*And all the others together with them took unto themselves
wives, and each chose for himself one, and they began to go in
unto them and to defile themselves with them, and they taught
them charms and enchantments, and the cutting of roots, and
made them acquainted with plants. And they became pregnant,
and they bare great giants, whose height was three-thousands
ells: Who consumed all the acquisitions of men. And when
men could no longer sustain them the giants turned against
them and devoured mankind. And they began to sin against
birds, and beasts, and reptiles, and fish, and drink the blood.
Then the earth laid accusation against the lawless ones.*

—The Book of Enoch, ch.7, p. 5

*And Azazel taught men to make swords, and knives, and shields,
and breastplates, and made known to them the metals of the
earth and the art of working them, and bracelets, and ornaments,
and the use of antimony, and the beautifying of the eyelids, and
all kinds of costly stones, and all colouring tinctures. And there
arose much godlessness, and they committed fornication, and they
were led astray, and became corrupt in all their ways. Semjaza
taught enchantments, and root-cuttings, Armaros the resolving
of enchantments, Baraqijal, (taught) astrology, Kokabel the*

*knowledge of the clouds, Araqiel the signs of the earth, Shamsiel the signs of the sun, and Sariel the course of the moon. And as men perished, they cried, and their cry went up to heaven.*

—The Book of Enoch, ch. 8, p. 5)

Pharmakeia: (Greek Word) Use of drugs, medicines, potions, or spells; poisoning, witchcraft; remedy, cure. (*Online Etymology Dictionary*)

The word *pharmacy* that we use here in our culture comes from the word *pharmakeia*, which literally means "witchcraft"! It is interesting to point out that the pharmaceutical's symbol or famous design happens to be two serpents. Is that a coincidence, or is it that they love to put the truth in plain sight? The symbol originated from the worship of false gods.

The pharmaceutical industry is deeply embedded into all our lives. Most of us grew up learning that whenever we get sick, we listen to the doctors and simply trust them for our health. However, what the population is not told is the sad truth about how doctors in America are trained by our professional institutions to prescribe medications to treat symptoms instead of being trained in nutrition and other holistic ways to cure diseases. Unfortunately for all of us, curing our diseases is not in the pharmaceutical industry's best interest since that would mean the end of them taking our money. For them, it is much more profitable to keep us sick and hooked on their very pricey medications, which most of them have terrible side effects for our health.

I began my relationship with the pharmaceutical industry as a teenager, when my beloved mother was ill with cancer. I found myself, along with her, putting our trust in all these professional doctors who seem to have our best interest at heart. We were devastated by the news that my mother had breast cancer, and we were told she would only have six months to live. Instantly they began doing chemotherapy sessions upon her, and I was the one who would drive her to the hospital and then take care of her at home. These chemo-

29

therapy sessions were pure torture for both my mother and me. She would come home extremely ill, she would experience hot flashes, and then she would be really cold; she felt nauseated most of the time and would throw up pure black vomit, which I then had to clean up. Her entire body ached so much, I had to give her long body massages to ease her pain.

The chemotherapy caused her hair to fall off, including her eyebrows. They also amputated one of her breasts, and her skin got really dry and wrinkled, making her look much older. She even shrunk in height. It was so torturous for us that she ended up trying new solutions in hope of another way to heal. She changed her diet, and we even went to New York, from Miami, to visit a spiritual healer who claimed he can heal people from cancer and other diseases with the touch of his hand. Although my mom did not die in six months, although she lasted three years, she suffered like no one I had ever seen suffered, and I wish no one to ever go through the suffering I witnessed her go through. Now that I am much older, I did some serious research about cancer and our Western health system, and to my horrific surprise, I have come to find out that chemotherapy is a huge scam. Maybe if my mother would have only done the holistic diet, perhaps she might still be here with me today.

This is a segment of a doctor and an author exposing the truth in a YouTube video titled *The Scam Called Chemotherapy*:

"A better thing to talk about, however, is in relationship between profits and cancer in the United States. There was a study that was published, I believe in 1994, it was a twelve-year program, twelve-year study, they looked at the adults who had developed cancer as an adult, not childhood cancer but adulthood cancer, is the main types of cancer that we get here in the US. They did a data analysis with these people all around the world who developed cancer as adults for twelve years and were treated with chemo, and they looked at their results, and they published their results in the *Journal of Clinical Oncology*, and the results, 97 percent of the time, chemotherapy does not work.

"So why is it still used? One reason and one reason only—money! If you go to a medical doctor and MD with a sinus infection, and that doctor prescribes an antibiotic, he gets no financial kick-back. Now if he prescribes five thousand of those antibiotics in one month, the drug company that makes it might send him to Cancun for a conference, but he gets no direct remuneration. With chemo-therapeutic drugs, it's different. Chemotherapeutic drugs are the only classification of drugs that the prescribing doctor gets a direct cutoff. So if your doctor prescribes chemotherapy for you, here is how it goes more or less: Doctor buys it from the pharmaceutical company for $5,000, sells it to the patient for $12,000, and insurance pays $9,000, and the doctor pockets $4,000 easily. And there ought to be a law!

"The only reason chemotherapy is used is because doctors make money from it. Period. It DOESN'T WORK! Ninety-seven percent of the time. If Ford Motor company made an automobile that exploded 97 percent of the time, would they still be in business? No! This is the tip of the iceberg of the control that the pharmaceutical industry has on us. When most people have no idea of this. I wrote a book, it's called *The MD Emperor Has No Clothes*. In my book, I have a bulleted list of ten questions that every cancer patient should ask their doctor. Ten questions. I had patients kicked out—literally kicked out—f the oncologist office because the doctor was PO that the patient was asking him those questions. These are just common-sense questions.

"Cancer treatment in the US, we have lost the war on cancer, we have lost the war on cancer, why? Because cancer is not a reduc-tionistic phenomenon, cancer is a holistic phenomenon. And when you try to bring a reductionistic methodology, like drugs and sur-gery, to bear on a holistic phenomenon, you will completely miss the boat, each and every time! You cannot do it! Medical doctors are like color blind art critics. They can see that, that is a boat, they can see the black-and-white outline, but they are completely blind to all of the colors and textures that make up the substance of the thing. It's no difference with cancer. The reason that people get cancer in the US and the reason that we have completely lousy outcomes is because medical doctors are driving the research bus. When women get together and do a 5k run for breast cancer, all of that money, you think any of that money goes to the nutritional research? You think any of that money goes to the homeopathic research or acupuncture or traditional Chinese medicine or naturopathic research? No, all of that money goes to drugs and surgeries, which DO NOT WORK! Now why aren't those women running for selenium? If every girl in this country took 200 micrograms of selenium, in one generation, we would eliminate breast cancer by 82 percent, and that is a big number. Why aren't we doing that? BECAUSE MEDICINE IN THE UNITED STATES IS A FOR PROFIT INDUSTRY AND MOST PEOPLE ARE COMPLETELY UNAWARE OF THIS AND MOST PEOPLE BOW DOWN TO THE ALTAR OF MD DIRECTED HIGH TECH MEDICINE AT THEIR OWN DEMISE!"[13]

Moreover in the year 2015, Dr. Farid Fata was sentenced after pleading guilty to multiple counts of fraud, money laundering, and administering cancer treatments to patients who were healthy and should not have received it.

There is another video in YouTube titled *Mike Adams speaks on Poisoning that is going on in the black community NaturalNews.com*! This video has been removed several times by YouTube; please watch it before it is removed for good. This brave and amazing scientist exposes how the government is trying to kill black people, and cancer is one of the ways. He also exposes how there is a link between vaccines and autism in young African American boys.

After my beloved mother was brutally murdered by the pharmaceutical industry with their fraudulent chemotherapy, I was left mentally disabled. The whole ordeal was too much for me to bear, and my mind was gone. I then became one more golden token for the pharmaceutical industry to gain their profit from. I was placed in an asylum and diagnosed with chronic schizophrenia. I was administered all these different types of highly toxic medications and was told that I would never be able to get off from them because if I did, I would go back to having schizophrenic episodes. They also told my parents that I would be in the institution for life because I was a threat to society and to myself, and there is no cure for schizophrenia. How convenient for them! The amount of money they gain from my

[13] Dr. Peter Glidden, BS, ND, author of the book *The MD Emperor Has No Clothes*, www.drglidden.com.

medical bills is massive, and even better, it is for a lifetime. Luckily for me, my father refused to let them to do that to me and took me out of the hospital without their approval and signed an affidavit taking responsibility for me and my actions. But I know not every patient is that lucky. I am deeply saddened to know how many lives are ruined and left to die in those hospitals because of the evil going on in our medical industry.

After my painful journey with my beloved mother, I then began a new one with my son. As a child, he got several seizures, several times, and the flu. I was taught by doctors to alternate Tylenol and Motrin every three hours while he was with fever to keep the fever down. Unfortunately I did this religiously every time he got sick for years. One day, the Holy Spirit taught me to put my trust in Him and to stop putting my trust in the medicine. He taught me to keep ice on my son to keep the fever down, but to let a little bit of the fever to do its job. I learned that if we maintain the fever too low, then whatever virus is in him will not be destroyed. It turns out that fever is the body's way to fight off the virus and bacteria. It is important to let the fever do its job. Once I did this, I saw that what used to take two or even three weeks for my son's cold to go away, now it only took two to three days.

I learned to make him natural remedies, such as boiling lemons, ginger roots, onions and garlic together, and then mix them with honey and cayenne pepper. This mixture gets rid of the cold, and even the flu, in twenty-four hours. It also boosts the immune system. I was able to even heal my son from influenza with this and lots of ice bags and, of course, lots of prayers, while I did not sleep all night long, monitoring his fevers. However, when I took him to the hospital, and they said he had the flu, they had given me a prescription for his flu, and it was Tamiflu. It turns out that I did my research on this medication, and many people have had serious side effects from this thing—hallucinations, suicidal thoughts, and even death. It is so painful for me to see how these medications are promoted in commercials as something good for you, and in the background, you are told how deadly they can be all at the same time. It seems to me that we live in the twilight zone. No! God created nature and plants and seeds and herbs and fruits so that we may heal with those types of things. He also gave us prayer and His power to be healed. There is no need whatsoever to gamble our health and lives to heal ourselves and live. That is nonsense!

I then realized that everything revolves around deception and the destruction of our immune systems, spirit, minds, bodies, and health. Thus I did my research on vaccines, and there are countless of testimonies on the Internet and countless of books written by real scientists and doctors telling us all that indeed vaccines do cause autism and many other health problems. They also show us what some of these vaccines contain in them and is disgusting. Also I just recently learned that they have fallen angel technology that just came out and are now going to put a hydrogel inside the coronavirus vaccines, and they will even put them in the testing kits for the coronavirus which will change our DNA into something that our Lord Jesus Christ will not recognize. This hydrogel will also continue to grow inside of our bodies once it is injected in us, and it is going to provide them with all sorts of information. It will show them when we sleep, when we have sex, when women are in their menstrual cycle, and all types of information of that sort. This is the beginning of the mark of the beast. It starts in the coronavirus testing kits, then the vaccines that will contain the RFID chips, and it will be one of the same and mandatory!

If you would like to learn more about this subject go to this channel, diamondisc, and look for her video titled *Celeste Solum: The BEAST is Here! 7/13/20*. Hopefully they do not censor her channel by the time you look for it. Because they are silencing all the truthers, and they will rid YouTube from people like her and only allow those who preach a fake gospel to be the ones on that platform. This lady used to work for FEMA for many years, and when she saw what they were planning to do, she quit, became a Christian, and is now exposing their plans.

Furthermore I learned that their vaccines also contain dead aborted babies' tissue inside of it. They literally keep the aborted babies alive so that they can get their heart tissue while it is still beating, and then use it on the vaccines, then they kill the baby.

That is as diabolical as it can get, and most certainly it is not in the Lord's will that we let them inject us with such an abomination. I have seen many whistleblowers confessing to these atrocities. People from all walks of life, starting with the man whom I discipled in Christ, who served Satan for over twenty years, from the testimony of Rebecca Brown from her book *He Came to Set The Captives Free*, from doctors, scientists, FEMA employees, etc. There are plenty of people who have dared to come out and expose these criminals. There is a woman called Deborah Tavares, and she has her own channel in YouTube titled StopTheCrime.net. This amazing lady has every single formal document you ever need to prove all the conspiracy theories you can possibly imagine because it is all in writing. She is a researcher, and she exposes the truth of what they are all doing against humanity like no one I have ever seen.

There is also a document on the Internet titled https://toresays. com/2020/04/18/lock-step-the-rockefeller-foundations-2010-plan-to-enslave-humanity-with-plandemic/. This article was read by the president of Africa unto his people, and he warned everyone to reject the Bill Gates coronavirus vaccine. There are several other world leaders who know the truth about the coronavirus and the depopulation agenda, and they too are warning their people to reject the Bill Gates vaccine.

In this article, you can clearly see for yourselves that this coronavirus was no accident or brought to us from a bat. This was created in a lab to usher in the New World Order, and like a puzzle, this virus allows them to put all their pieces in place for their agenda. They have many things to accomplish with this virus, but their main goal with this virus is to vaccinate everyone in the globe, and the vaccine will be more deadly than the virus itself. It also has a link to the deadly radiation from 5G technology. When they turn on 5G, people will be dying a lot faster. It will contain a tracking system where we will lose all our freedoms, and the RFID chip is a part of this health system. Once you implant the RFID chip in your body, you lose your salvation. There is no turning back. It's a done deal! Thus do not accept this vaccine or the RFID chip. If you must lose your life for you to reject it, then give it up. You will live in eternity in heaven with the Lord.

**For whosoever will save his life shall lose it, but whosoever will lose his life for My sake, the same shall save it. For what is a man advantaged, if he gains the whole world, and lose himself, or be cast away? (LUKE 9:24–25)**

There are hundreds of thousands of testimonies of people who were seriously injured after a vaccine, or even killed. There are hundreds of stories of parents, siblings, spouses, etc. who lost a loved one 'cause of a vaccine. There are several countries who are trying to prosecute Bill Gates because of vaccine injuries and fatalities that he administered to the people there. Watch the documentary called *Vaxxed*.

I saw a testimony of a woman who went to the doctor to vaccinate her baby boy, and while the doctor left the office for a moment, she claims that she heard a voice say to her to not do it. She heard a voice say to her to not vaccinate her son because it was not good for him. But she ignored the voice and went ahead and did it. A day later, he stopped talking and was completely changed. He got autism! She felt so guilty for ignoring the voice that she made it her life's mission to cure her son. She did a lot of research, and thus she reversed the autism in her son entirely through an organic diet! This is, by far, one of the most powerful testimonies I have seen that confirms that vaccines do cause autism and that the food we eat have everything to do with our mental health.

Why is it that they spend millions of dollars to advertise in TV commercials Coke, Pepsi, fast food, alcohol, and all kinds of things that are full of sugar and bad for our health? Instead of spending all that money to promote the things that we should be eating instead to heal our body. Because there is an agenda to depopulate the world, people, please open your eyes! If they really cared to heal us, and to keep us healthy, it would begin with the things that are constantly bombarding our minds through the TV. It would also be mandatory to teach children in public schools about nutrition. But is not. And most ridiculous to me is that instead of training doctors to heal their patients with food, they only train them to learn to prescribe toxic medications. All the years they spend studying in colleges and universities, and they do not learn about healing the body through food. This should be a huge red flag that something is majorly wrong in America and the education system.

I learned that there are many doctors who have come out of the Western health medical field and became holistic and focused on educating other doctors and people on how to heal the body with food and other holistic things. I also learned that many of these doctors have been mysteriously killed or put in jail or stripped from their license or persecuted in some way. There is a book titled *A Plague of Corruption* by Judy Mikovits, PhD, and Kent Heckenlively, JD. I highly recommend this book, which is a best seller. This book, among many others out there, exposed the truth about the pharmaceutical industry, and this woman paid a very high price to get this information out.

About the authors of this book:

> Judy Mikovits, PhD, spent twenty years at the National Cancer Institute, working with Dr. Frank Ruscetti, one of the founding fathers of human retrovirology, and has coauthored more than forty scientific papers. She co-founded and directed the first neuroimmune disease institute using a systems biology approach in 2006. Dr. Mikovits lives in Southern California with her husband, David.

> Kent Heckenlively, JD, is a former attorney, a founding editor of Age of Autism, and a science teacher. During college Heckenlively worked for US Senator Pete Wilson, and in law school he was a writer and an editor of the school's law review and spent his summers working for the

US Attorney's Office in San Francisco. Kent and his wife Linda live in Northern California with their two children, Jacqueline and Ben.

What people are commenting about this book:

Anthony Fauci, Bill Gates and Big Pharma don't want you to read this book. Get *PLAGUE OF CORRUPTION* now and learn the truth about public health industrial complex's decades of research fraud and vaccine cover-ups.
—Michelle Malkin, New York Times bestselling author and political commentator.

The breathtaking story of an extraordinary scientist who discovered the most likely cause of chronic fatigue syndrome, only to witness a cover-up and character assassination emanating from the highest levels of the scientific community. An incisive critique of what's wrong with science today, and yet a hopeful portrait of how science still has the means to find the truth. It leaves you overwhelmed by the insidious methods and players corrupting science, but hopeful for truth-seekers in the scientific community like Dr. Mikovits who are persevering against all odds.
—J.B. Handley, co-founder of Generation Rescue and author of How to End the Autism Epidemic

What this book teaches more than anything else is that science can be a dangerous game. The notion that science is precise and unambiguous is wrong. When there is doubt, there is the potential for powerful interested parties to make life miserable for scientist with integrity. Throughout the book, intrigue is seamlessly intertwined with fascinating revelations about the still poorly understood science behind the potential role of retroviruses in mysterious debilitating diseases like chronic fatigue syndrome and autism.

—Dr. Stephanie Seneff, Senior
Research Scientist, MIT Computer Science
and Artificial Intelligence Laboratory.

This book is a jaw-dropping excursion through the lies of Big Money, Big Government and Big Pharma. God bless Dr. Mikovits for her courage in sharing this story!

—Max Swafford, author and educator.

The reason why I am writing all these details from this book is to show you how there are plenty of respectable scientists and professionals who agree with all I talk about in my book. There is something fundamentally wrong in our health-care system in America, and they are lying to us, and the consequences of not exposing the truths are dire. Our eternal lives are at stake, and this is why I am writing this book. People need to stop blindly trusting doctors and scientists that are serving Satan and money.

There is plenty of evidence of what I am trying to say here. YouTube is full of channels that are focused on healing our bodies from all types of incurable diseases, such as herpes, autism, mental illness, etc. with natural medicine. The elite have convinced the American people that the only way to good health is through them and their toxic medications, and that is just not true. Unfortunately most people do not do their research, and they just trust everything they see on TV or hear in the mainstream news when all these channels are owned by the same people who are behind the pharmaceutical industry.

Here is a list of other YouTube channels that are doing a great job at exposing the things they are doing to destroy us: A Call for an

Uprising, Dabhoo 777, Israeli News Live, diamonddisc, Godshealer 7, Kerry Ann Giddens, HolySpiritWind-Jeff Byerly, Mike444, etc.

**But he was wounded for our transgressions, He was bruised for our iniquities: the chastisement of our peace was upon him; and with his stripes we are healed.** (ISAIAH 53:5)

It is time to lift the veil from the people's eyes concerning the lies that are being told to the masses, and it is time to learn to trust our Lord and Savior for the healing of our bodies and the things that He gave to us to be healed.

# CHAPTER 4

My Testimony

Writing has been a long life passion of mine. Since I was fourteen years old, I indulged myself in long hours of journal writing. I was in search for the truth. I longed to understand the mysteries of the universe. I longed to satisfy my thirst and hunger for knowledge and truth through my pen and paper. I experienced many supernatural events since I was a young child. I knew that there was more to life than what our natural eyes saw. I had many encounters with ghosts or, as I now think, demons. I was in constant fear and paranoia because I used to have spirits confront me all the time. Sometimes I would feel them around me, or they would literally grab me, choke me, and even sexually molest me. Other times I used to just see them, and many times, I would see the lights in my home randomly turn off by themselves or items around me fall and break. As I grew older, I began to write about these experiences and ponder about what was going on. Who were these entities that seemed to enjoy tormenting me or spooking me so much?

**And ye shall know the truth, and the truth shall make you free. (John 8:39)**

In 1995, I received a phone call on February 9. My best friend called me, crying, letting me know a good friend of ours passed away in the early hours of the morning in a car accident. He was hit by a drunk driver who was speeding by the expressway and seemed to not have noticed my friend Michael (not his real name) who was in the emergency lane of the expressway, trying to fix the tire of his girl-friend's car. When I heard the news of his passing away, I was in total disbelief. I felt my heart sink in fear, and suddenly just pure sadness flooded my entire being. How can this happen? He was so young? Why did this happen to him? *This is not fair*, I thought. He was not ready to die!

Even though I was not a godly teenager at all, I had been taught that we must not die in a sinful lifestyle. I grew up in a Catholic home, and I was taught about heaven and hell and sin. Even though no one in my home or community lived godly lives or set an example of holiness for me to follow, I still thought that if we died in the middle of a lifestyle of partying, having sex without being married, using drugs, drinking alcohol, using foul language, not reading the Bible, not going to church regularly, not praying regularly, not obeying the Lord's commandments, etc., I genuinely believed that we do not go to heaven when we die in that condition.

**This I say then, walk in the Spirit, and you shall not fulfil the lust of the flesh. For the flesh lusteth against the Spirit, and the Spirit against the flesh: and these are contrary the one to the other: so that ye cannot do the things that ye would. But if ye be led of the Spirit, ye are not under the law. Now the works of the flesh are manifest, which are these: Adultery, fornication, uncleanness, lasciviousness, idolatry, witchcraft, hatred, variance, emulations, wrath, strife, seditions, heresies (changing the word of God or twisting it for convenience), envyings, murders, drunkenness, revellings, and such like: of the which I tell you before, as I have also told you in time past, that they which do such things shall not inherit the kingdom of God. (Galatians 5:16–21)**

I guess I did not fear much for my own salvation at the time because no one in my life really feared the Lord either, and everyone was living liberal lives. That was the only way of life I really knew. I also thought of myself as "not so bad" since at that time, I was not using drugs or having sex or doing a lot of the things that my friends were doing. I also was the only one I knew that would go to Catholic mass on Sundays, from time to time. Sometimes I would go with my parents, but I remember going alone too. Since I was comparing myself to my friends, I thought that I was not so bad! I also thought that because I was so young, death was not anywhere near my path, thus it was okay if I had some fun in my youth.

**There is a way which seemeth right unto a man, but the end thereof are the ways of death. (Proverbs 14:12)**

Moreover, when I heard about my Michael's passing, I knew that he lived his life like most of all of the people I knew; thus I felt fear creep up within me like a spear piercing through me.

Oh my! Where is he now? What has happened to his soul? I was so scared that he did not make it to heaven. I was so terrified that he was now lost for eternity, and there was just nothing that anyone could do to help him or to get him out of hell. I also thought that perhaps his soul was still roaming the earth, lost, afraid, and confused. I imagined him looking at all of us but not being able to communicate with anyone and not being able to get any rest either. I felt this deep sadness that was something I had never experienced before. I also felt hopeless because this situation was one that had no solution. He was gone, no more of my friend. He no longer existed. Just like that. In a blink of an eye, from one moment to another, this person no longer existed in the earth, and there was nothing anyone can do to change it. Nothing seemed any sadder for me at the time than that.

**Whereas ye know not what shall be on the morrow. For what is your life? It is even**

**a vapour, that appeareth for a little time, and
then vanisheth away. (James 4:14)**

During this time, I was already falling into depression. My
mother had been extremely ill with breast cancer, and I had been her
caretaker for two and half years prior to this phone call. I was overwhelmed by the amount of labor that I was subjected to do 'cause
of her illness and because of having to see her suffer so much daily.
I had to drive her to do her chemotherapies and watch her suffer
greatly after each session. It was taking an emotional toll on me. I
had just graduated high school and started Miami Dade College. I
was majoring in psychology, but I was also thinking about majoring
in journalism. I was not sure which route I was going to take yet, but
I started my classes.

But after my friend's passing away, everything just became too
much for me to bear. I literary was plunged into a full-blown depression. I also got obsessed with writing in my journals even more than
what I already was. I began writing to Michael. I began trying to
contact him through my journals. I wrote about how I thought that
he was lost, and perhaps even around me, reading what I was writing
and wanting to communicate with me.

**There shall not be found among you any-
one that maketh his son or his daughter to
pass through the fire, or that useth divination,
or an observer of times, or an enchanter, or a
witch, or a charmer, or a consulter with familiar spirits, or a wizard, or a necromancer. For
all that do these abominations the Lord thy
God doth drive them out from before thee.
(Deuteronomy 18:10–12)**

**Regard not them that have familiar spir-
its, neither seek after wizards, to be defiled
by them: I am the Lord your God. (Leviticus
19:31)**

Moreover, I went out one day and hung out with a friend of mine who was studying photography. I had done modeling in my high school years, and he had asked me if I would be his model for one of his photo shoots. I decided to do it, even though I was not working anymore. I was focused in school and the care of my ill mother, and I had much sadness in my life to do anything else. But I thought this might help me feel better, so I went to his place.

After the photo shoot, he offered me to smoke marijuana with him. Up until that day, I had always steadfastly refused every single person who had offered me a joint. It was almost an automatic response to tell them, "No, thanks, I don't smoke." Unfortunately that day, when he offered me this joint, my mind went somewhere else. I thought about my friend who passed away in the car accident prior to that moment. I told myself, *Look at him, he died so young. Life is so short. Perhaps I should just try weed for once since we never know when we will die. I should just see what all the fuzz about weed is all about.*

Sadly after that thought, I stretched out my hand and grabbed the joint and smoked. *There, I did it! I finally smoked weed,* I thought to myself. Unfortunately I loved it! I loved the way it made me feel and think. Thus I began to smoke a lot after that. Even though I did not have any money to buy it, it was no problem for me to get it. My brother always had some at home, and all our friends always had and would gladly give it to me for free.

When I would smoke, I noticed that my mind would think differently. I do not know how to explain it. I would just go deeper into thought. I wrote differently in my journals, and when I would write as I was high, it was a different experience. It was as if I would enter a trance. A spiritual trance. I was already tapping into that realm without the weed, but once I started smoking, it was as if I had a breakthrough and entered some sort of spiritual portal.

**For rebellion is as the sin of witchcraft, and stubbornness is as iniquity and idolatry. Because thou hast rejected the word of Lord, he hath also rejected thee from being king. (1 Samuel 15:23)**

**Be sober, be vigilant, for your adversary
the devil, as a roaring lion walks about seeking
whom he may devour. (1 Peter 5:8)**

Furthermore, I was still in college and taking all my classes. But now I was studying my books while being high on weed. I loved reading my psychology books as I was high. It was just so much fun for me. I was still taking care of my mother also. I was spending more time in my journals as well. As my mother was slowly dying in front of my face, day after day, I was dwelling on my friend's death as well. Thus death became my sole focus. I wanted to understand what the meaning of life is. Since one day we will all die, I desperately wanted to know where my friend's soul was. Also I was curious about several other people in my life that had passed away as well and lived careless or liberal lifestyles. Finally I also wanted to know, where was my mother's soul going soon?

**And I saw a great white throne, and him that sat on it, from whose face the earth and the heaven fled away; and there was found no place for them. And I saw the dead, small and great, stand before God; and the books were opened: and another book was opened, which is {the book} of life: and the dead were judged out of those things which were written in the books, according to their works. And death and hell were cast into the lake of fire. This is the second death. And whosoever was not found written in the book of life was cast into the lake of fire.**

**—Revelation 20:11–15)**

# CHAPTER 5

## Losing My Identity

**Before I formed thee in the belly, I knew thee; and before
thou camest forth out of the womb I sanctified thee,
and I ordained thee a prophet unto the nations.**

**—Jeremiah 1:5**

I found myself spending most of time on my journal writing. I also found myself writing, most of the time, to Michael. This became everything to me. I would drive to the cemetery and spend hours and hours crying over his grave and writing to him in my journals. I do not believe I have ever cried harder and longer than during these days. I was just so brokenhearted that he was gone, and the thought that he may not be in heaven would only sound louder and louder in my mind with each passing day. I remember how everyone in his funeral would comfort one another by saying to one another that he went to a better place; that he now was resting in peace. I just could not believe that. I found no comfort in hearing those words. I genuinely thought of them as a deception.

I had not been too close to Michael during the time he died. We had dated a few years prior to his death, but we both drifted away from each other. He had a girlfriend, and I also dated other guys after him. But when he died, his time with me on earth was magnified in my mind to the maximum. I recalled over and over all the memories

47

we once shared and found it very strange that one day, he had given me an incredibly unique light-blue rock in a chain as a gift. He told me it was his gift so that I never forget him, and he told me that the rock meant—eternal life. I thought now that he had died that it was quite ironic that his gift to me meant eternal life.

I also remembered that one time I dedicated to him the song from the band U2, which is titled "Who's Gonna Ride Your Wild Horses," which lyrics say, "Who's gonna drown in your blue seas? Who's gonna taste your saltwater kisses? You are an accident waiting to happen. You are a piece of glass left there on the beach. Well, you left my heart empty as a vacant lot, for any spirit to haunt." At the time when we were dating, and I dedicated to him this song, I did it because we loved listening to this band together and because he was very flirtatious with other girls. I knew he was a womanizer. He was handsome, and many girls liked him, and he liked them. I knew that keeping him as my boyfriend was probably not going to happen. And sure enough, he left me for another girl. However, now that he passed away, I was dumbfounded that out of all the songs I could have ever dedicate to him, I dedicated to him a song that described with much precision what I was experiencing now that he is gone. *What a coincidence?* I thought.

I would play that song over and over and just cry and weep for hours and hours. I would also listen to all the other songs he and I used to listen to when we dated. I became so obsessed with him that without intending to do it, I fell in love with him. All that was in my mind, all day long, was his name, his image, our memories together, and my worry about where his soul was. I forgot about everything else. His memory consumed me all day long. And my concern about his soul was eating me up inside.

I strongly started to believe that his spirit was with me. I strongly sensed his spirit hovering over me as I wrote. I began to talk to him in my journal, as if he were next me. I began to ask him to give me signs that he was with me. I started to write to him, as if to try to comfort him. Because in my mind, he was suffering. In my mind, he was afraid and confused and lost and needed to feel consoled by someone. I began to write to him, describing to him what I thought it was that he was experiencing now that he passed away but was stuck in this world as a spirit. I wanted to make him feel as if even though he felt utterly alone, he was not. I wanted him to feel that someone was trying to figure out his situation and trying to see if there was any hope of taking him out of it.

I would do all this while taking care of my ill mother and while getting high on weed. This was a formula for disaster. I did not realize that what I was doing was opening many doors for the devil to come in and take ahold of my mind. I was naive, ignorant, and way too curious to be stopped. Like a train wreck, I wrote myself into a deep abyss!

> My people are destroyed for lack of knowledge: because thou has rejected knowledge, I will also reject thee, that thou shalt be no priest to me: seeing thou has forgotten the law of thy God, I will also forget thy children. (Hosea 4:6)

> Lest Satan should get an advantage of us: for we are not ignorant of his devices. (2 Corinthians 2:11)

> For though we walk in the flesh, we do not war after the flesh: For the weapons of our warfare are not carnal, but mighty through God to the pulling down of strong holds; casting down imaginations, and every high thing that exalteth itself against the knowledge of God, and bringing into captivity every thought to the obedience of Christ; and having in a readiness to revenge all disobedience, when your obedience is fulfilled. (2 Corinthians 10:3–6)

Taking my thoughts captive to the obedience of Christ was opposite to what I was doing. I was letting all my thoughts roam around and be as free as can be. I was submerging myself in every thought that was popping up in my mind and letting my imagination run as wild as it can. With no care in the world, I was doing the things that Satan wanted me to do so that he can take control of my mind. And little by little, as I delighted myself in forbidden knowledge, Satan took over. I remember one day, after I had finished writing in my journal for hours, I told my mother while she was lying in bed, "Mom, I feel as if I am no longer the one writing in my journals, I feel that I am just reading what my hand writes."

Later I discovered that what I was doing has a name—automatic writing. I discovered that many famous people practice this. They invoke demons to take over their minds and allow them to write through them, and this is how they get inspired to write scripts for film, novels, songs, and all kinds of forms of entertainment. I also learned that many psychics and mediums use this technique to read people's future.

**All scripture is given by inspiration of God, and is profitable for doctrine, for reproof, for correction, for instruction in righteousness: That the man of God may be perfect, thoroughly furnished unto all good works. (2 Timothy 3:16–17)**

Just as God can inspire His children to write the Bible, the devil also can inspire his children to write just the same way. We are all created in the image of God; thus we are all eternal and spiritual.

**And God said, let us make man in Our image, after Our likeness: and let them have dominion over the fish of the sea, and over the fowl of the air, and over the cattle, and over all the earth, and over every creeping thing that creepeth upon the earth. So, God created man in His own image, in the image of God created Him; male and female created He them. (Genesis 1:26–27)**

We all are vessels in this world, and we choose who to allow to inspire us to do what we do. We choose who we allow to express their ideologies through our lives.

> **Now therefore fear the Lord and serve him in sincerity and in truth: and put away the gods which your fathers served on the other side of the flood, and in Egypt; and serve ye the Lord. And if it seem evil unto you to serve the Lord, choose you this day whom ye will serve; whether the gods which your fathers served that were on the other side of the flood, or the gods of the Amorites, in whose land ye dwell: but as for me and my house, we will serve the Lord. (Joshua 24:14–24)**

I was living my life separated from God. Even though I considered myself a good and loving person, and I went to church as a Catholic, I was practicing sin daily. Because of that, I was considered a child of Satan and not a child of God. I needed to repent, to turn away from my sins and reconcile with God.

> **For all have sinned and come short of the glory of God. (Romans 3:23)**

I was spiritually blind, and I did not know this. There was a veil on my eyes that prevented me from seeing my true spiritual condition on front of a Holy God.

> **He that practices sin is of the devil; for the devil sinneth from the beginning. For this purpose, the Son of God was manifested, that he might destroy the works of the devil. Whosoever is born of God doth not practice sin; for his seed remaineth in him: and he cannot sin, because he is born of God. (1 John 3:8–9)**

**To open their eyes, and to turn them from darkness to light, and from the power of Satan unto God, that they may receive forgiveness of sins, and inheritance among them which are sanctified by faith that is in Me. (Acts 26:18)**

After long hours of writing to Michael, after weeks and months had passed by, after dwelling on his memory and desiring to see him again with no other desire in my mind, things began to take a crazy turn.

One day I went over to my friend's house, whose names are Jesus and Lissette. I went there with one of my cousins and my best friend. We always hung out at their house and smoked weed together. But this night was very strange. After we all got high on weed, I heard Jesus starting to speak bizarre things to us. Honestly it has been over twenty years since this thing happened to me, and I am trying my best to recollect the memories, but there are a lot of things that I forgot. All I remember was that they were talking about celebrities that they knew that worship the devil. They spoke about how the celebrities call Lucifer their father and how they pledge their allegiance to him. There were more conversations about all that going on that night that were scaring me, but for some reason, they were having fun talking about it. Then it was as if a switch was turned on, and everyone's demeanor changed at the same time.

Everyone began acting weird, and it was as if they all knew something that I did not. Suddenly I heard Jesus talking about how we were all meant to meet in this life and how that moment was like a divine meeting. He went on saying that we all knew one another before we were born and that we were all supposed to perform some sort of work here on earth together. Then I would stare at my cousin and best friend to try to see if they thought Jesus went nuts on us, but instead they were all on the same page as him. It was all so surreal! They all had a weird smile on their faces, and they were all making me feel as if I was clueless of something serious, and they had to update me on it. My friend Jesus having that name on his uniform was not helping me either. All this time I could not stop reading his name on his shirt and think of Jesus Christ. He took me over toward the living room and stared into my eyes in the most bizarre manner.

Many weird things went on that night, and after this event, it seemed to me that things in my life only became weirder and weirder. Another day after this day, I was hanging out with my cousin again, and she was introducing me to some of her friends, and to my shock, one of her friends said to me, "You are Desiree?" Then she looked at my cousin and said, "The famous Desiree?"

I do not know what my cousin replied, neither do I know why she said that. But she ended up treating me as if I were a celebrity, and I do not know why. She really thought I was famous, and she sure made me feel as if I was.

One day, I was overwhelmed at my house and decided to drive to Miami Beach in hopes that I can clear my mind by sitting in front of the ocean and just meditate. It was a nice afternoon, and I drove there. I was in the parking lot of the beach when suddenly, I saw this elderly man, who seemed to be poor or perhaps even homeless. He had a red rose in his hand, and he was shouting really loud, "Jesus is coming! Jesus is coming! Jesus Christ is coming!"

I was astonished by this man because it just seemed to coincide with all the sequence of crazy events that were happening in my life, and it was scaring me. I went down to the beach in hopes of getting away from this strange happenings and spiritual encounters, but it was just following me everywhere I went. I parked my car and walked out cautiously since I could see this old man approaching me. He came all the way toward me and did not stop saying that Jesus Christ was coming, then he handed me his red rose and left.

I found it very strange, to say the least. I walked toward the sand with my rose in my hand. I was on my way to spend some quality time with nature and just meditate and clear my thoughts. But as I approached the sand, I saw two African American people who seemed to be a couple. They had long dreadlocks and were dressed nicely; they seemed really cool to me. It was a man and a woman who seemed to be young adults, and they were standing in front of me and between the ocean and me. They were holding incense in one hand and marijuana joints and horoscope books in the other. They were smiling at me, almost as if they had been expecting me. They saluted me and greeted me and asked me if I would like to smoke weed with them, and I, of course, said yes. I smoked with them and thought to myself that it was such a cool treat to be able to smoke weed right before going to meditate.

I was not really expecting to get high at that moment, but since the opportunity came to me, well, I thought it was amazing! After I was smoking with them and getting to know them a little bit, talking about the horoscopes, the incense, the universe, and weed, I noticed, by the corners of my eyes, other people approaching us. Suddenly what had been a circle composed of three of us became a reunion of five of us. Two more men joined us. First it was this white male in his young adult years as well, who was a magician—out of all the things he could be. I actually freaked out at first when I looked at him because I saw the face of one of my ex-boyfriends on his face as he came over. It then disappeared.

This magician guy was holding cards in his hands. He came over really enthusiastic as he joined us and took over the meeting. He began saying to all of us that this was a divine appointment and that we were destined to meet that day. He then looked at me and grabbed my hand and kissed it, then said to everyone there, "Isn't she beautiful?" Then he told all of us, "Did you know that Jesus was coming back as a woman?"

At that moment, my heart sunk within me, and I no longer felt any excitement. I felt as if I was a two-year-old child who had just lost my parents and was left all alone with a bunch of strangers. Fear crept in me like a sharp knife, and I did not know what to do or think. I have never felt so vulnerable up until that moment. Confusion never seemed so scary as that day.

I had gone to the beach that day in hopes of clearing my mind from so many things that were confusing me, and ended up getting the most confused I have ever felt in my entire life. After the magician guy said that and began handing us his magic cards, then the other man approached and joined us. This was an Indian-looking young man; he was wearing a bunch of crucifixes on his neck. There were so many of those crucifixes on his neck that it was very bizarre.

He came and stood among us, and then the magician man, who seemed to be the leader of this meeting, looked at him and then looked at me, as if he was sort of introducing us to each other and as if we were supposed to meet. Then the Indian man reached out his hand for me to grab and take me for, what it seemed to me, a walk away from the group and by the sand alone, with each other. But instead of me grabbing his hand, I turned away and ran for my life. I got in my car and drove off to the other side of the beach. Far away from all those people.

I was truly startled and confused by that whole event. I parked my car again and went toward the beach once again, in hopes of getting some time to myself. Now it was starting to get dark and no longer daylight. As I walked in the sand and looked at the water, I hallucinated again. I saw, far away, in the ocean what seemed to me a "pirate ship." I was stunned by the ship that sat on the water in front of my eyes and could not believe it. It was so real. I then looked up at the sky, and I saw a cloud in the shape of a huge cross and a little boy hugging the bottom of the cross; it was beautiful! I then was so amazed by all the things that I had seen that I became emboldened in my mind to dare to try to walk on water. I looked at the shore of the beach and thought that perhaps if I had faith, I could walk on top of the water as Jesus did. Thus I tried it, and of course, instead of my feet gliding above the water, my boots sank in, the waters consumed them, and that was the end of that.

Then I just started to walk on the sand, and suddenly I felt an arm gently grab my arm and envelop my arm in his arm. I could not see anyone, though; I just felt that someone was there, and indeed, not only did I feel an arm grab my arm, but it began to pull me faster than how I was walking. It made me run a little. But it was very gentle, and I thought that maybe it was Michael, or perhaps maybe it was Jesus. Who knows? I was so confused, as you can see. I laughed as I walked rapidly with this mystery ghost who was revealing himself to me, and that was all that I remember from that night. I then drove home. This event took me into a much deeper level of confusion within me.

Then another day, my friends took me out for a girls' night out. One of my friends was getting married, and we went together to celebrate that she was soon going to get married. They took me to the Chippendales strip club. Going to a male strip club was something I had never done before. I was not too thrilled to be there either. It was not appealing to me at all. However, I wanted to honor my friend and share that moment of her life with her. When we were there, I do not think I was having too much fun. All I had in mind was my Michael. Right from the moment I left my house that night, I can clearly remember that things were different for me now. This was my first time going out to a social gathering since Michael had died. I remember getting in the car with my friends who came by my house to get me. We started to smoke a joint, and when I started to feel high, I not only felt high from the weed, I felt Michael's spirit with me like never before. It was such an intense sensation that his soul was there with me, and I was delighted about it.

After we left the club, we then went to one of my friend's house to hang out. We smoked more weed, and then I had to go use the bathroom. When I went to the bathroom, I was hearing a song in the background that reminded me of Michael a lot. It's called "Missing" by a group called Everything but the Girl. This song came out during the days he passed away, and the lyrics made me think of him a lot.

These are the lyrics to the song:

> *I stepped off the train, I'm walking down your street again, and passed your door, but you don't live there anymore. It's years since you've been there, and now you've disappeared somewhere, like outer space, you've found some better place. And I miss you, like the deserts miss the rain and I miss you, like the deserts miss the rain. Could you be dead? You always were two steps ahead of everyone, we'd walk behind while you run! I look up at your house and I can almost hear you shout down to me where I always used to be, and I miss you like the deserts miss the rain. And I miss you, like the deserts miss the rain. Back on the train, I ask why did I come again? Can I confess, I've been hanging around your*

*old address, and years have proved to offer nothing*
*since you moved and you're long gone, but I can't*
*move on...and I miss you.*

As I was washing my hands, remembering him as I listened to the song, I looked at myself in the mirror. Suddenly the strangest thing occurred. I noticed that half of my face was looking like Michael's face. As I stared at the mirror intently, I then realized both my hands were involuntarily lifting upward. Then they involuntarily clapped together above my head. I was not in control of my body movements at all. I was just a spectator in front of the mirror. I remember when my hands met with each other on top of my head, I broke down in a deep and intense cry. Suddenly crying was all I could do. My friends came and grabbed me out of the bathroom and sat me down. I then remember, as I was sobbing in the most intense manner I had ever cried, I was involuntarily rubbing my thighs and saying repeatedly, "It feels so good to feel again." And again, as I would feel my legs, I would say, crying intensely, "It feels so good to feel."

That night, I stayed crying the entire night after that happened. My friends all stayed there with me too. In the morning, they took me to a church called Unity. I do not know much about this type of church. I had never been to one of them. I think they have to do with the New Era. One of my friends was part of them. When I went in there, I was exhausted from crying. We all sat in a circle. Then they made us stand up and hold hands together. Suddenly they were all inhaling and exhaling deeply, at the same time, as we held hands. When I first experienced their first breath, I was immediately plunged once again into an agonizing burst of tears. It was so much that I had to sit down, and my friend even had to sit with me and hold me so I would not fall to the floor, crying.

I did not know what was happening to me. I felt such pain in my heart, and it was overwhelming me to the fullest. They all kept on doing those breathing exercises, as I just wept in my friend's shoulder. When the whole service was over, someone was handing out little messages for everyone to pick out. I picked out mine, and it read, "You are everyone's mirror."

I read it and then the lady who gave it to me said, "You have no idea how beautiful you are. You are very special." She also said to me that I had chosen in heaven to do the role I had to fulfill here on earth; she said I had volunteered to take a very painful path here on earth.

I was so confused. Who are all these people? What does it mean that I am everyone's mirror? Why do I feel such horrendous pain? Why am I crying so much? Where am I? What is this place that they brought me in? And finally, why has Michael possessed me in this manner?

I left the church, and my friends finally dropped me off home. Life was forever changed for me after that night. Things only got weirder and weirder for me. One day, my mother was in her room, and my sister was next to her. My mom called me over and began saying, "Desiree, poor Desiree, you have always had so many misfortunes in your life!"

And she grabbed me and hugged me super tight as she was continuing to say how sorry she was that life had been so cruel to me. I will never forget her hug. It was the strongest hug my mom or anyone ever gave me. As she hugged me, and I heard her words, I began to weep in her arms. Then my sister came and began to comfort me too. My mom then continued to speak to me. "Desiree, don't you know? Don't you know that we are the Trinity?" She then stayed silent and just stared in my eyes. I then stared at my sister to try to understand what in the world my mother was telling me.

And my sister grabbed my hand and caressed it and said, "Yes, Desi, we are the Trinity."

I felt pain hearing those words because they simply made no sense to me. But why were both my mother and sister telling me that we were the divine Trinity? What was it that I did not know about the truth that they seemed to know? I was so confused. I felt fear. Lots and lots of fear. It was as if I was slowly drifting out of my reality, and it did not feel good at all. I remembered my mom when she told me the story of how she could not have children when she first wanted to be pregnant. She told me that she and my father tried getting pregnant, but it was to no avail. Thus she went to Mexico. She went to pray to the Virgin of Guadalupe. She told me that she knelt and walked a long path toward the statue of this Virgin, on her knees, and that when she arrived at her feet, she made a covenant with her. My mom vowed to the Virgin of Guadalupe that if she would grant her a child, she would dedicate that child to her. Then my mom said that as soon as she came back home from that trip, she found herself pregnant with her first child, which was my sister.

Then my mom told me that on her third month of pregnancy, the Virgin appeared to my mom in her dreams and that the Virgin handed over my sister to my mom. My mom said that in the dream, my sister looked exactly the way she turned out to look in real life. My mom then told me that she then got pregnant with me and that the same way that it happened in her first pregnancy, the same thing happened with her second one. On her trimester of my mom's second pregnancy, my mom had a dream again with the Virgin of Guadalupe. In the same manner, the Virgin handed me over to my mom. My mom said I looked the same way too as in real life, except for my eyes. She said in the dream, my eyes were blue. In real life, my eyes are brown, but from time to time, they turn hazel and light. Finally my mom told me that the same thing happened with my brother in her pregnancy. She had a dream in her trimester of pregnancy, and the Virgin handed over my little brother to her, and she saw him the same way he looked in real life.

When my mom and my sister were telling me that we were the Holy Trinity, I remembered the story of the Virgin of Guadalupe. I also remember how my father told me that when I was born, he knew a lady that was very spiritual, and she had told him after she met me, shortly after I was born, that she saw in the Spirit that I was going to do something huge for this world someday. He told me that story a couple of times through my childhood, and this came up in my mind at this moment as well.

Thus I felt fear. I was confused of who I was. I was uncertain of the truth about my identity. The whole concept of thinking that my mother, my sister, and I were the Trinity was insane! But since my mother and sister were dead serious while they were telling me this, and seemed to believe it, I was terrified and confused.

Thou shalt have no other gods before me. Thou shalt not make unto thee any graven image, or any likeness of anything that is in heaven above, or that is in the earth beneath, or that is in the water under the earth: Thou shalt not bow down thyself to them, nor serve them: for I the Lord thy God am a jealous God, visiting the iniquity of the fathers upon the children unto the third and fourth generation of them that hate me; and shewing mercy unto thousands of them that love me, and keep my commandments. (Exodus 20:3–6)

What say I then? That the idol is anything, or that which is offered in sacrifice to idols is anything? But I say that the things which the Gentiles sacrifice, they sacrifice to devils, and not to God: and I would not that ye should have fellowship with devils. Ye cannot drink the cup of the Lord, and the cup of the devils: ye cannot be partakers of the Lord's table and of the table of devils. Do we provoke the Lord to jealousy? Are we stronger than He? (1 Corinthians 10:19–22)

Ye are of your father the devil, and the lusts of your father ye will do. He was a murderer from the beginning, and abode not in the truth, because there is no truth in him. When he speaketh a lie, he speaketh of his own: for he is a liar, and the father of lies. (John 8:44)

And no marvel; for Satan himself is transformed into an angel of light. (2 Corinthians 11:14)

Unfortunately out of ignorance, my mother dedicated my siblings and me to Satan without knowing. Sadly she was tricked into it, thinking that she was dealing with the Divine Virgin that gave birth to our Lord and Savior, but the truth is that she was only dealing with Satan, who deceived her and dressed up as an angel of light.

**For there is one God, and one mediator between God and men, the man Christ Jesus. (1 Timothy 2:5)**

After this event with my mother and sister, my whole belief system about my identity was utterly shattered. I now went on a quest to try to understand who I really was. I had no idea what Satan was preparing for me. I was soon going to find out just how skillful of a deceiver Satan really is.

# CHAPTER 6

## Falling Down the Rabbit Hole

I began to experience a strong sense that Michael's spirit was not only always with me, but that he was trying to speak to me through different ways. I felt excited at first, since I had written so much in my journals, trying to accomplish the exact phenomenon I was experiencing now. I wanted Michael to reveal himself to me since I strongly suspected that his soul was with me. However, my mother was getting sicker and sicker, and the emotional toll of taking care of her was starting to show. I was burning out from all the physical labor that I did every day caring for her, and my mind was starting to deteriorate from the lack of sleep and from all the writing in my journals, and from all the grief and strange spiritual experiences I was enduring. Also my mother and sister telling me that I was part of the Trinity was not a good thing at all for me either, as you can imagine.

My sister took notice that I was not doing well, and she decided to take me with her to her home in Orlando, from Miami which was where I lived. She allowed me to take my best friend from my middle school years, who I will name Louise, since she and I used to pretend that we were like the movie *Thelma and Louise* (not her real name). This trip was the tip of the iceberg in my mental downward spiral out of control. Since the moment we sat in the car and began to ride to Orlando, it was as if I was on a bad acid trip, even though I was not on any drugs nor had I ever tried acid before. I only heard about what that drug did to my friends, but I respected the power it seemed to have on the mind and stayed away from it; however, I was smoking weed. As usual!

When I sat in the front seat, the trip started out nice. The sky was blue and clear, and it was a beautiful day. However, a couple of hours into the trip, it began to rain hard; the sky now was turning dark, and there was lightning and thunder. Then the radio was playing Nine Inch Nails, which is a band that Louise and I used to love, but the lyrics to their songs are extremely wicked and evil, and this was when the trip began to feel really bad for me. I started to think that Michael was speaking his feelings about his life, now as a spirit, through these songs; I began to feel extremely sorry for him. The lyrics to many these songs are about feelings of frustration and anger, hatred and restlessness, fear and confusion, etc. One of my favorite songs is titled "Terrible Lies."

Moreover, as we kept on driving, we began to enter Orlando, and it was dark and raining, and then I could see all the billboards promoting Disney World, which played into giving me more conviction of what Michael was trying to tell me. I saw one billboard that was advertising the Halloween Horror Nights from Universal Studios. The imagery of this billboard was quite disturbing to me, and as we kept on going, more and more disturbing-looking imagery was just popping up from everywhere around the expressway. Those billboards, combined with the music and the rain and lightning and thunder, were just a cocktail of pure fear and sadness for my vulnerable mind and soul.

By the time we got to my sister's home, I was extremely saddened and fearful with only Michael in mind. My concern that he was lost in the spiritual realm, surrounded by evil, wicked demons tormenting him was now greatly intensified. My sister lived in a nice three-bedroom home with a pool that was in the yard, but it was enveloped by a huge net to keep pests outside of the water. When I went in to her house and settled in, I decided to go in the pool to try to feel better from the four hours' ride we just had. Even though it was nighttime, my sister did not mind me going in, and I changed into my bathing suit. I put on my Counting Crows CD and began walking toward the pool as I heard the music playing. I was listening to a song titled "Time and Time Again." As I walked toward the backyard, listening to the lyrics of this song, it was as if the whole world just stopped, and I was left all alone with Michael. In my mind, Michael was carefully picking each of the songs I was listening to, and he was expressing how he felt to me through each song. And so, as I was walking toward the water, I was hearing the words:

> *I wanted so badly somebody other than me, staring back at me. But you were gone, gone, gone, I wanted to see you walking backwards and get the sensation of you coming home. I wanted to see you walking away from me, without the sensation of you leaving me alone. Time and time again, time and time again, time and time again, I can't please myself. I wanted the ocean to cover over me, I want to sink slowly without getting wet. Maybe someday, I won't be so lonely; and I'll walk on water every chance I get. Time and time again, time and time again. I can't please myself. So, when are you coming home sweet angel? Your leaving me alone? All alone? Well, if I'm drowning darling, you'll come down this way on your own. I wish I was traveling on a freeway, beneath this graveyard western sky. I'm gonna set fire to this city, and out into the desert, yeah, we're gonna ride. Time and time again, time and time again, time and time again. I CAN'T PLEASE MYSELF, AND I CAN'T PLEASE MYSELF AND I CAN'T PLEASE NOBODY ELSE AND time again... I can't please myself... No, no, no.*

As I was hearing those lyrics, great sadness took over me, and I was convinced this was how Michael was feeling that very moment, and he was utterly tormented. I felt as if he was a ghost, and he was trying to come back to life as it used to be for him, but it was not possible anymore. I found myself walking really slow and entering the pool with a huge heartache inside me. As I submerged myself in the pool, I kept walking toward the middle of the pool, and the light of the moon was lighting up the net that was surrounding the entire patio with the pool inside. I stopped in the middle of the pool and stared at a shadow that was right in front me, which looked exactly like a shadow of a huge Virgin. I involuntarily moved my arms together and placed them as in the form of prayer and just stayed completely still and gazed into this bizarre shadow in front of me, in the form of a Virgin, listening to this emotionally charged sad song and glaring into the moonlight. I must have stayed like that for a while because later, I noticed my sister was not too happy to see me acting like that. She was very worried about my mental state by now.

The next day, Louise offered me to smoke weed with her, and so I did. We then went to play basketball at the court that was in my sister's neighborhood. As we were shooting hoops and just playing around together, I was not thinking about anything. I was trying to just have fun. I loved playing sports with my best friend; we always played many sports together, and it always cheered me up and made me escape all sad thoughts. However, this time was different. This time, as we were playing ball, after a couple of shots at the hoop, I noticed Louise was looking different. She was acting a bit strange. She was out of her character. Suddenly I saw her looking at me as if she knew something that I did not know. She smiled weirdly at me, called out my name, and saluted me as if we had just greeted each other for the first time that day. I automatically knew in my mind that what was happening was that Michael took over her. It was not Louise anymore. It was Michael inside of her, talking and playing basketball with me. I was delighted to the maximum! I will never forget the excitement I felt within me when I saw this unfold! Finally he's back! Michael was there and was hanging out with me! I felt as if I was skydiving. The adrenalin rush of that moment was like nothing I had ever experienced before, or ever again for that matter. All I had ever wanted, for months now, was to have him with me again. And finally, I got it!

That whole day was amazing. At nighttime we all went out. We went to Pleasure Island, and we were inside the clubs of this park in Orlando. I went in one of the clubs, and Louise began to speak to me about the picture frames that were on the wall of this specific club. There were a couple of them. But I only remember one that she pointed out to me. It was a picture frame that said the words "World Famous Psychologist" on it. She then went ahead and told me in her out-of-character and new personality and mannerism, which was exactly like Michael's, "Desiree, you see this right here? This is going to be you in the future!"

I was so happy about that! I thought that Michael was now telling me that I was going to become a world-famous psychologist, and that was thrilling for me to think of since becoming a great psychologist was what I have always longed to be. We had a lot of fun that night, and I had forgotten all about the sadness and the worries of his soul being tormented. I thought that if he could take over my friend's body and talk to me through her, he was powerful and had supernatural abilities. I thought that he was going to somehow figure out a way to be okay, and in his process of doing that, he was going to host me around this new reality and give me a lot of happy memories. Boy, was I wrong and very naive!

My sister drove us back home after a weekend at her place, and now I was in a much worse mental state than when she first got me. Funny how her intentions had been to take me away for a weekend to help me to clear up my mind and fix myself. The total opposite occurred! I was now in a mental breakdown. The veil from my reality to a different reality was officially broken, and there was no way for me to go back to the way things were. Satan had officially taken over not just my mind but everything that was happening around me. Like a master of puppets, he was pulling the strings of everyone that I would come in contact with, and I was in for a show. He was orchestrating all these different events for me to be astonished by him, taking me on an emotional roller-coaster ride to then throw me down from the highest peak of it. Like a mouse walking into a trap, I was being led to destruction, and I had not the slightest clue of what I was walking into, neither was there any way to stop me.

By now I was so convinced that Michael was alive and talking to me, and that he loved me and that I could trust him. It was the perfect setting for the enemy to strike his fatal blow, and I was too blind and ignorant to see it. I was also surrounded by people who did not know the Lord Jesus Christ truthfully; they did not obey His Word or even read it. Thus all these people in my life were host bodies for the demons to use and deceive me. The stage was being set for my eyes to witness the wonders of the enemy of my soul, and I could not be more excited to see it! Unknowingly I surrendered wholeheartedly to Michael's spirit and decided to cater to his every need. Unknowingly after that experience in my sister's home, I officially made him my lord and god, and there was nothing I would not do for him. I was seriously devoted to serving him and dedicating to him all my time, energy, and love. I was a woman in love with a ghost!

> **Wherefore, my dearly beloved, flee from idolatry. (1 Corinthians 10:14)**

> **And thou shalt love the Lord thy God with all thy heart, and with all thy soul, and with all thy mind, and with all thy strength: this is the first commandment. (Mark 12:30)**

By making Michael my idol, I had no time to love God. Michael truly became my god, and I gave the devil the legal right to do with me whatever he desired.

> **Neither give place to the devil.**

> **—Ephesians 4:27**

# CHAPTER 7

*❦*

# Hypnotized Under A Strong Delusion

When Michael passed away, his mother had invited all of his friends to her house and gave us all his belongings. I took some pants and shirts that she gave me, and they fit me well. After I got home from Orlando, I put on his clothes, and I always wore his chain that he gave me. I went to smoke weed by myself at a nearby park that I used to love to go to. It was a beautiful lake with benches all around it and trees, a trail to walk by the side of the lake, green grass everywhere you looked, lots of ducks, a waterfall in the middle of the lake, and there were houses and apartments surrounding the whole place. I grew up in that area, and that was my sanctuary, to sit down and just be one with nature. It was late at night, and I had been sitting down there, smoking weed all by myself. I was talking with Michael.

Suddenly I heard in my mind, Michael asking me that he wanted to go visit his mother. He was asking me to drive to her house and knock on her door. I said, absolutely no way! I knew that was insane! But he kept on insisting that he longed to go see her. He made me feel sorry for him. And after going back and forth in my own head about it, I finally got convinced to do him the favor. I got up and, like a zombie, walked into the parking lot and turned on my car and drove to his house. It was like one o'clock or two o'clock in the morning. I knocked on the door, and she came out. When she looked at me, I was out of control of everything concerning my words and actions. It was truly no longer me but Michael in me. She let me inside the house, and she sat down, and I knelt down by her lap, placed my hand on her heart, and said, "Mom, it's me, Michael."

Honestly I do not remember what she said or did. I am sure she freaked out. I am sure that I horrified her and made her cry. But I truly do not remember. I only remember up until that moment that I said those last words to her. I remember leaving her home and getting into my car, but I also do not remember the ride home either. I was possessed!

After that event, none of my old friends wanted to be near me. I was known as Satan's child after that, and everyone became very afraid of me. I do not blame them!

Another day, I was hanging out with one of my brother's friend. My brother and I were close friends, and we would have a lot of friends come to our home. His friends were not aware what was going on with me at all. Thus they were not scared of being around me. I was smoking weed with one of his friends, and we went to his place. He had a guest in there from New York. Another young man. He too was smoking weed with us. When my brother's friend left to use the bathroom, the other guy—who I had no clue of who he was nor did he know me—said to me, "Desiree, do you know that you are the devil!"

So before I go on saying what happened next, let me refresh your memory on how Satan pulled the greatest stunt in my life to deceive me. I always heard from my father, as I was growing up, that when I was born, a friend of his who was a "witch"—she was into Santeria, the Spanish religion which is witchcraft—well, she told him when she first met me that one day, I was going to do something really great for this world. My father told me this over and over as I grew up. Then my mother shared her story about how she could not get pregnant and made a covenant with the Virgin of Guadalupe and how the Virgin granted her wish and handed me over to her. Then when I was fifteen years old, I had gone to a psychic, and she read my hands. This woman did not know me. That was the first time we ever met. She told me a lot of things that came to pass, and she also said things that were false.

That is what the devil does. He gives you some truth so that he may deceive you. Anyways this psychic lady said that she saw that my mom was ill with cancer, and she then said to me, "Don't worry, she is not going to die from the cancer."

Unfortunately she was wrong. She did pass away. Unless the demon in her was insinuating that she was going to die from the chemotherapies instead of the cancer, in that case then she was right. Then she said to me that she saw that my father was a heavy drinker. She told me to tell him that if he didn't stop drinking alcohol, he would surely die. Well, there she was right. He died from drinking too much alcohol. She told me to tell my brother to stop doing drugs and to warn him that when we consume too many drugs, we can end up having children with birth defects. Luckily his kids came out healthy. That was a good advice, nevertheless. Then she said that she saw that I liked to do something with my hands. She then asked me if I liked to write. I said, "Yes, it's my favorite thing to do!"

She then said to me, "Keep writing, don't ever stop because you are going to do something in the future that has to do with writing." Then she said in an astonished manner, "Oh my, you are going to be famous! You are going to write a best-seller novel!"

She then said that I was going to solve a puzzle about the world! I was completely shocked! *Well, that is as exciting as can be!* I thought. She then continued speaking in a really excited manner, and she said that my life was going to be like a fairy tale and that I was going to make a movie too and that it had to do with my friends. She said I was even going to win a Nobel Prize! By now I was absolutely thrilled! Wow! How cool is all that! She then moved on to tell me that I was going to get married to a blond guy with blue eyes, and that I was going to be very happy with him. This part completely shattered me because the reason why I even met with this psychic was to find out if I was ever going to get back with my last boyfriend that I had, whom I was still in love with. He broke up with me after seven months of dating, and I was devastated. He had black hair and brown eyes. Thus all that great emotion I felt when I heard all those amazing things quickly vanished after she said I was going to marry some blond guy with blue eyes. After she spoke to me and I paid her, we never saw each other again.

But I surely never forgot about her or her words to my life. Then after this event, the devil took me to the beach one day and connected me to a bunch of strangers, who one of them told me that I was Jesus, and then he told everyone else about how Jesus was coming back as a woman. Then the devil possessed my mother and my sister, and in my most vulnerable moment of life, he made them tell me that we were the Holy Trinity. Then the devil took me to a church called Unity which is all about the New Age Movement, and he used someone to tell me that I was "everyone's mirror." In the middle of the emotional roller-coaster ride between these events and the moment where the devil told me that I was Lucifer in the flesh, I also went from thinking that I was Marilyn Monroe reincarnated or someone of great importance reincarnated. So like a brilliant master deceiver, Satan patiently groomed me and prepared me for this moment where a total stranger just randomly came to me and said to me that I was the devil.

The devil was working on my identity since I was a young child. Telling me things to build my ego large and then breaking my ego into tiny little pieces. He had taken me up so high to then be able to violently throw me down from there. He is smart, I must say. A genius! He is also very patient, as you can see. He does not seem to be in a hurry; he will work in a person's life an entire lifetime, to then crush him in the end to the fullest capacity.

So back to the moment where I was in my friend's apartment, alone with his friend who was a stranger to me. We were in the living room, while my friend was in the bathroom. After that guy said to me, "Desiree, do you know that you are the devil!" My mind went straight to my journals. I just saw page after page, flipping one by one, and I remembered many of the things I would spend hours writing all by myself. Many of my writings were very dark. I was exploring forbidden knowledge and with no guidance from the Lord, and the conviction about how sinful all that writing was hit me like a rock that day. I remembered something I wrote when I was in the seventh grade. I once wrote in dark pencil ink and big letters, "I hope everybody f—— dies!"

I was angry, and truthfully, I do not remember why I was mad. But I wrote that, and it was bad. In that split second of recollecting all those memories, when I remembered that specific page and that horrible statement that I put on paper with pencil, I automatically felt a sense of conviction of guilt. *Oh my god! I am the devil! I am the devil!* I thought. I thought that was why I would write so many strange supernatural things, I thought that was the reason I has so many dark supernatural experiences with demons, with ghosts, and with spirits. I thought that it was my fault that so many people in my life died. I thought that because of me writing that statement in the seventh grade, since I was the devil, I caused many people to die. I blamed myself for Michael's death, I blamed myself for the death of those who died prior to him dying. I blamed myself for my mother's cancer, etc.

It was all so clear now—I was Satan! All that happened in my mind in seconds after the guy told me that I was the devil, and instantly, I found myself bowed down to the fullest capacity, on the rug, in the middle of the living room. As I had my arms fully stretched forward all the way away from my head, and as I felt my face squashed totally upon the floor, I heard a very dark demonic voice coming out my mouth and saying to God, "I am sorry."

I sensed and visualized God standing on front me, looking down on me with great indignation, with His mighty arms crossed, as if extremely angry with me. This moment for me felt as if I truly died. I was horrified to the max! I have never felt so much fear in my entire life. I felt the inside of my chest completely depleted from anything good. It was a cold and deep void within me that lingered inside of me. I was paralyzed with fear. And since when I said that I was sorry to God, the sound of my voice was not mine but a demon's voice, I was that much more convinced that indeed I was the devil, and there was no way out to deny that fact. After God knows how long I was on my knees on that floor, I finally got up and went home, but after that day, I was never the same again. I felt that I died. Now I was not just worried about Michael coming back to life. I was now in Michael's same situation which I had envisioned him in. I felt as if I was dead and a ghost and living among the dead with no hope of coming back to normal. I wrote myself into Michael's shoes, and now I had no idea how to come out.

One day I was in my room, and I looked at myself in the mirror, and my face was completely demonic-looking. I was so scared of my own self. This, of course, only made me believe much more that I was Satan. Another day, I remember that I walked around the house, and I felt like a beast, not human at all. I felt like a wild animal. I don't really know how to explain it, but I was disgusted with myself. I was in a total state of panic. I could not sleep, smile, or even eat. I lost a lot of weight and looked pale and malnourished. All I could do was cry and walk around smoking cigarettes while asking God, "Why do I have to be the devil?" I asked over and over, "Why me? Why me?"

My poor father would just look at me in horror and not know how to help me. He did pray for my sanity to come back to me, but he was truly horrified. My mother and siblings were scared for me too, but my father was the one who saw the worst of it all. My mother was too ill, and my siblings were out of the house most of the time. My sister didn't even live with us anymore.

I used to lie in bed in a fetal position and just rock myself back and forth and wonder how hell was going to consume me. I used to read the book of Revelation in the Bible over and over again, just to understand what the future held for me as I was Satan and destined to be in the lake of fire forever. I would go outside and look at the sun and wonder if that was the lake of fire and visualize myself burning in it. I would look at myself in the mirror and scratch my skin mercilessly and tell myself over and over that I hated myself.

One day I decided I would end my life and not because I thought that if I killed myself, I would end my misery since I was sure that I would go to hell. I decided to kill myself after much thinking about just how much suffering I was causing my parents and my siblings. I thought that I did not deserve their love and care, and that if I killed myself, I would do them all a favor. I also thought that the world deserved for me to die; since I was the reason everyone was cursed, I should not be here. Thus I literally drank an entire brand-new bottle of Tylenol. I was terrified of going to hell, but I did it anyway! Luckily for me, the Lord didn't allow me to die. I did become sick, and the next morning, I could not see well. My vision was blurry. But thankfully, I did not die. And thankfully, I never tried killing myself ever again.

Well, now that killing myself was out of the question, I didn't know what to do with my life. I found myself absolutely hopeless. What was going to be my incentive to do anything good in this world if in the end, I would end up in hell? It made no sense. What good will it do for me to try to live a good life and be productive in anything if I was evil and the antichrist? I felt I was in a dead end. I didn't have anyone to turn to either. No one would understand and believe that I am the devil. Even though I was sure I was. It was so horrible! The fear was endless. I didn't smile or sleep for an entire year after this young man told me that I was the devil.

One day—I remember it was in the afternoon—I was lying down in my bed, and suddenly I was startled by something that took over my body. I was paralyzed by this entity and could not move at all. Then I suddenly heard in my right ear—really loud—the words *Jesus Christ, Jesus Christ, Jesus Christ* three times. It was loud and like if someone placed a speaker outside my ear, which caused my ear to vibrate with the sound of the words spoken. After it was over, I was released from the entity that had me paralyzed, and I walked out of my room and out of my house. I was walking once again like a zombie. I walked toward the Catholic Church next to my house. I don't know why I did that, but I did. Then it turned out that it was open, and there was no one inside of it. I walked in the church and went to the altar. I grabbed the Holy Communion that they had there and drank and ate from it. Then I was as if dead. I lay down on the altar, and once again, I could not move. My hands were then folded together on my chest, as you see when someone is in a casket at a funeral. All of this happened without me being in control of any of it. I was possessed. Then I eventually got out of my trance and walked back home.

Another day I came out of my home in the middle of the night, once again like a zombie. I was in my pajamas and barefoot. I began walking around the entire neighborhood, and I was feeling as if someone was holding a gun to my back. I was with my hands crossed in a prayerlike manner and felt much fear. I envisioned lots of ghosts or demons following me. I walked around the whole neighborhood like that and then came back home.

I used to get in serious fights with God during these days. I cursed Him for having created me. I used to tell Him that if He knew that I was going to become Satan, then why would He create me? I used to argue with Him all day long that it was not fair. I didn't want to spend eternity in hell. I blamed Him for my existence. I was angry with Him to the max. I used to also feel jealous of everyone in my life. I would see my brother sleeping, and I would envy that he can rest because I could not do that. I forgot what sleeping felt like. I would see my mother, and even though she was dying of cancer, I envied that she can still go to heaven someday, and I could not. I even envied my little Yorkshire, I wished that I could be her instead of me. I wished over and over that I was never born. I desired with my most inner being to enter back into my mother's womb.

I thought about all the souls who were already in hell and thought that perhaps this was the way they all felt right now. I was convinced that my experience, even though I still was alive on earth, was no different than those in hell. Psychologically this is what they are experiencing. They have no hope. They are full of anger, fear, confusion, sadness, and regret. They hate God for their existence, and they desire with all their might that they had never been born, but there they are, existing. Existing to feel nothing but pain and torment! Truly a nightmare!

By now I forgot all about Michael. Now all my attention and focus were on me. I could not take my eyes off myself, and I grew to hate myself more and more each day. My beloved mother finally passed away, and I was too numb to even cry for her. I did not go to her funeral either. I really just wished I would die too and have the privilege to be saved. But that was never going to happen because I was the devil, and there is no repentance for Satan. He must pay for what he did, and it turned out that I was him!

# CHAPTER 8

·❦·

# Born-Again in Christ

It was not long after experiencing those bizarre events that I ended up losing my mind for good. I was Baker Acted one day by the police after freaking out on my parents and going crazy on them while playing my Nine Inch Nails CD full blast in our living room and singing their songs from the top of my lungs. I knocked out one of the cops that came into my home and left in handcuffs to the Jackson Mental Health Hospital in Miami. There I fought with five or six different men for a while until they injected me with a tranquilizer and strapped me onto a bed for an entire night. I was then diagnosed with chronic schizophrenia, and they gave me a bunch of insane medications, such as lithium, Zoloft, and other ones that were making me act like a true zombie. I remember I became slow and sluggish and was just not myself anymore.

I went in and out of the mental institutions several times throughout that year. Sometimes it was involuntarily. One time I saw myself so out of control, I volunteered to get in there. My parents had no idea how to help me or what to do. A lot of bad things were also happening to me during these days because I was surrounded by evildoers, and they were taking advantage of me since I was so drugged up by the psychiatric medications and since I also was so intensely possessed and did not know what I was doing, nor did I have control of my own body.

One day I almost died from smoking weed out of a bomb pipe. I had been drinking beers and alcohol and then went on to smoke weed, and mixing that with my psychiatric medications was a formula for disaster. My heart began speeding, and I truly felt that I was going to have a heart attack. I went to my father's room and told him how I felt and told him I was surely going to die that day. But my father had no idea that I was smoking weed and drinking alcohol that day, and he just thought I was talking crazy, as I usually sounded, so he brushed it off as if it was not serious and began joking to me, saying that I was not going to die that day and that I was going to grow old, and he began acting as an old lady and making fun and saying that I was going to take care of him when he was really old.

Even though I knew he was kidding, I felt no comfort. I was sure I was going to die and that was the day I was going to enter hell and abandon all hope for good. I ended up having a seizure in my father's bed, but he never noticed. But to my surprise the next day, I was not in hell or dead. But I did learn that day that my psychiatric medications were just as dangerous as all the other drugs I was using, and that surely, I would be able to die solely on them.

I lost all sense of reality. I only thought that I was the devil and that I was going to burn in hell forever. That was all I thought. I also thought that demons were trying to kill me and that they were after me. Being in the institution only made me get worse. Everyone there was just as crazy as me. Even though I was nineteen years old, I was placed in the forty-year-old-and-older section. They said I was too messed up to be with my same-age group. I ended up getting addicted to smoking cigarettes in this place because the meds that they were giving me were making me feel really accelerated sometimes, and I saw that smoking cigarettes would calm me down.

I met a woman in there who was pregnant, and she told me that her baby's father was a Satanist, and that in her dreams, he would appear to her and try to kill the baby in her womb. She was truly scared and tormented and afraid of falling asleep. I was also afraid of falling asleep. I believed that if I slept, the demons would come and take my soul and that I would die. Thus I would force myself to not fall asleep. I used to pace back and forth through the hallways of this hospital and be super anxious the whole time. I felt like a wild animal in a cage. I longed to get out of there more than anything else. I felt trapped and extremely desperate for sunlight and fresh air. I once even felt that I could not breathe, and I was out of breath. I think it had to do with the fact that I was smoking way too many cigarettes, and my lungs were beginning to fail me. I begged the doctors on my knees to let me go outside. But they would not. I was truly tortured in this place.

We all noticed that they would overmedicate us to keep us sedated and calm. The workers were mean-spirited too. They used to manhandle me all the time and sort of provoke me to anger. I guess working in there all day long must make someone turn mad themselves. Because sometimes the staff looked and acted just as insane as the patients. I never learned to appreciate nature and the outdoors more than when being locked up in this place.

After going in and out throughout the year, they finally gave the verdict to my father. They told him that I would never be normal or healed again. They told my father that I was a threat to society and to myself and that I should stay locked up in their mental facility for the rest of my life. They also told him that I could never get off from my medications 'cause if I did, I would only get worse. How convenient was all that for the pharmaceutical industry! They were setting themselves up to collect a lot of money from having me in there for the rest of my life and consuming their medications. Thankfully my father rejected this sentence upon my life and chose to sign an affidavit saying that he would take full responsibility for my life. He then took me back home and continued to administer to me the medications, but he refused to have them lock me up for life. Thank God for my father, he saved me from the medical cartel that rules upon America. I would have rotten in there as they would have gotten richer from my pain and misery!

During this season of my life, everyone got away from me. Everyone except this one guy that knew me since we were young. I will name him Frank (not his real name). This guy was around my life since elementary, but I did not really get to know him well until this season of my life. He was different. He looked different too. He was a white male, my same age, and had blond hair and blue eyes. However, he had a lot of tattoos. He had a tattoo of a teardrop under his eye. He had a tattoo of a spider on his arm, a tattoo of a spiderweb around his nipple, a tattoo of a scorpion on his neck. His appearance was a bit shocking, to say the least. He was an artist. He liked to write dark poetry and was good at it. He liked to listen to heavy metal and rock and roll. He played the guitar and sang. He also liked to drink and do drugs.

Ironically this guy was the only one who stuck around me throughout these days. I was so lonely and scared that I found myself leaning on him for support. But he was not well in the head either. He definitely had serious emotional and mental issues. But no one was crazier than me! I had confided in him everything going on in my head. He also read a lot of my journals. He found them fascinating. He was a writer; thus he was appreciative of my writing style. I was a dark writer as well. Just not into the poetry thing. He would write poetry about me and my life that would painfully pierce my ears and wound my heart with crafty words of truth and horror. His mother became a born-again Christian and an ex-girlfriend of his also became a born-again Christian, and they both would evangelize him all the time. He would tell me that I was not crazy like everyone else was saying. He would tell me that what I had were demons and that I needed to be liberated from the demons by the power of Jesus Christ. Those words comforted me greatly for short moments. But then I would be reminded, in my mind, that I was the devil, the antichrist, and that for me, salvation and liberation was not possible.

He ended up introducing me to his ex-girlfriend who was now a Christian. She was beautiful in every way. She would speak the Gospel of Christ to me, and it was amazing. But sadly, I would not be able to receive her words for my life because I always thought I was the devil. They took me to her church, and I met more Christians, and they prayed a lot for me and talked to me about the Word of God. I would listen but feel tortured inside of me. I even would hear curse words to God as they were preaching, which would only convince me that I was Lucifer even so more and that I was just pure evil and that I could never be saved.

Frank was sort of schizophrenic himself. One moment he was really nice to me and trying to encourage me, and the next moment he would look at me really angrily, slap my thighs as we sat next to each other, and tell me straight to my face, "You are going to pay, Lucifer!"

One moment he was assuring me that I had demons, and the next moment he was assuring me that I was the devil. He would change back and forth from personalities as if he was possessed himself. When he would get mean-spirited toward me, it was the worst feeling. He would really convince me that I was the devil. His poetry was darker and darker too with each passing day. And there was no stopping him from reading it to me. My relationship with him gradually became very toxic. He would get drunk and get really mean toward me. But he was all I had at the time, and even though he was the one person who would scare me the most, he was also the only person who would make me feel better at times. It was simply insane!

Most of the people in my life did not approve of my friendship with this guy. They all knew that I was mentally ill and that he seemed to have some type of mental issue as well. But there was nothing they could do. I became inseparable from this guy. He was my toxic crutch and the only link between Christ and me. Incredibly he was the one person that showed me the path to Christ. He was a double-edged sword. He confessed to me, after a while of being together, that he and his friend, who was also a longtime friend of mine, they had planned to do something bad to me. They had planned to get the cross that was placed on the side of the road where Michael had died, and they were going to submerge it with gasoline and throw the cross inside the window of my room and set my room on fire! He told me they went as far as ripping that cross out of the grass where it was, and they came over to my house at nighttime, ready with the gasoline and the matches. He confessed that they saw my father in the garage and that after much thinking about it, they ended up changing their minds and not doing it at all. They went back home. I was horrified! But I can totally see them trying to bring that plan into fruition because that is how crazy some of these people I used to know were. I do not know why Frank decided to confess that to me either, but he did.

Moreover, I was getting evangelized over and over by all these Christians, but even though I would try hard to believe that I could receive forgiveness and salvation, it was to no avail. I would get on my knees on the carpet of my home and beg God to forgive me, but then I would hear the same things in my mind that would block me from receiving His forgiveness. I heard myself cussing God over and over, and I would then feel ashamed and guilty and unworthy of His mercy and forgiveness. It was an overwhelming battle between the demons, making me think I was the one cussing God in my mind and then me trying to receive His forgiveness in the midst of all those evil thoughts. I had so many different voices speaking horrible things to me in my mind that were tormenting me to the point that I would pull my hairs and pray that I can get silence. I wanted the voices to stop, but they were only getting worse by the day. It was as if I had a radio turned on in a bunch of different channels all at the same time and speaking negative things.

In this church that I was attending, they evangelized me a lot, but I was still very captive. One day, they had a huge event in Fort Myers, and they paid for me to go there. It was a huge conference with a lot of Christians. I had never gone to anything like that. I went and it was incredible. Thousands of Christians were there, and the worship and praise were intense. I was able to really feel the presence of God in this place. I ended up going on my knees and crying for hours as everyone sang. The pastor of my church said he had never witnessed anyone crying like I did that day. I had not cried for like a whole year or even more. I remember thinking of my mom during that long cry. I had not cried for her at all since she passed away. I also felt angered toward God for taking my mother away from me, and that day it was released through tears.

There was an evangelist called Angel Baez from Puerto Rico as the main guest speaker. He was amazing. I will never forget this man. He chose ten people, out of thousands, to give a personal prophetic word. I was one of them. He approached me and began to say, "Thus says the Lord, I chose you, you did not choose Me, many things that have happened in your life were never My will, but because of your wrong choices, they happened."

He said to me that one day, I will hear the voice of God as he heard it. He said to me that he saw that I had a lot of writings in my home and that God was telling him to tell me to burn those writings because the devil had authority with my life through them and that as long as I kept those journals, the devil would keep me in bondage. I was blown away by all the things he told me, and I could not believe how he knew about my journals. Then I kept asking him, "How in the world do you hear the voice of God?" I was so curious.

He said that he cannot explain it, but that he knew for certain that one day, I would know the voice of God the same way he knew it. He then was led by the Holy Spirit to give me his book, written by Watchman Nee, called *The Spiritual Man*. This book ended up being the best book I have ever read besides the Bible. It took me years to read it, but I ended up reading it more than five times, and it helped me to overcome so many things and get so close to God. I highly recommend all my readers to buy and study this book. In this book, you will learn how to overcome sin and walk in the Spirit and not in the flesh. This book also teaches the full Gospel. Most churches teach half a gospel. Sadly most churches are in extremes. The liberal churches only know to teach about forgiveness and grace and love, and the legalist churches only know to teach about condemnation, rules and regulations, and judgment. In this book, you will learn the full Gospel and see the balance of both extremes and understand how it is that God is both love and a consuming fire.

I was completely changed after this event. The best thing about the whole event was that it helped me to believe that I was not the devil, I was not the antichrist of the world, and I was able to be saved. Finally after going back and forth in my mind between thinking I was forgiven and then thinking I could not be forgiven, I finally received forgiveness and learned that perhaps I was not the enemy of human-ity after all. It took two years for that moment to arrive. I had envied everyone I knew because of thinking that they all had the option to receive eternal life, but I did not have that option. I remember wish-ing to even be a girl that was paralyzed for life; she was someone that

I knew, and when I saw her in that painful condition that she was in, because of a terrible car accident that she had, I still thought she was much better than me. I still wished to be in her shoes than in mine. There was nothing worse in my mind than to not be saved. There is nothing worse in this life than to die and go to hell, and that is still my mentality to this day.

I rather be the most poor person on the planet, the most mistreated and rejected and hurt human being in this world but end up in heaven, than to enjoy all the riches and wealth of this world and to be famous and live a luxurious glamorous lifestyle to then die and find myself lost in flames of fires and in a bed of worms eating me alive for eternity. It truly is a privilege to be saved, and I am truly thankful for all the pain and sacrifice that our Lord Jesus Christ/ Yeshua Hamashiach went through to give us eternal life.

**For God so loved the world, that He gave His only begotten Son, that whosoever believeth in Him should not perish, but have everlasting life. (JOHN 3:16)**

**For what shall it profit a man, if he shall gain the whole world, and lose his own soul? Or what shall a man give in exchange for his soul? Whosoever therefore shall be ashamed of Me and My words in this adulterous and sinful generation; of him also shall the Son of man be ashamed, when he cometh in the glory of His father with the holy angels. (MARK 8:36–38)**

**Where their worm dieth not, and the fire is not quenched. And if thy foot offend thee, cut it off: it is better for thee to enter halt into life, than having two feet to be cast into hell, into the fire that never shall be quenched: Where their worm dieth not, and the fire is not quenched. And if thine eye offend thee,**

**pluck it out: It is better for thee to enter into the kingdom of God with one eye, than having two eyes to be cast into hell fire: Where their worm dieth not, and the fire is not quenched. (MARK 9:44–48)**

# CHAPTER 9

―――――― ⌗ ――――――

# My Liberation from Demons

**Behold, I give you unto you power to tread on serpents
and scorpions and over all the power of the enemy:
and nothing shall by any means hurt you.**

**—LUKE 10:19**

When I came back from the Fort Myers Christian conference, I grabbed all my book bags filled with journals from years of writing, and I burned them all in a barbecue in my backyard. It was not easy for me to do that. I really loved those journals. But I knew that it was the right thing for me to do.

Then I was brought into a new church where they practice liberation of demons. In this church I was delivered from a legion of demons. Then I was trained on how to liberate other people from demons as well. I was trained in everything that had to do with spiritual warfare, intercession, and deliverance. The pastors of this church had been in the occult all their lives, and then they were saved and trained to deliver others and to train them to also deliver others. After my liberation, I threw away all of Michael's clothes, his chain that he gave me, and anything that reminded me of him. Even though it was painful to do that, and I felt guilty to let him go, I knew that if I did not do that, I would never get healed either. I had to let him go and not look back. I was tired of the torment that I had endured, and I was determined to get better. I was also convinced to the maximum that we do not fight against flesh and blood but against demons, and that I needed to be self-disciplined if I intended to defeat them. Because they were powerful. More powerful than me, that is for sure! I knew that if I did not obey God fully and learn to walk in the Spirit, they would return and kill me.

**Finally, my brethren, be strong in the Lord, and in the power of His might. Put on the whole armor of God, that ye may be able to stand against the wiles of the devil. For we wrestle not against flesh and blood, but against principalities, against powers, against the rulers of the darkness of this world, against spiritual wickedness in high places. Wherefore take unto you the whole armor of God, that ye may be able to withstand in the evil day, and having done all, to stand. Stand therefore, having your loins girt about with truth, and having on the breastplate of righteousness; And your feet shod with the preparation of the gospel of peace; Above all, taking the shield of faith, wherewith ye shall be able to quench all the fiery darts of the wicked. And take the helmet of salvation, and the sword of Sprit, which is the word of God: Praying always with all prayer and supplication in the Spirit, and watching thereunto with all perseverance and supplication for all saints. (EPHESIANS 6:10–18)**

**And these signs shall follow them that believe; In My name they shall cast out devils, they shall speak with new tongues; and if they drink any deadly thing, it shall not hurt them; they shall lay hands on the sick, and they shall recover. (MARK 16:17–18)**

After my liberation, I also never took any more psychiatric medications and never went back to any mental institution nor did I ever have any new mental breakdowns or schizophrenic episodes. It's been over twenty years since I was liberated from demons, and even though the pharmaceutical industry had sentenced me to a lifetime under their medical care, taking toxic medications for the rest of my life that were going to kill me, and even though they said to my father that I was supposed to live the rest of my life in their mental health facilities because I was a threat to society and myself and that I was never going to be cured from this, I am healed! By the grace and power of the Lord Jesus Christ/Yeshua Hamashiach, all those doctors were *dead wrong*!

> **But He was wounded for our transgressions, He was bruised for our iniquities: the chastisement of our peace was upon Him; and with His stripes we are healed. (ISAIAH 53:5)**

I also graduated from Miami Dade College in 2010 with an associate degree in psychology, and I also graduated from The Institute of King Jesus in Miami, Florida, as a Christian minister. I was going to study and get my bachelor's in psychology in Liberty University, and I studied online for one semester, but I was not able to finish for circumstances that were outside of my control, and then when I tried to go back, the Lord told me that it was not His will because the enemy has infiltrated almost all of His churches and schools, and they have twisted the Scriptures and changed the Gospel, and then He asked me to stay at home and study His Word alone and with His Holy Spirit only. Thus after attending church regularly since 1997, in 2012 He pulled me out of all churches and all schools and showed me just how much violence they have done unto His Word and true Gospel.

I have, in more detail, what I learned with the Lord as my only Teacher in my first book, titled *We Were Deceived*. We are living in the end of days, and Satan is not wasting his time. The Bible is full of warnings about not allowing anyone to deceive us during these days and that many were going to rise and say that they were Christ, but they were imposters.

**For many shall come in My Name, saying, I am Christ, and shall deceive many. (MATTHEW 24:5)**

Deception is everywhere, and the pharmaceutical industry is one of the most powerful tools that Satan has used to keep people in bondage. Schizophrenia is not a disease. It's a legion of demons. And I am proof of that! I must say, I do not believe every mental problem is a demon. I do know that sometimes, someone can be mentally ill from having a brain tumor. Thus everyone seeking a mental health diagnosis should have a brain scan done first to see if there is a tumor causing the symptoms. Sometimes a physical injury in the brain or a seizure can also cause mental illness, which this will also be shown in a brain scan. But sadly, most doctors do not do brain scans when diagnosing their patients, and I believe this is a huge mistake. They are trained to medicate people and not to cure them. I am so sorry to say, but it is the truth. Many doctors have come out and said this truth, but they are then persecuted and even stripped from their medical license.

Moreover, diet has a lot to do with mental health. If someone is always eating toxic foods, they are most likely deteriorating in their minds as time passes by. The vaccines, chemtrails, fluoride in our waters, the pesticides in our foods, the high frequencies in our music and TVs, the radiation from Wi-Fi and other technologies are all factors that also contribute to our mental decline. Lastly the traumas, rejections, lack of affection from people, mistreatments, neglect, and abuse are also part of how the mind can become mentally ill. Thus there are many reasons why a person may be experiencing mental illness, and there are things in our lives that we can do in the natural to help ourselves get better, such as detoxing our bodies from the vaccines, foods, water, and air we breathe through organic food and the right supplements and vitamins, and drinking water without fluoride in it. We can also decrease the number of hours we spend behind the screens or listen to sounds that have good frequencies. There are frequencies in sounds that literally damage our minds.

Do your research on the sound frequencies and ask yourselves, if there is not a conspiracy against humanity, then why in the world did they change the frequencies in our mainstream music to 440hz when it's known that that this frequency damages our brains? Instead of giving us 432hz which heals us and edifies us. Everything in the mainstream media, including the churches, are all under their control and designed for our destruction. We can also stay away from entertainment filled with sin, such as sexual perversion, foul language, violence, hate, discord, and all those things that cause anxiety and bad toxins in our bodies. And obviously, learn to walk in the Spirit and not in the flesh, learn to serve God and not the enemy because if we serve Satan, we are most certainly going to become mentally ill at one point in our lives.

> **But it shall come to pass, if thou wilt not hearken unto the voice of the Lord thy God, to observe to do all his commandments and His statutes which I command thee this day; that all these curses shall come upon thee, and overtake thee: The Lord will smite thee with madness, and blindness, and astonishment of heart. (DEUTERONOMY 28:15, 28)**

In conclusion, I do not think everything in mental illness is a demon, but I do believe that demons take advantage of whatever the mind is put through to take control of it. The mind is the battlefield where this spiritual battle is waged, and the demons are always looking for a loophole to be able to control it. They do not care of how to get the person's mind, whether through a physical injury, a tumor, a trauma, poison in our bodies, etc. It does not matter to demons what the cause of the open door is, they only care to find an open door, and they will go in. Many of the pharmaceutical medications give the demons the legal right to take control of the person's mind even more so. Therefore, you can see that many of these mentally ill people never get better and take these medications for a lifetime. Those medications are not designed to cure anyone but to keep them in captivity.

> **And when He was come to the other side into the country of the Gergesenes, there met Him two possessed with devils, coming out of the tombs, exceeding fierce, so that no man might pass by that way. And, behold, they cried out, saying, What have we to do with Thee, Jesus, thou Son of God? Art thou come hither to torment us before the time? And there was a good way off from them an herd of many swine feeding. So the devils besought Him, saying, If thou cast us out, suffer us to go away into the herd of swine. And He said unto them, Go. And when they were come out, they went into the herd of swine: and, behold, the whole herd of swine ran violently down a steep place into the sea, and perished in the waters. And they that kept them fled, and went their ways into the city, and told everything and what was befallen to the possessed of the devils. And, behold, the whole city came out to meet Jesus: and when they saw Him, they besought Him that He would depart out of their coasts. (MATTHEW 8:28–34)**

In 2008, I had a bizarre experience. I was on my way home from a Christian event. I was with a man who had a prophetic mantle from the Lord, and he was prophetically anointed. We had gone to this event together. We were enthusiastic about God during the drive home because of how awesome that event had been. We were praying in tongues and just seeking God as I drove back home. We had a CD playing powerful anointing worship, and the presence of God in my car was tangible.

After a while of driving and praying, I heard the guy prophesy to me, saying that God was saying to me that He knew how much I hurt for the death of my friend Michael. He said that He saw all the tears I shed for him and that He knew I never really got over his death and that it still pains me. He said that because of that, He was going to do something. Then I saw the guy change his demeanor, and he looked horrified, and then I heard him say over and over again, "Oh no, I don't want to go there, please, don't take me there..."

I was quite confused as to why he was saying that, to say the least. He had been praying the whole time with his eyes closed, and it was just so weird that he said those words. After he said those words, though, he looked as if he fainted in the front seat of my car next to me. I was scared by now because he also seemed to be having a seizure; I did not know what was happening to him. Then shortly after, he began to act as if he got possessed. He began to repeat the words, "I feel peace, I feel peace, I feel peace," over and over again. It seemed to me that he must have said those words hundreds of times. Then he sat up and looked as if something was on front of him, and he said, "It's okay, you are in my presence now!"

The way I heard this made me imagine God saying this through him, but I did not know why or to whom God was saying that to? But then I saw the guy had one of his arms as if paralyzed. I think it was his left arm. He looked as if he was hurt. Physically hurt. Then after I had pulled over to the side of the road and waited to see what was happening, the guy came back to himself and told me, "Desiree, I cannot move my arm, and your friend Michael was pulled out of hell!" Then he told me that I would have three confirmations to let me know that it really did happen.

Well, it turned out to be that the part of the body that was paralyzed in this guy that I was with happened to be the same part of the body that was mostly hit by the car that hit Michael. It took a while for this guy to be able to get back motion in his arm. Then I had more than three dreams with Michael after that event. The first dream I had was that I was in a two-story house on the second floor, and I saw Michael going up the stairs and then coming toward me, and he gave me a hug, then he said that he knew that I truly loved him and that now he was going to be serving me and the government (which I knew he meant the kingdom of God).

Then months later, I had another dream where he came up and gave me a little paper and told me that this was his new address. Then I opened the paper to read it, and it was Ezekiel 1:26. I did not know what this verse said, so I looked it up.

**And above the firmament that was over their heads was the likeness of a throne, as the appearance of a sapphire stone: and upon the likeness of the throne was the likeness as the appearance of a man above upon it. (Ezekiel 1:26)**

Thus Michael lives in heaven, in front of the throne of God and in His presence.

I had more dreams of him where he gave me prophetic messages and other dreams that were personal.

In 2013, I had been discipling a man who served Satan in the Illuminati for over twenty years. I met this man in the school of the church I was attending. As I taught him many things about God and my testimony, he also taught me many things about his life in the Illuminati and his testimony. This man was discipled in jailed by a fallen angel. He mentored me in many things concerning the plans of the enemy for humanity in the future. He also confirmed to me that this conspiracy against humanity is a real deal. He was taught to hate Christians and Jews the most. He also exposed to me that he would meet with some of the leaders and principals of a very known and prestigious Christian university, and they were all meeting together as Satanists. This was when I was confirmed that I should not go back to study for my bachelor's in any Christian university. Well, during this time, I had a dream with Michael.

In this dream, he came up to me and this man whom I was discipling in the Lord and handed me a blueprint. Then he told me that the guy I was mentoring was going to help me vindicate his death and bring his killers to justice.

In the beginning of 2020, I had a dream that Michael came to me and said that by the end of this year, we will see an asteroid impact.

After my journey with Michael and Jesus and the demons, I learned many people have died and gone to hell and come back to tell us about it.[14] In God's mercy, He allows these people to go there, whether in real time or after they die, so that they may tell us the truth about the afterlife when we are not saved. I believe that Michael's death may not be in vain if I tell his story the way I know it. And yes, indeed the guy that was in the Illuminati taught me so many things that I needed to know. Unfortunately he passed away a couple of years ago, but he really was a huge honor and a blessing to me, and the things he taught me are priceless.

Furthermore, I also saw a movie called *Fallen*, from 1998, with actor Denzel Washington. I was blown away with the similarities that were displayed in this movie and what I experienced with Michael after he died. I asked myself if it's possible that other people go through similar experiences with people who die as I did? Obviously this movie proves that, indeed, what I went through is something that others have already experienced as well. Because Hollywood is always showing us truth that is hidden in plain sight. Most of their films are either the truth about the spiritual world we do not see or the truth about evil schemes being done in secret or the plans of the devil for our future, or their films are mocking the sacred things of God so as to desensitize us to the holiness of God.

In 2015, the Lord gave me a dream. In this dream, I saw a TV and a surfer. The surfer was surfing a huge wave, and on his way down from the wave, he ended up coming out of the screen and into my living room in front of me. Then I saw a guy skiing in snow. Just as the surfer, he was going down from a high mountain, and at the end of the mountain on the way down, he popped out of the TV screen and into my living room. He was standing right in front

---

[14] www.testimoniesofhell.com.

of me. When I awoke, the Holy Spirit revealed to me that the time had come where we will see the movies become our reality! Many of our favorite movies are nothing but the plans the enemy has for humanity.

# CHAPTER 10

## The Psychiatry Scam

There is a documentary in YouTube titled *The Drugging of Our Children*. It is one hour and forty-three minutes long. This is what it says in the description box:

> In the absence of any objective medical tests to determine who has ADD or ADHD, doctors rely in part on standardized assessments and the impressions of teachers and guardians while they administer leave little room for other causes or aggravating factors, such as diet, or environment. Hence, diagnosing a child or adolescent with ADD or ADHD is often the outcome, although no organic basis for either disease has yet to be clinically proven. Psychiatrists may then prescribe psychotropic drugs for the children without first making it clear to parents that these medications can have severe side-effects including insomnia, loss of appetite, headaches, psychotic symptoms and even potentially fatal adverse reactions, such as cardia arrhythmia. And yet, despite these dangers, many school systems actually work with the government agencies to force parents to drug their children, threatening those who refuse with

the prospect of having their children taken from
the home unless they cooperate.

This is one of the best documentaries exposing the truth about
the psychiatric industry I have ever seen. Please take time to watch
the entire thing. Here you will learn to see that the depopulation
agenda is indeed truly happening and how the elite truly took over
our education system and are using it to make our children drug
addicts since a very young age. Mental illness is their business, and
they truly have no intention in curing it. Instead they work relentlessly to make us all mentally ill as early as possible in life. It literally
is a medical mafia!

Moreover, American psychiatrist Leon Eisenberg, who was
known as the father of ADHD, stated in his last interview before his
death that ADHD is a fictitious disease.

There is a psychiatrist named Dr. Peter Breggin who has a
YouTube channel dedicated to expose the truth about the things that
are wrong with our psychiatric industry. He also has written several
books. I will transcribe one of his videos, *Psychiatric Drugs Are More
Dangerous Than You Ever Imagined.*

"This is Dr. Peter Breggin, and this is another of my simple
truths about psychiatry, and the subject today is that psychiatric
drugs are much, much more dangerous than you've ever, ever been
led to believe by the doctors who are prescribing them. I genuinely
believe that if most people knew how dangerous this psychiatric
drugs really were, most people will never start on them, and I also
believe that if most prescribers had even the faintest idea how dangerous they were, they would stop prescribing them. Well, how is it that
so many people could be ignorant about psychiatric drugs? Well, the
truth is because they all are getting their information from the drug
companies. I mean, when was the last time you saw a car company
leap up to tell people way in advance that they have had some deaths
on the road from their bad brakes? When was the last time that car
companies would admit culpability and say yes, our accelerators are
sticking and running people down?

"Well, I can tell you that drug companies are even worse. They go to all kinds of extremes to avoid letting you know and to avoid letting your doctor know how dangerous the drugs are. I know this because I have been a medical expert in dozens of lawsuits against drug companies. I have looked inside drug companies and seen what they are really doing. I was appointed by a court in Indiana to be the scientific expert of over 150 lawsuits against Ely Lily. Suits alleging that the drug Prozac can cause violence, suicide, mayhem, mania psychosis, so I know what goes inside. I know as much as anyone about how dangerous the drugs are.

"So let me just give you a little brief outline of material you can find in the first half of my book *Psychiatric Drug Withdrawal*. Obviously the second half is intended to help you come outside of psychiatric drugs because it can be very dangerous to come off drugs. It's dangerous sometimes, even more than starting the drugs. Let's take a look at the stimulants that you may be taking as a college student or as a parent that you may be giving to your children. Follow-up studies on people who were started on stimulants as children show that they have shrinkage of brain tissue, measurable on brain scans. They have reduced height and weight. They have been incarcerated more often than other people. They go into mental hospitals more often. Their suicide rate is increased. Every single one of these facts, documented by follow-up studies, of what happens to you if you get started on stimulants and one particular well-done study is the rate of cocaine abuse, is greater when you become a young man or woman. If you have been put on stimulants as a child, that is because the stimulant drugs are so similar to cocaine in their effects.

"All right, let's look at another group. The sedatives and sleeping pills that you are taking like Sonata, Ambien, and any one of the prescription sedatives use for sleep, we now got two or more studies showing that they shorten life span. You can google them. You can google practically anything that I am telling you. But you get more accurate direct data from *Psychiatric Drug Withdrawal*. Now what about the benzodiazepines, the tranquilizers like Xanax, Valium, etc.? They are very addictive. Did you know that people taking Xanax and controlled clinical trials, after a mere six weeks, a large percentage of them cannot get off from them? After a mere six weeks, they become addicts to Xanax. Great for the drug business, great for the psychiatrists or prescriber who just wants to write prescriptions; terrible for you!

"These drugs now, several studies show, like Xanax and others, they cause shrinkage of the brain too. Coming off from them can also be an absolute horror story! It can be harder to get off those drugs than to get off opioids. They leave people who try to come off from them with horrendous insomnia, horrendous anxiety, aches and pains in their bodies, such pain in their feet that they can't stand up. That is just too much pain, weird feelings throughout their body. And then the realization as they come off that their minds are not working as well. That they have memory loss from the past, they have more trouble learning.

"Now I know this is hard, you know it's hard for me to even talk about it. But it's really time to face up just how dangerous these drugs are. So we have looked at the stimulants and the sleeping pills and the benzos, now the antipsychotic drugs which are not really antipsychotic drugs, they are just lobotomizing drugs that have been given to some people for sleep. All of these drugs are very damaging to the brain, they virtually wreck a part of the brain called the basal ganglia. They cause a dreadful disorder tardive dyskinesia. I have a done a video on the simple truth of tardive dyskinesia. They are shortening the lifespan. We have evidence of people who are put on a lifetime dose of this antipsychotic drugs for whatever reason, whether it's to help you sleep at night or because you are hallucinating or have a lot problems, twenty-year shortened life span. And we know some of the ways life spans are being shortened because, especially these newer antipsychotics, so-called second generation, very typical antipsychotics, they are even worse than the older ones and causing a metabolic syndrome. People get obese, they get diabetes, they get pancreatitis, they get elevated cholesterol, blood pressure is off, and then since the drugs also cause heart arrhythmia, and in combination with all the other comes more cardiovascular damage, that is one of the way in which people are having shorten life spans on these drugs.

"The mood stabilizer, so-called, which is just emotionally flattening drugs, most of them were originally antiseizure drugs. The one we studied for the longest time is lithium. If you stay on lithium for a lifetime, as your doctor tells you to, you are at grave risk of severe mental problems in the form of memory difficulties, learning new materials, conducting your affairs like you have your whole life.

"None of these drugs are good for your brain. All of these drugs are bad for your brain, and it should not be of any surprise. These drugs are producing multiple biochemical imbalances in brains that do not have any biochemical imbalance, until a physician or prescriber puts you on these drugs. Now please, do not just stop taking your drugs. Because the ultimate tragedy is that coming off those drugs can be catastrophe, people can become suicidal, they can get violent, and some of the drugs you can get seizures, some of the drugs can drop your blood pressure if you are coming off, so you know, get good information. I put everything I know about it in the book *Psychiatric Drug Withdrawal.* Get good information, get some good clinical supervision, work with your family or friends. The shorter time you are on psychiatric drugs, almost certainly means that you will have a better quality of life."

That was one of his many insightful videos. Peter R. Breggin, MD, has been called "the conscience of psychiatry" for his many decades of successful efforts to reform the mental health field. His scientific and educational work has provided drugs and ECT, and leads the way in promoting more caring and effective therapies. He is the author of dozens of scientific articles and more than twenty books, including the best seller *Talking Back to Prozac* (1994, with Ginger Breggin), *Medication Madness: The Role of Psychiatric Drugs in Cases of Violence, Suicide and Crime* (2008), and *Psychiatric Drug Withdrawal: A Guide for Prescribers, Therapists, Patients and Their Families* (2013). Dr. Breggin's videos include current commentary and education about psychiatry as well as important historical footage.[15]

---

[15] Breggin.com.

Please consider learning from this man if you are someone who is suffering from mental illness or if you know someone who is suffering from mental illness. Also learn the Bible and walk by faith and learn to be led by the Holy Spirit so that He may lead you to complete healing of your mind and emotions. I can attest to everything this doctor said as being 100 percent truth. I was once very mentally ill, and I was institutionalized in an asylum. I can attest that staying in that hospital was only going to ensure that I would never get healed and that I would die young. The way they treated me, the way they drugged me, the way they fed me in that place was going to take me to the grave very early in life, and they were going to laugh all the way to the bank as I drowned in their toxic medications. It's time the people are awakened to the truth of our health-care system here in America. Many other countries outside of the US are aware of the scam going on in here, yet it seems that most Americans are too distracted and sedated to realize what they have done to so many generations. Many doctors are waking up from all types of fields and blowing the whistle. I am hoping that many more would come, and together we can save lives and stop the crimes that the elite are committing against humanity in the name of health care!

There is an article in Science Daily[16] titled "Cannabis use in adolescence linked to schizophrenia."

> Psychoactive compound in cannabis may trigger the brain disorder, researchers say. April 26, 2017. American Friends of Tel Aviv University. A new study points to cannabis as a trigger for schizophrenia. The research finds that smoking pot or using cannabis in other ways during adolescence may serve as a catalyst for schizophrenia in individuals already susceptible to the disorder.

I just wanted to mention this article before I close this chapter because it turns out that I had never expressed any schizophrenic

---

[16] https://www.sciencedaily.com/releases/2017/04/170426124305.htm.

symptoms up to when I was nineteen years old and shortly after I began experimenting with marijuana. Thus I believe this study to be true because I had my first schizophrenic episode shortly after I started to smoke weed, and they were getting worse and worse each time I smoked weed. Thus legalizing marijuana may also not be in humanity's best interest. It might just be one more thing they are doing to depopulate us instead.

# CHAPTER 11

—— ❦ ——

# The Link between the LGBT Community and the Pharmaceutical Industry

I am going to transcribe a video from a man named Walt Heyer. He is an author and public speaker who formerly identified as transgender. He is the author of several books, and through his website, SexChangeRegret.com, Heyer raises public awareness about those who regret gender change and the tragic consequences suffered as a result. He shared his story and warned against implementing radical hormonal and surgical interventions for gender dysphoric children.

And it begins like this:

"Well, thank you, Ryan, for putting this panel together. It's a topic that everybody brings different perspective to, and if you haven't come into the conclusion yet, this is very complicated, and it has many different layers. And I am not sure that we are going to be able to get to all of them, but we definitely need to open up a discussion about it.

"I lived eight years as a female, named Lory Jensen, after undergoing gender reassignments surgery in April of 1983. I started as a four-year-old kid in 1944, so I am bringing into this conversation today seventy-four years of firsthand experience in some way, either living it or trying to deal with it or trying to recover from it, and it's important, I think, to understand that everything that we've heard today is damaging to children, and I was damaged by this, and I have some very strong points of view. So I hope that don't take exemptions to them. They come out of pain, they come out of real-life experience. I am not trying to be hurtful to anybody, but I think that I have a website called sexchangeregret.com, and we get letters from either the parents or the transgenders themselves asking for help after they have lived the life like I did, for five, six, fifteen, eighteen, twenty, all the way up to thirty years, and they are saying, 'Well, can you help me detransition? This was the biggest mistake of my life.'

"I've met with people personally. We've had the honor and pleasure of working with people who are now detransitioning, just recently a school teacher, a pharmacist, and a good friend named Jamie Shewp. I think is important for us to realize that there is actually nothing good about affirming a young boy, four years old, like my grandmother did me. The moment you affirm a child like my grandma did, putting me in a purple chiffon dress and telling me how cute I was, how wonderful I looked, is at the very same moment that you are affirming that young person, you are telling them that there is something wrong with them. That you are not right. That is child abuse! We need to begin calling it what it is. It's not affirming a child, it's causing them to be depressed and anxious about who they are.

"And then we go on to inject hormone blockers into them and begin altering their body. Can we begin to understand today from this discussion how destructive this is to the psyche? It's no wonder they end up with separation anxiety and bipolar disorder, dissociative disorders, schizophrenia, and many other disorders that they want you to ignore. They want to block any child from having access to psychotherapy. The only reason that I am able to speak to you today is because after forty-six years of dealing with this issue, I was able to detransition in 1990. After, I had extensive psychotherapy. The very same psychotherapy that they are trying to prevent people from having. Why? Because they don't want them to detransition. Because somebody like me puts a real bad mark on the idea that it's all good. Because it is not.

"I have recently written a book, *Trans Live Survivors*, that has the stories in them. It's painful to get these e-mails from people whose lives have been totally torn apart, men like myself who was married, had two children, had a career. I was an executive for American Honda Motor Company. One of those therapists who was an advocate for gender-change surgery told me that, 'What happened to you as a child, wearing that purple dress, the only way to solve that is to have cross-gender hormones and undergo reassignment surgery, that's the solution.'

"Well, I trusted his expertise because Dr. Walker had actually written the original international standards of care for treatment of gender identity disorder or gender dysphoria. I am here because he was wrong. I am here because those standards of care have morphed into what they are using today. They haven't changed much. Yeah, they have gone through revision after revision, but the basic idea is that when somebody comes in, they can self-diagnose their gender dysphoria. We are manufacturing transgender kids.

"We are manufacturing their depression, their anxiety, and it's turned into this huge industry that people are profiting from after kids' lives are completely torn apart. The most vulnerable people in our society, and adults are tearing their lives apart. It's really beyond my understanding why we are even having this discussion because it should not be happening. I don't believe any doctor who injects a young person with hormone blockers should have a license to do so. I would prefer that they not have that ability. And I hope that people begin to realize this and begin to speak up about it. There is absolutely nothing good about affirming somebody in a cross-gender identity because it destroys their life.

"We won't see the consequences of what they are doing today until ten or fifteen years later, and there will be somebody else, speaking up like I am, saying, 'It was horrible what they did to me, they never should've done it!'

"The people are suffering, we are not trying to minimize their suffering, but why do we abuse them with hormone blockers and cut their bodies apart as a way to affect treatment? It's insane actually! It doesn't make any sense. If we are just to pause and take a sober breath, it's insanity! When will we finally grasp this? Christina Olsen, a research psychologist at Washington University, and I wrote the article public discourse, published in 2017, June. She said, "We do not know who the transgender kids are?" One way or the other, we don't know who they are. Do you get that? We don't know who they are. That should sink in, they cannot identify who trans kids are except by them saying so.

"There is no test. There is no proof. A parent can actually cause a kid to be gender dysphoric by affirming them. The APA, which an article is going to come out in the Daily Signal in the next couple of days that I just finished last night. The APA and their handbook in 2014 says, 'Kids are not born transgender!' And yet we are treating them with medical treatment as if they were and trying to alter them. They are not born that way. I want to say it again. We are manufacturing transgender kids. None of us should be a part into altering a kid's mind, psyche, and sending them down a path where they are going to sit up here and say how their life was torn apart. I am the fortunate one. I got sober. I am thirty-three years sober. I drank heavily and used cocaine as a way to try to mask the pain from having undergone the surgery as a way to cope with what Grandma did in a purple dress.

"It confused me, that when I was a little boy, four, five, and six years old, I began to want to be affirmed, I began to enjoy being affirmed, I became addicted to the affirmation and the attention. I mean if a kid wants to steal all of the attention out of the room, all they have to do is to say, 'I am a transgender.'

"They can suck the life out a room in a heartbeat. And the focus is right on them. And they can get anything that they want, can't they? Nobody calls them out. Nobody says, 'How did you come to this conclusion?' Well, we know how they came to the conclusion. Schools are giving them books, they are indoctrinating them, parents are encouraging them, online they are in chat rooms, suggesting groups of kids become transgender.

"It's a fad. Yes, there are people who are autogynephilic, but there are also people who are deeply troubled. Over 50 percent of the people that I have worked with, hundreds of people that I have worked with over the last ten years, were sexually abused. Boys who are abused at a young age come to the conclusion that the only way they can prevent themselves from being sexually abused again is to cut off their genitalia and become females. In their minds, that is their defense mechanism for sexual abuse. Girls who are sexually abused want to be men as a way fend off any intruder or sexual abuser because they will no longer be attractive for sexual abuse. Whether it's men or women, vast majority of them were abused as children. Many of them I sit with and talk with privately are in their thirties, forties, and fifties before they are ever able, for the first time, to disclose they were sexually abuse. It's too painful.

"I was sexually abused at nine years old, multiple times, by my uncle. When I told my parents that I was sexually abused, they said, 'Oh, Uncle Fred, would not do that.' Wrong! They said I was a liar. So now I had worn a purple dress as a four-year-old. I had been sexually abused, and now I am liar. You know it's not a real good way to start off life, and you are not even nine years old yet. We got to start helping the young people, and when people ask for help from me, I have one simple thing I always ask them. Tell me what caused you to not want to be who you are? One hundred percent of the time, they can tell me. They can tell me. I am feeling the pain right now of them sharing with me some of these stories because even I weep. They're ugly, they're horrible. They're so deep, nobody wants to talk about it. But we better start talking about it. We are ruining an entire generation of young people, and it's serious business. I am not pulling any punches anymore, and you should not either. Thank you."

This was published in a channel called The Heritage Foundation on April 4, 2019. It is titled *He Used to Be Trans—Here's What He Wants Everyone To Know.* You can see this clip on this link: http://www.youtube.com/watch?v=bnP_W.

This was a very long conference with many professional scientists and well respected and educated people who bring to light many important topics that are not being shown in the mainstream media. Please take time to listen if you are someone who struggles with gender identity or if you know someone who struggles with this issue. Also please take time to see this if you are a doctor or therapist and if you are an LGBT activist. Some of the topics that were discussed in the seminar were: "The Medical Harms of Hormonal and Surgical Intervention for Gender Dysphoric Children," "Doctor's Gave Her Daughter Hormone Treatments (And She Couldn't Stop Them)," "Medical Risks of Hormonal and Surgical Interventions for Gender Dysphoric Children," "What Doctors Aren't Telling the Parents of Gender Dysphoric Children (And What Happens to Those People Who Dare To Speak Up)," "Former Transgender Activist: Transitioning Is Dangerous—Especially for Youth." This is the link to the entire event, https://youtu.be/bnP_WoeNuwA. This should be all over the mainstream media if we lived in a world where the ones in control would truly care for our well-being. But it's not. On the contrary, the media works relentlessly in trying to silence these people and works relentlessly on putting the opposite messages about this topic in their programs. Please put on the thinking hat. It's time to come to the realization that the mainstream media suppresses the truth and feeds us with lies. This is only one more confirmation of that.

I would like to share that I have been walking with the Lord for more than twenty years now. I have also dealt with demons since I was very young. I can attest that there is such a thing as a homosexual demon. I have seen liberations from this spirit, and I have personally met several people who were homosexual since they were born and were delivered by a minister, and now they are happily married with the opposite sex and living holy lives. This spirit can be transferred unto the womb of the mother. I met a man who was homosexual his entire life, and he was set free by our Lord Jesus Christ, and he was revealed that the way he acquired this spirit was one day, his mother, while she was pregnant with him in the belly, she went to visit a witch doctor who happened to also be homosexual. This witch placed his hands on her belly and declared that she was going to have a girl. The Lord revealed to this man that the witch placed a spirit of homosexuality on him while he was in her womb at that very moment.

This spirit can also be transferred from generational curses, just like schizophrenia can be transferred from generational curses. Dr. Rebecca Brown wrote a book title *Unbroken Curses*. I highly recommend this book so that you may learn how to pray and break generational curses against your life and your descendants.

A lot of people try to argue that these things have nothing to do with demons because science shows that is something to do with the brain. Well, let me tell you something. I know that my brain was utterly different when I was ill with schizophrenia. I had a brain scan done. Yes, it is true that it shows that the brain from a schizophrenic person, and perhaps even from someone who is homosexual, may not be considered normal. However, that is because the demons can actually change the structure of your brain. They do affect the neurons and cells and chemicals in our brain. Does not the Bible tell us that the mind is the battlefield?

> **For though we walk in the flesh, we do not war after the flesh: (For the weapons of our warfare are not carnal, but mighty through God to the pulling down of strong holds;) Casting down imaginations, and every high thing that exalteth itself against the knowledge of God, and bringing into captivity every thought to the obedience of Christ. (2 Corinthians 10:3–5)**

In the same manner that the demons physically harmed my stomach on the day that I was delivered from them (it took me weeks to feel my stomach back to normal, after those demons resisted coming out of my body and seemed to hang on for dear life, from the inside of my womb), in the same way, they also damaged my physical brain. But glory to God that He healed my stomach and my mind and physical brain and put it all back to normal. That is what happens, the demons change our minds and brains in the spiritual and in the natural, and God heals it in the spiritual and in the natural as well. It's that simple!

I also want to add that I have seen testimonies of people from Hollywood who converted to Christ and were saying that in Hollywood, they were paying them money to pretend they were gay, even though they were not gay. Yes, because Hollywood, which is used by Satan and the rulers of this dark world, is wanting to make homosexuality the new trend. You know mainly why? Because sin is the devil's food. Satan and his demons have legal rights to our lives through sin. The more we sin, the more we empower them to do as they please. Thus they work relentlessly into making all types of sin a trend and cool. Not just homosexuality; they are in the business of promoting fornication, drunkenness, drugs, gluttony, vanity, greed, lawlessness, promiscuity, lying, cheating, stealing, killing, and just about all of the things that you all see on TV, movies, video games, shows, etc. They are in the business of making sin something cool to do or to be. But they don't show you all the negative sides to all of that. It's a huge deception!

**And the great dragon was cast out, that old serpent, called the Devil, and Satan, which deceiveth the whole world: he was cast out into the earth, and his angels were cast out with him. (REVELATION 12:9–12)**

I would like to end this chapter with a dream the Lord once gave me. I had a dream where I was a guest at a wedding. The people that were getting married were two men. After they said their vows to each other, and after they kissed, they then walked toward two chairs and sat in front of each other. I then began to see, in horror, how one of them would cut of the toes of the other one, and then he would place the toes that he cut off in different parts of the same foot where the toes had been removed. It was barbaric! He literally cut off all the ten toes from both feet and rearranged them completely different from where they used to be. Then I saw the feet of the man whose toes were cut off from, and I saw the toes were sown back to his feet but in a different manner from how they originally were. When it was finished, the man's feet looked dead. The toes looked as if they were frozen and could not move by themselves anymore. It just looked completely wrong and as if now this man would be disabled by the lack of mobility from his toes. The feet looked like a statue's feet. When I woke up, I could not understand what that dream was, but later on throughout the week, I began doing research and ran into this video of transgender surgeries. It was showing how they literally cut off parts of the person's body and then place the parts that were cut off in a different area of the body. I was blown away because the surgery was exactly like my dream. Then I understood the dream.

All of these surgeries cause serious harm to the person receiving them. Their bodies will never be the same again. It is so unnatural! And it may even cause those areas of the body to stop functioning right. Like in my dream, it looked lifeless and motionless. Like a statue. This must stop! The people must understand that we really do have a conspiracy against humanity, and they are in control of the mainstream media, the education system, the economic system, the entertainment industry, and the medical industry. Healing us is not in their best interest. Making us crazy and sick is what gives them billions of dollars of profit, and killing us is what their goal is. It is written in eight different languages in the Georgia Guidestones. People need to be educated by the right doctors. It takes as much faith to believe and trust the fake doctors in the media than it does to believe the true doctors that are being censored by the media. Why are so many choosing to trust our government and media and the doctors that they pick and choose to educate us, instead of listening to all these other professionals who are putting their lives in danger to expose the truth about what these criminals are doing to all of us? Open your eyes, people, and do your research before it's too late. Choose the truth and stop loving lies because it destroys lives, and it will make you lose your salvation and send you to hell.

**For I am not ashamed of the gospel of Christ; for it is the power of God unto salvation to everyone that believeth; to the Jew first, and also to the Greek. For therein is the righteousness of God revealed from faith to faith: as it is written, the just shall live by faith. For the wrath of God is revealed from heaven against all ungodliness and unrighteousness of**

men, who hold the truth in unrighteousness;
Because that which may be known of God
hath shewed it unto them. For the invisible
things of Him from the creation of the world
are clearly seen, being understood by the
things that are made, even his eternal power
and Godhead; so that they are without excuse:
Because that, when they knew God, neither
were thankful; but became vain in their imaginations, and their foolish heart was darkened.
Professing themselves to be wise, they became
fools, and changed the glory of the uncorrupt-
ible God into an image made like to corrupt-
ible man, and to birds, and four-footed beasts,
and creeping things. Wherefore God also gave
them up to uncleanness through the lusts of
their own hearts, to dishonor their own bodies
between themselves: Who changed the truth of
God into a lie, and worshipped and served the
creature more than the Creator, who is blessed
forever. Amen. For this cause God gave them
up unto vile affections: for even their women
did change the natural use into that which is
against nature: And likewise also the men, leaving the natural use of the woman, burned in
their lust one toward another; men with men
working that which is unseemly, and receiving
in themselves that recompense of their error
which was meet. And even as they did not like
to retain God in their knowledge, God gave
them over to a reprobate mind, to do those
things which are not convenient; Being filled
with all unrighteousness, fornication, wickedness, covetousness, maliciousness; full of envy,
murder, debate, deceit, malignity, whisperers,
backbiters, haters of God, despiteful, proud,

boasters, inventors of evil things, disobedient
to parents, without understanding, covenant
breakers, without natural affection, implaca-
ble, unmerciful: Who knowing the judgment
of God, that they which commit such things
are worthy of death, not only do the same, but
have pleasure in them that do them. (ROMANS
2:16–32; Leviticus 18:22–24; Genesis 19:1–
11; 1 Corinthians 6:9–11; 1 Timothy 1:8–11;
Hebrews 13:1–5)

# CHAPTER 12

## America's Frontlines Doctors

I will now transcribe a forty-minute-long video that was posted on YouTube and was deleted repeatedly because it was said to violate their community standards. Famous people such as President Trump, Trump Jr., and Madonna also posted this video in their social media, and it was also deleted. This is not a Republican versus a Democrat issue that is being debated. This is also not about favoring Donald Trump or trying-to-make-him-look-bad type of thing. All that is just a trick to make people think of those things, and like that, they will dismiss all the truth that these doctors spoke here. Our freedom of speech is being taken away from us as they also hide truths that will set us free and save lives. Please remove all thoughts about the president or the liberals about the elections or the political charade going on. They want you to focus on that. This is not about any of that. This is about the truth that they are all hiding from all of us. Focus only on what every single doctor said in this clip and then come with your own conclusion about it, separate from any politics.

And the video begins like this:

"All the expertise that is out there all across our country. We do have some experts speaking, but there are lots and lots of experts across the country, so some of us decided to get together. We are America's Front Lines Doctors. We are here only to help American patients and the American nation heal. We have a lot of information to share. Americans are riveted and captured by fear at the moment. We are not held down by the coronavirus as much as we are held down by the spiderweb of fear. That spiderweb is all around us and is constricting us and is draining the lifeblood of the American people, American society, and American economy. This does not make sense!

"COVID-19 is a virus that exists in essentially two phases—the early-phase disease, and there is the late-phase disease. In the early phase, either before you get the virus or early when you have gotten the virus, if you've gotten the virus, there is treatment. That is why we are here to tell you. We are going to talk about that this afternoon. You can find it on Americasfrontlinesdoctors.com, there is many other sites that are streaming on live in Facebook. But we implore you to hear this because this message has been silenced. There are many thousands of physicians who have been silenced for telling the American people the good news about the situation, that we can manage the virus, carefully and intelligently, but we cannot live with this spiderweb of fear that's constricting our country. So we are going to hear now from various physicians. Some are going to talk to you about what the lockdown has done to young, to older, to businesses, to the economy, and how we can get ourselves out of this cycle of fear."

DR. HAMILTON. Thank you, Dr. Simone, and thank you all for being here today. I am Dr. Bob Hamilton. I am a pediatrician from Santa Monica, California. I have been in private practice there for thirty-six years. And today I have good news for you. The good news is that children, as a general rule, are taking this virus very, very well. Fewer are getting infected, those who are getting infected are getting hospitalized in low numbers, and fortunately the mortality rate of children is about one-fifth of 1 percent. So kids are tolerating the infection, and very frequently they are actually asymptomatic. I also want to say that children are not the drivers of this pandemic. People were worried about initially if children were going to actually be the ones to push the infection long, the very opposite is happening. Kids are tolerating it very well, they are not passing it on to their parents, they are not passing it on to their teachers. Dr. Mark Woolhouse from Scotland, who is a pediatric infectious disease specialist and epidemiologist, says the following, "There has not been one documented case of COVID being transferred from a student to a teacher in the world."

"In the world, I think that is important that all of us who are here today realize that our kids are not really the ones who are driving the infection. It is being driven by older individuals, and yes, we can send the kids back to school. I think without fear. And this is the big issue right now, as Congressman Norman alluded to, this is the really important thing to do. We need to normalize the lives of our children. How do we do that? We do that by getting them back in the classroom. And the good news is that they are not driving this infection at all. Yes, we can use securing measures. Yes, we could be careful, I am all for that, we all are, but I think the important thing is we need to not act out of fear. We need to act out of science, we need to do it, we need to get it done. Finally the barrier—and I hate to say this—but the barrier to get getting our kids back in school is not going to be the science, it's going to be the national unions, the teachers' union, the National Education Association, and other groups who are going to demand money.

"And listen, I think it's fine to give people money for PPE and different things in their classrooms, but some of their demands are really ridiculous. They are talking about—where I am from in California, the UTLA, which is the United Teachers of Los Angeles— is demanding that we defund the police. What does that have to do with education? They are demanding that they stop, or they shut all private charters schools. Privately funded charters schools, these are the schools that are actually getting the kids educated. So clearly there are going to be barriers, the barriers will not be science, they will not be barriers for the sake of the children, it's going to be for the sake of the adults, the teachers, and everybody else and for the unions. So that is what we need to focus our efforts and fight back. So thank you all for being here, and let's get our kids back in school."

"Hello, I am Dr. Stella Immanuel, I am a primary physician in Houston, Texas. You know, I actually went to medical school in West Africa, Nigeria. I took care of malaria patients, treated them with hydroxychloroquine and stuff like that. So I actually used these medications. I am here because I have personally treated over 350 patients with COVID. Patients that have diabetes, patients that have high blood pressure, patients that have asthma, old people—I think my oldest patient is ninety-two years old and a seventy years old—and the results all have been the same. I put them on hydroxychloroquine, and I put them on zinc, and I put them Zithromax, and they are all well. For the past few months, I have taken care over 350 patients and have not lost one. Not a diabetic, not a somebody with high blood pressure, not somebody with asthma, not an old person. I have not lost, not one patient! And on top of that, I have put myself, my staff, and many doctors that I know on hydroxychloroquine for prevention. Because by the very mechanism of action, it works early and as a prophylaxis. We see patients, ten to fifteen COVID patients every day. We give them breathing treatments. We only wear surgical masks. None of us have gotten sick. It works! So I came here to Washington, DC, to say, America, nobody needs to die! The study that made me start using hydroxychloroquine was a study that they did in united air NIH in 2005 that say it works.

"Recently I was doing some research about a patient that had the hiccups, and I found that they even did a recent study in the NIH which is in our National Institute of Health. They actually had a study, go look it up, type hiccups and COVID, and you will see it. They treated the patient that had hiccups with hydroxychloroquine, and it proved that hiccups is a symptom of COVID. So if the NIH knows that treating the patient with hydroxychloroquine proves that hiccups is a symptom of COVID, then they are definitely know that hydroxychloroquine works.

"I am upset, why I am upset is that I see people that cannot breathe, I see parents walk in, I see diabetics sit in my office, knowing that this is a death sentence. And they can't breathe, and I hold them, and I tell them, it's going to be okay, you are going to live! And we treat them, and they live. None has died! So if some fake science, some person sponsored by all these fake pharma companies come out and say, 'Oh, we have done studies, and they found that it doesn't work, I can tell you categorically, it's fake science!' I want to know who is sponsoring that study? I want to know who is behind it? Because there is no way I can treat 350 patients and counting, and nobody is dead, and they all did better. And you are going to tell me that you treated 20 people, 40 people, and it did not work? I am a true testimony! So I came here to Washington, DC, to tell America, nobody needs to get sick! This virus has a cure! It is called hydroxy-chloroquine, zinc, and Zithromax! I know you people want to talk about masks, hello? You don't need masks. There is a cure! And you don't want to open schools? No, you need people to be locked down. There is prevention, and there is a cure! And let me tell you something, all you fake doctors out there that tell me, 'Oh yeah, I want a double-blinded study,' you sound like a computer, double blinded, double blinded… I don't know if your chips are malfunctioning, but I am a real doctor. I have radiologists. We have plastic surgeons, neurosurgeons, like Sanjay Gupta saying, 'Oh yeah, it doesn't work, and it causes heart disease.'

"Let me ask you, Dr. Sanjay Gupta, hear me, have you ever seen a COVID patient? Have you ever treated anybody with hydroxy-chloroquine, and they died from heart disease? When you do, come and talk to me because I sit down in my clinic every day, and I see these patients walk in everyday, scared to death! I see people driving two or three hours to my clinic because some ER doctor is scared of the Texas Board, they are scared of something and they will not prescribe medication to these people. I tell all of you doctors that are sitting down and watching Americans die, you are like the good Nazis, the good ones, the good Germans that watched Jews get killed and did not speak up. If they come after me, they threaten me—I mean I have already gotten all kinds of threats—or they are going to report me to the bots, I say you know what, I don't care! I am not going to let Americans die! And if this is the mountain, if this is the hill where I get nailed on, I will get nailed on it. I don't care. You can report me to the bot, you can kill me, you can do whatever, but I am not going to let Americans die. And today I am here to say that, America, there is a cure for COVID! All this foolishness does not need to happen. THERE IS A CURE FOR COVID! There is a cure for COVID! It's called hydroxychloroquine, it's called zinc, it's called Zithromax! And it is time for the grassroots to wake up! And say no, we are not going to take this any longer! We are not going to die! Because let me tell you something. When somebody is dead, they are dead. They are not coming back tomorrow to have an argument. They are not coming back tomorrow to discuss the doctors' double-blinded study and the data. All of you doctors that are waiting for data, if six months down the line you actually found out that this data shows that this medication works, how about your patients that have died? You want a double-blinded study when people are dying is unethical. So, guys, we don't need to die. There is a cure for COVID."

"Oh my god, Dr. Immanuel also known as warrior. Before I introduce the next guest, I just want to say that I wish that all doctors that are listening to this bring that kind of passion to their patients, and the study that Dr. Immanuel was referring to is in virology which talks about a SARS viral epidemic that affects the lungs that came from China, and they did not know what would work. The study showed that chloroquine would work. It sounds exactly that it could have been written three months ago. But in fact, that study in virology, which was published by the NIH, the National Institute of Health, where Dr. Anthony Fauci was the director. Again the official publication of the NIH in virology, fifteen years ago, showed that chloroquine—we use hydroxychloroquine and is the same—a little safer. It works, they proved this fifteen years ago.[17] When we got this novel coronavirus—which is not that novel—it's 78 percent similar to the prior version of CoV-1. Not surprisingly, it works! I am going to introduce the next speaker."

"I am Dr. Erickson. Dr. Gold asked me to talk about the lockdowns and how effective they were, and do they cause anything non-financial? They always talk about the financial, but you have to realize that lockdowns, we haven't taken a $21 trillion economy and locked it down. So when you lock it down, it causes public health issues. Our suicide hotlines are up 600 percent. Our spousal abuse, different areas of alcoholism are all on the rise. These are public health prob-

---

[17] https://www.palmerfoundation.com.au/deadly-cover-up-fauci-approved-hydroxychloroquine-15-years-ago-to-cure-coronaviruses-nobody-needed-to-die/.

lems from a financial lockdown. So we have to be clear on that fact that there is. It's not like if you just lock it down, and you have consequences to people's job. They also have consequences—health consequences at home. So we are talking about having a little bit more of a measured approached. A consistent approach. If we have another spike, you know, coming in cold and flu season, let's do something that is sustainable. What is sustainable? Well, we can socially distance, wear the masks, but we can also open the schools and open businesses. So this measured approached I am talking about is not made up. It's going on in Sweden, and their death rate is about five to sixty-four per million, UK full lockdown, six hundred deaths per million, so we are seeing that the lockdowns aren't decreasing significantly the amounts of death per million. Some of our Nordic neighbors have less death for a variety of reason, I don't have time to go into that today. Okay, so what my quick message here is in a minute or two is just that we need to take an approach that is sustainable, a sustainable approach, which is slowing things down, opening up schools, opening up businesses, and then we can allow the people to have their independence and their personal responsibility to choose to wear masks and socially distance as oppose to putting index on them, you know, kind of controlling them. Let's empower them with data and let them study what other countries have done and make their own decisions. That is what I would like to share, thank you."[18]

"Are there any questions?"

Someone replies to the doctors, "Who are you guys? We are so excited. I am from the South Dakota. I am so glad you guys are preaching this message."

Dr. Simone spoke again. "You know South Dakota did something very interesting and is very interesting seeing that you are from there. So the governor did not restrict access to hydroxychloroquine, and I believe that you were the only state in the union that did that, and there have been studies out there that attempt to show that it doesn't work. They are inaccurate because they give the wrong time,

---

[18] http://toresays.com/2020/04/18/lock-step-the-rockefeller-foumdations-2010-plan-to-enslave-humanity-with-plandemic/.

the wrong dose, the wrong patient, either too much or the long time, so South Dakota did better because it had access to hydroxychloroquine. Thank you so much."

Someone else from the audience now speaks. "Okay, someone we love gets sick with the COVID, and you say that the hydroxychloroquine is restricted here, how do we get access to it?"

Dr. Simone answers, "That is the number 1 question we are all asking every day. I want you to know that you are not alone, I have many congressmen ask me, 'How can I get it?' So the congressmen can't get it, it's tough luck for the average American Joe getting it. It's very difficult! You have to overcome a few hurdles. Your doctor has to have read the science with a critical eye and have eliminated the junk science, many studies have been retracted as you know. And number 2, the pharmacists have to not restrict it. Many states have empowered their pharmacists' to not honor physicians' prescriptions. That has never happened before. They're interference with the doctor-physician relationship with the patient, when the patient talks with the doctor honestly, and when doctors answers the patients honestly have been violated. So you have a very difficult time as the average American. Some of the information we will share, later this afternoon, is to show that mortality rates in countries where it's not restricted and the mortality rates where is restricted. So I have friends all over the world now because of this. And in Indonesia, you can just buy it over the counter. It's in the vitamin section. And I am here to tell the American people that you can buy it over the counter in Iran because the leaders in Iran, the males in Iran think that they should have more freedoms than Americans. I have a problem with that! My colleagues have problems with that. We don't like to watch patients die!"

Someone replies, "So, Doctor, if people have problems, they should be picking up the phone, and they should be calling their state, and their federal representatives and senators and say, 'We are the American people, and we demand this!'"

Someone else from the panel of doctors speaks, "Let me say this. Thank you, Julie, that is the exactly right, if you hear this and if you are concerned and wondering why you may not be able to get access to it, we need to make four calls. Call your governor, call both of your senators, and call your congressmen. And tell them that you want to know why you are not able to get access to a drug that doctors are telling you will help in this and help us reduce the numbers of hospitalizations and reduce the number of deaths. Urge them to read Dr. Harvey Riches' study from Yale. He is the Yale professor of epidemiology, and from there you will find other studies."

Someone else from the audience spoke, "How do people trust the data that they are looking at every day? The numbers are so variable, and when you look at John Hopkins, CDC, which provides COVID deaths in different categories that is related to pneumonia and other things, so how do we get the right information?"

Dr. Simone replies, "So the only number that I think is worth paying any attention to—and even that number is not so helpful—but it's mortality because that is a hard and fast number, so any case number is almost irrelevant. And that is because there is a lot of inaccuracies with the testing, and also even if the tests are accurate, most people are asymptomatic or mildly asymptomatic. So it's not that important to know. So the case number, which we see rising all the time in the news, is basically irrelevant, and if you have told us a few months ago that was the number that the media was going to go crazy over, we all would have just laughed at that. I mean, that is essentially herd immunity. There's lots of people out there who have tested positive without symptoms or with very mild symptoms. So the only number that is worth paying attention to is mortality. When you look at the mortality, this is a disease that unfortunately kills our most frail members of society. People with multiple comorbid conditions. Specifically diabetes, obesity is a big one, we don't talk about that, but it is, it's a fact. Coronary artery disease, severe coronary artery disease, people like that, and also if you are older is a risk factor, but the biggest risk factor is if you have comorbid conditions, if you are young and healthy, then this is not…you are going to recover. If you under sixty with no comorbid conditions, it's less deadly than influenza. This seems to come as great news to Americans because this is not what you are being told. I would say the answer is that is very difficult to get accurate numbers."

Someone in the audience asks, "If you had a message to Anthony Fauci, what would you say to him?"

A woman among the doctors says, "Listen to the doctors, listen the frontlines doctors. Have a meeting with the frontlines doctors, and maybe I need to say that into the microphone. My message to Dr. Anthony Fauci is to have a meeting with these frontlines doctors who are seeing real patients, they are touching human skin, they are looking people in the eye, they are diagnosing them, and they are helping them beat the virus, they are the ones who are talking to the patients. Have meetings with them and do it every single day and find out what they are learning about the virus firsthand. And it's important to understand that we have doctors here who are not emergency room doctors; they are preventing patients from even hitting the emergency room. So if they are only listening to emergency room or ICU at the very tragic end of a person's life, they are not getting the full story. They need to come back and hear the earlier portion, and they also need to understand what the lockdowns and the fears are doing to patients around this country because there are a lot of unintended consequences, which the doctors can speak about."

Dr. Stella Immanuel takes the microphone. "Let me say something. My message to Dr. Anthony Fauci is when is the last time you put a stethoscope on a patient? That when you start seeing patients, like we see on a daily basis, you will understand the frustration that we feel. And you need to start feeling for the American people like we do, America's frontline doctors, how we feel, and need to start realizing that. They are listening to you, and if they are going to listen to you, you gotta give them a message of hope. You gotta give them a message that goes with what you already know—that hydroxychloroquine works!"

Someone from the audience asks a question to Dr. Warrior, or Immanuel, "You mentioned before the remarkable results that you had treating your own patients. I believe you said 350 patients were taken care of by you."

She says, "Yes, sir."

He continues, "Have you been able to publish your findings and results?"

She replies, We are working on publishing right now, we are working on that. But here is what I will say, people like Dr. Samuel published the data, and my question is, and? That will make you see patients. There is enough data around the world. Yes, my data will come out. When that comes out, that is great! But right now, people are dying, so my data is not important for you to see patients. I am saying that to my colleagues out there. That talk about data, data, data—"

Dr. Simone takes the microphone. "May I just interject. There is a lot of published data on this, not every clinician needs to publish their data to be taken seriously, the media has not covered it! There is a ton, I have a compendium on Americasfrontlinedoctors.com There is a compendium of all the studies that work with hydroxychloro- quine. The mortality rate was published in Detroit less than month ago, in the Fourth of July weekend, they published it. Mortality by half in the critically ill patients. The patients who get it early is esti- mated that one-half to three-quarters of those patients would not be dead. We are talking seventy thousand to one hundred thousand patients would still be alive if we had followed this policy. There is plenty of published data, I am sorry that is not out there."

Dr. Stella Immanuel speaks, "Dr. Rich published data recently, so there is a lot of data out there. They don't need mine to make those decisions."

The person asks Dr. Immanuel one more question, "What was the little girl that was nine years old, otherwise healthy and was reported that she died of COVID-19, so I was curious, from your perspective, do you feel that this little girl died from other conditions and was wrongly accredited to COVID-19, or is there some other reason why she would have died?"

Dr. Immanuel answers, "I would not be able to say that till I look at the little girl's literature and the little girl's history and what- ever happened. I know I have taken care of a lot of family members, and I see a lot of children, and they usually get a lot of mild symp- toms. But I cannot talk about a kid that I have not looked at.

Dr. Hamilton takes the microphone "What was the issue of the child again?"

The person replies, "She was nine years old."

The doctor says, "Okay. So listen, there are children who are dying of this infection. And the reality is that when they do die, they seem to have comorbidities, really you kind of have to look at each individual case, uniquely, there have been a little over thirty patients in the entire country in the age category of fifteen and below who have died of COVID. Frequently they do have comorbidities like heart disease, they have asthma, they have pulmonary issues, so we don't know the answer to this nine-year-old girl. Tragically she passed, and she is no longer with us, but there is probably—if you dig into it—there is probably a story behind it."

Someone asks, "Dr. Hamilton, have you seen any patients for having adverse side effects from the schools that have been closed, from depression, from suicide?"

Dr. Hamilton responds, "I think it's common knowledge that with the schools not being open, when you think about what you experience in junior high and in high school, what do you think about? You think about parties, and you think about football games, socializing, those are the things we think about, but those are all being shut down, folks, nobody is having fun anymore. And I will tell you that these are critical years of life to be out mixing with other kids, other people, and that is being shut down. So yes there are lots of comorbidities that go along with shutting down. We are talking about anxiety, we are talking about depression, loneliness, abuse is happening. Special needs kids in particular are not doing well either. So there is a long list of complications that occur when you quarantine and lock down people."

Someone in the audience then says, "So in extension of what you were just talking about, we hear all these studies and all these rumors that moms are afraid to go back to work because they are not letting their children in schools, they are scared that if moms go back to work, the children going to school will infect the elderly grandparents, etc."

Dr. Hamilton responds, "So this is the big issue because people are afraid, not that their children are going to get particularly ill, because I think that they are learning the truth about that this infection is being tolerated well by children, but certainly they look at their particular environment, their unique family, and I think that in some situation, that may be an appropriate fear. However, I do think that as a general comment, a general rule through the country, kids can go back to school. Maybe a few kids here and there, their living situation, who they are being cared for, that can be a potential problem. But again, for younger children in particular, they are not the ones passing on the disease to the adults."

Someone from the audience speaks, "So what about the hydroxychloroquine as a prophylaxis? Maybe Dr. Immanuel can speak about that."

Dr. Immanuel speaks, "We talk about that we can't open our businesses, can't go to school, and parents are scared to get treated... Personally I have put over one hundred people on hydroxychloroquine as prophylaxis. Doctors, teachers, people from the health-care workers, my staff, me, I see over fifteen to twenty patients a day. I use a surgical mask. I have not been infected. Nobody I know has been infected, that is around me. So this is the answer to this question. You want to open schools, everybody, get on hydroxychloroquine. That is the prevention for COVID. One tablet every other week is good enough. And that is what we need to get across the American people. It's prevention and it's cure. We don't have to lock down schools, we don't have to lock down our businesses. There is prevention and there is cure. So it's not talking about masks, it's not talking about lockdown, it's not talking about all these things. Put the teachers on hydroxychloroquine, put those that are high risk on hydroxychloroquine. Those that want it, if you want to catch COVID, that is cool, but we should be given the right to take it and prevent it. So that is the message. We don't...all this stuff that we are putting together is not necessary. Hydroxychloroquine is the prevention for COVID!"

Someone from the audience asks her, "Earlier I heard you say that hydroxychloroquine, that the drug is the cure but also you said that is measured with zinc and other... You also said that other doctors have used it, but they use it on the wrong dosage, so I keep hearing that the drug, but then what is the right dosage? What is the right mixture?"

Dr. Immanuel replies, "That you will discuss with your doctor." Another doctor takes the microphone. "Yes, that is a great question because the fear of this drug has driven the whole political situation that has driven the fear towards this drug, so let's address that. This drug is super safe. It's safer than Aspirin, Motrin, Tylenol, it's super safe all right. So what the problem is in a lot of the studies, they did very, very, high doses, massive doses, all through the country. They did the remaps studies, the Solidarity Trial, that was the World Health Organization Trial and also the Recovery Trial. They used 2,400 milligrams in the first day. All you need is 200 twice a week for prophylaxis. They used massive toxic doses, and guess what they found out when you use massive toxic doses—you get toxic results. The drug doesn't work when you give toxic doses. It's a very safe drug, it concentrates in the lungs. Two hundred to seven hundred times higher than the lungs, it's an amazing drug because in the bloodstream, you are not going to get high levels, but you get massive levels in the lungs, so you are going to find yourself, if you are prophylaxes, that as soon as the virus gets there, it's going to have a hard time getting through. Because the hydroxychloroquine blocks it from getting in. And then once it gets in, it won't let the virus replicate. Bring in zinc, and zinc will mess up the copy machine, called the RDRP, so with the combination of drugs, it's incredibly effective in the early disease by itself, it's incredibly effective as a prophylaxis, so I hope that answered the question."

Dr. Simone speaks, "Yes, I want to emphasize on something that the doctor just said because I love the question, this is a treatment regimen that is very simple, and it should be in the hands of the American people. The difficult aspect of this is because at the moment, because of politics, it's being blocked from doctors prescribing it, and it's being blocked from pharmacists releasing it. They have been empowered to overrule the doctor's opinion. Why is this not over the counter as you can get it in much of the world. Almost in all Latin America, in Iran, in Indonesia, in Sub-Saharan Africa, you can just go and buy it yourself. And the dose, my friends, is 200 milligrams twice in a week and zinc daily. That's the dose. I am in favor of it being over the counter. Give it to the people! Give it to the people!"

Dr. James Tedaro takes the microphone, "I just want to add a couple of comments that Dr. Gold was saying. If it seems like there is an orchestrated attack that is going on against hydroxychloroquine, it's because there is! When have you ever heard of a medication generating this degree of controversy? A sixty-five-year-old medication that has been in the World Health Organization's safe essential list of medications for years. It's over the counter in many countries, and what we are seeing is a lot of misinformation. So I coauthored the first document on hydroxychloroquine as a potential treatment for coronavirus. This was back in March, and that kind of kicked off a whole series of storm on it. And since then, there has been a tremendous amount of censorship on doctors like us and what we are saying. A number of us have already been censored. That Google document that I coauthored was actually pulled down by Google. And this is after now, many studies have shown that it is effective and that it is safe. You still can't read that article. And there is also this misinformation out there, and unfortunately this has reached the highest orders of medicine.

"In May, there was an article published in the *Landis*, this is one of the world's most prestigious medical journals in the world. The World Health Organization stopped all their clinical trials on hydroxychloroquine because of the study. And as independent researchers like us, who care about patients, who care about the truth, that dug into this study and determined that it was actually fabricated data. The data was not real. We did this so convincingly, this study was retracted by *Landis* less than two weeks after it was published. This is almost unheard of, especially for a study of this magnitude. So I apologize to everyone for the fact that there is so much misinformation out there. It's so hard to find the truth, and unfortunately, it's going to take looking to other places for the truth. That is why we formed Front Line Doctors here to try to help get the real information out there. Most of my thoughts I actually publish on Twitter, Twitter is being great lately, James Tedaro (Mdtodaro) but I also have a website, medicineuncensored.com, which contains kind of a lot of the information about hydroxychloroquine. I think it's much more objective than what is going on in other media channels. Facebook and YouTube have taken the most draconian measures to silence and censorship the people, and this is coming from the CEO from YouTube as well as Mark Zuckerberg, saying anything that goes against what the World Health Organization has said is subject to censorship, and we all know that the WHO has made a number of mistakes during this pandemic. They have not been perfect by any means. Twitter, although they have some flaws and faults and flags some content, they really still remain one of the main free platform to share dialogue and intelligent discussions, regarding this information. And many of us here today actually connected on a social platform and mediums like that."

Dr. Joe Adapo speaks, "I am a physician in UCLA, and I am a clinical researcher also. I am speaking for myself and not on behalf of UCLA. I am thinking of the people who are behind the screen who are watching what you guys are broadcasting, and I want to share with you because there is so much controversy, and the atmosphere is so full of conflict right now that what this group of doctors is trying to do, fundamentally, is really to bring more light to this conversation about how we may manage COVID-19 and the huge challenge. And that is what this is, that is what it's ultimately about. And bringing light to something means thinking more about tradeoffs, about—one of my colleague said—"unintended" consequences, and I actually think that is not even the right word, the right word is *unanticipated consequences*. Really thinking about the implications of the decisions we are making in this really extraordinary time that we are in.

"I am sure people are listening to some of the discussion about hydroxychloroquine and wondering, 'What are these doctors talking about?' And you know these are doctors that take care of patients who are certified, went to great med schools, and all of that. You know, how can they possibly be saying this, you know I watch CNN and NBC, and they don't say anything about this, and that is actually the point! There are issues that are moral issues, and there really it should be a singular voice, you know. So for me, you know, issues

128

related to whether people are treated differently based on their sex or race or their sexual orientation, I personally think those are moral issues, and there is only one position on those. But COVID-19 is not a moral issue. COVID-19 is a challenging complex issue that we benefit from having multiple perspectives on. So it's not good for the American people when everyone is hearing one perspective on the main stations. There is just no way that it's going to be of service.

"So the perspective most people have been hearing is that hydroxychloroquine doesn't work, right. That is the perspective that most people have been hearing on the mainstream television. And I believed that perspective too, until I started talking to doctors who would look more closely—like some of the physicians behind me here—who would look more closely at the data and the studies. So it is a fact that several randomized trials have come out so far—that is our highest levels of evidence—and have shown that hydroxychloro-quine, their findings have generally been that there is no significant effect on health. There is no significant health benefit. So that is fact that the randomized controlled trials have come out so far. In fact, there were two or three big ones that came out over the last two weeks and internal medicine, *New England Journal of Medicine*, and I think one other journal. It is also a fact that there have been several observational studies, so these are just not randomized controlled trials, but patients who are getting treated with this medication that have found that hydroxychloroquine improves outcome.

"So both of those things are true. There is evidence against it, and there is evidence for it. It is also a fact that we are in an extraor-dinary challenging times, so given those considerations, how can the right answer be to limit physicians' use of the medication? That can't possibly be the right answer. And when you consider that this med-ication, before COVID-19, had been used for decades by patients with rheumatoid arthritis, by patients with lupus, by patients with other conditions, by patients who traveled to West Africa and needed malaria prophylaxis. We have been using it for a long time. But all of the sudden, it's elevated to this area of looking like some poi-sonous drug. That doesn't just make sense! And then when you add on to that, the fact that we've had two of the biggest journals in the world—*New England* and *Landis*—as my colleagues say, retract studies that found out interestingly that hydroxychloroquine harm patients, right, both of these studies, and they had to retract these studies, it really is unheard of. That should raise everyone's concern about what is going on. So at the very least, we can live in a world where there are differences of opinions about the effectiveness of hydroxychloroquine but still allow more data to come, still allow physicians who feel like they have expertise with it, use that medication and still talk and learn and get better at helping people with COVID-19. So why we are there is not good, it doesn't make sense, and we need to get out of there."

Dr. Stella Immanuel speaks, "Listen, let me just put a little bit of that, I have seen 350 patients and counting, put them on hydroxychloroquine, and they all got better! This is what I will say to all those studies, they had high doses, they were given to the wrong patients, I will call them fake science! Any study that says hydroxychloroquine doesn't work is fake science! And I want them to show me how it doesn't work? How is it going to work for 350 patients from me, and they are all alive, and then somebody say it doesn't work? Guys, all them studies is fake science!"

This was the end of the whole conference. Now why would social media ban this video from their platform? There is plenty of information here to prove that these are real doctors with real studies and real results? There is only one answer why the media would not want this on their platform, and it's that they are hiding the truth, and they are all working together with those who plan to depopulate our world. They are also using this virus to usher in the vaccine that will plunge humanity into transhumanism. They want to inject us with alien technology that will change our DNA; they will also get us sicker with this vaccine and weaken our immune systems that much more, and some will die from it. They want to patent humans with their code to own us. We will be merged with AI. We will lose our humanity and become like a GMO type of human.

I will go into more detail about this in my next chapter. But I just want to explain that the main reason that they don't want to give hydroxychloroquine is because they want to scare us to death into accepting their diabolical vaccines, and then we will belong to them. Aside from them trying to kill us, they want to control us through fear and lies; they also want to bankrupt our nation and drive everyone mad with all the lockdowns. They want civil unrest, and they want to patent humans with a different DNA. They also want us to accept the mark of the beast, which is the RFID chip, and it will be in the vaccines. This is the reason for all the hush-hush and censoring!

*A Plague of Corruption* by Judy Mikovits is a must-read! This woman confirms everything these doctors said here in her book.

# CHAPTER 13

## The Credentials

America's Frontline Doctors who were in the Washington, DC, conference video which went viral in social media and was then banned by YouTube, Facebook, and Twitter, these are their credentials:

Simone Gold, MD—Emergency medicine specialist in Los Angeles, California, and has over thirty-one years of experience in the medical field. She graduated from Rosalind Franklin University of Medicine Science—The Chicago Medical School in 1989. She is affiliated with Centinela Hospital Medical Center.

Dr. Bob Hamilton—Pediatrician from Santa Monica, California; medical school: UCLA Geffen School of Medicine, Los Angeles, California; internship: UCLA Geffen School of Medicine, Los Angeles, California; residency: UCLA Geffen School of Medicine, Los Angeles, California.

Dr. Stella Immanuel—Primary care doctor in Houston, Texas, went to medical school in West Africa, Nigeria, has practiced in Louisiana and now resides in Texas where she has treated more than 350 COVID patients who all were cured.

Dr. Dan Erickson, DO—Emergency medicine specialist in Bakersfield, California, and has over sixteen years of experience in the medical field. He graduated from Western University of Health Sciences—College of Osteopathic Medicine of the Pacific, Western University of Health Sciences medical school in 2004 (while both degrees mean your doctor is a licensed physician, their training differs slightly, and each has a unique perspective on care. "An M.D. follows an allopathic medical training path, whereas a D.O. follows osteopathic").

Dr. James Todaro, MD—An ophthalmology specialist, received his medical degree from Columbia University—Vagelos College of Physicians and Surgeons in New York, and completed his surgical training with four additional years of residency in ophthalmology.

Dr. Joe Ladapo MD, PhD—Physician at UCLA and clinical researcher, internal medicine, American Board of Internal Medicine, 2011. Residency internal medicine: Beth Israel Deaconess Medical Center—East Campus, 2009–2011; internship internal medicine: Beth Israel Deaconess Medical Center—East Campus, 2008–2009; degree: Harvard Medical School, MD, 2008 Harvard University graduate, School of Arts, Sciences, PhD, 2008.

Unfortunately but not surprisingly, Dr. Gold was fired after that video was posted on social media, and I believe they also shut down their website, America's Frontline Doctors.

Thus their master plan is to intimidate all doctors from speaking the truth and punish those who dare to speak by firing them and making them an example for the rest of them. Then they are coming up with a new plan to replace all "disobedient" doctors with robotic ones.[19]

Truthfully with the way things are rapidly changing here in America, I even wonder if I should even continue writing this book. Will they censor it too? Will all my work be in vain? But I feel the Holy Spirt urging me to not stop, and thus by faith, I am sitting here for hours and hours, without collecting any money from anyone for doing this, and hoping that my work will wake up the sleeping masses before it's too late.

What is happening in the medical department with the good and caring doctors has also been happening with our police force. I have heard testimonies of police being fired for intervening and for stopping another cop from killing or brutally assaulting an innocent person. There have been several cops that lost their jobs and posted

---

[19]  https://www.brookings.edu/blog/usc-br.

in social media the reason why they were fired, and it's disgusting. I have also heard from an insider that the police applications to start working with them, the ones that have résumés that show the person to be sound-minded and good, those are being thrown into the garbage, and they are choosing to hire the ones that are more of a "villain" type of people. They are looking and keeping résumé that seem to show that these people are more willing to obey unethical commands. I also learned that they have been training our police to disarm the American people from their guns by force. They have trained them to go in their homes and kill people if they have to, to take their guns away.

America, as sad as all this seems to be, we must come out of denial and accept that the truth is that our nation is in the wrong hands. Our nation has been under the rulership of really evil people for quite a while, and if the evidence that I put here in this book doesn't wake you up, then nothing will!

Moreover, Dr. Cameron Kyle-Sidell also made a YouTube video at the beginning of the coronavirus stating that he felt the ventilators that were being put in many of the patients were actually doing more harm than good.[20]

I also heard the author of *A Plague of Corruption* stated that many of the measures that were being used to treat the patients, or to prevent us from getting the virus, were actually doing the opposite of what they were supposed to be doing. She, along with other doctors, warned that if we all get locked up in our homes for too long without exchanging bacteria and germs as we usually do, without challenging our immune systems, or getting enough vitamin D and exercise, inevitably our immune systems will go down. They all said that wearing the mask all day long and outdoor was insane as well, claiming that we are going to be breathing toxic air, and that by doing so, we can actually even activate viruses that we already have in our systems from previous vaccines that have been placed in us. They all also said that anyone who ever received the flu shot in their lifetime will automatically get a positive result when testing for COVID because all

---

[20] http://youtu.be/Ykp0H8DenqQ.

the flu shots contained coronaviruses. They all warned us that after they reopen up the states, we were going to see a lot of people get ill, not because of the virus but because they now have a much-weaker immune system! This information was all in the documentary titled *Plandemic*, but of course, it has been removed, and all I can tell you is to please purchase the book *A Plague of Corruption* before that is also censored.

Dr. Richard Urso, an ophthalmologist, is another doctor coming out in social media, claiming that he also has cured many COVID-19 patients with hydroxychloroquine and that when he tried to get the word about this out there, he was intimidated into losing his license and was persecuted. He confirmed that indeed they are trying to suppress the truth about this and that for doctors to speak up, it may cost them their jobs.[21]

I remember when the outbreak first began in China, a young Chinese doctor blew the whistle on what they were doing with this, and unfortunately, he was killed. A couple of other Chinese people came out in social media, exposing the truth about what they were really doing, and they went missing. One of the ladies said that they were literally burning people alive and lying to the world, claiming that they were dead from the virus. This is a massive cover-up for genocide, people. Please open your eyes!

There was another doctor from Florida who claimed that he has cured many COVID patients with hydroxychloroquine, but that now, when his patients go to the pharmacists, they are blocked by them from getting the drug. The doctor was in shock since he has also prescribed this medication to hundreds of patients with lupus, and they were on it for decades, and none of them have any side effects from the drug. Yet now you cannot get the drug at the pharmacy stores like they used to be able to do. Why? This doctor also mentioned the news was making it seem as if the hospitals in Florida were all filled with patients and out of beds, but that was just not the truth. He said that the hospitals in Florida, many of them were so slow in business that many of the staff had been laid off, and because

---

[21] https://youtu.be/66Jhq-zGV88.

of lack of staff, there were not enough patients being able to be seen. But there were plenty of beds.

He also mentioned about many of the testing labs being busted for fraud. They were claiming 100 percent positivity rate when in reality, it was found that it was only 10 percent. I personally met a waiter in Florida that shared with me that one of his colleagues went to register at one of these labs for testing for the virus and went home. He then received a call telling him that he tested positive for the virus. The problem with that is that he never went back to take the actual test. He had only registered to go take it. Then I saw in social media, a lot of people claiming that this was happening to a lot of people in Florida.

I am going to interject now a little, considering the politics of all this. These people are so slick that they have managed to brainwash the masses and divide us into two categories: the Liberals and the Conservatives. They want to make us believe that this fraud is all about the elections, and this is all about taking Trump out of office. By making you all think this way, they can make you dismiss all logic about all the evidence out there from all these whistleblowers and focus on the smoke screen of the elections. This is not about Trump, people! First of all, to all those Trump supporters who believe that God chose him to make America great, you have been majorly deceived! Trump is part of their sick psychological game! He is a psyop and a double agent. He is one of them. Trump is a Freemason, an Illuminati puppet that they put in office so the world can hate Christians passionately! He was never placed in office by God; God allowed it because America turned their backs on Him, and thus, Trump is their judgment! Unfortunately the mainstream church of Christ sold herself to the love of money and fame. They allowed the Scriptures to be majorly twisted and have turned blind eyes to all of God's warnings to repent through His true prophets.

The elite already know that Trump won't be there much longer. They already know that Obama will rise to power once again, and the elections won't matter either, even though they really never matter since our presidents are not elected; they are selected by the elite, and they make us think we have a choice. It's all a sick game, and the world is a stage, people! They are in total control of Trump and the one coming after him. And because of sin and unrepentance, God is allowing all this.

They wanted to attach Trump to all truthers and Christians so that then everyone else thinks we are all nuts, since—I am sorry to say—Trump is a nutcase! Trump's mainstream media, fake Christian leaders are also Illuminati puppets and knowing that they are the ones whom he claims to listen to should be enough evidence to know he is not being led by God. Trump comes out in record supporting the RFID chip. In one of his campaigns, he talks about how he is working hard at chipping the immigrants; he campaigned in favor of being against vaccines to gain the trust of the evangelicals, but now he is pro vaccine and soon to force the COVID-19 vaccine on the military and the rest of the nation. He also has implanted a lot of 5G towers all across our nation, and many of us know 5G technology is fatal to our health. I have seen people who worked installing them all over the country and then quit because they realized they were installing something that was going to cause people to get cancer and tumors and all types of sicknesses. They posted their video on social media, and of course, it was removed.

I know that 5G technology also makes the coronavirus that much deadlier! Well, if Trump would really be God's man, he would not be promoting these things or forcing them down our throats! He is a lukewarm Christian, and the Bible warns that if we are lukewarm, He will vomit us out of his mouth.

**So then because thou art lukewarm, and neither cold nor hot, I will spue thee out of My mouth.** (REVELATION 3:16)

I know that Trump shared the video of the doctors in Washington, DC, in his social media account, and then he looks like the good guy 'cause he tried to tell us the truth, but they did this by design. The moment Trump attached himself to these doctors, half of the nation automatically did not want to even hear what all these doctors had to say. Automatically every Trump hater out there just dismissed any truth coming out from these doctors just because Trump supported them. Then they even began making fun of Dr. Immanuel because Trump praised her, and she is the most Christian of them all. I saw that they were trying to make her seem as crazy as Trump seems to be to most of the world, and that is just not the truth. But this is the psychological operation of mind control going, people.

Since before Trump was elected, the Lord revealed to me that he was an impostor, as all the prosperity preachers out there are. I wrote in detail the deception in the church in my first book, titled *We Were Deceived.*

The devil is a skillful liar. He uses some truth to convince you of his lies. Trump is one example of that; he uses some truth to deceive. Satan also is an expert at doing good deeds to cover up his evil ones.

> **For such are false apostles, deceitful workers, transforming themselves into the apostles of Christ. And no marvel; for Satan himself is transformed into an angel of light. Therefore, it is of no great thing if his ministers also be transformed as the ministers of righteousness; whose end shall be according to their works.**
> **(2 CORINTHIANS 11:13–15)**

Satan is very clever, and I see him as playing chess. In order to push his agenda, he knows how to give up some of his things, he knows how to do "good deeds" to seem righteous, so at the same time, he can get away with the real evil deeds that matter to him. Such as implanting the world with the RFID chip, which is the mark of the beast, such as injecting us with poisonous chips and vaccines with alien technology to change our DNA, to destroy our health and to keep a tracking device inside us, to enslave us, and in this way, he gets to patent and own us, like GMO humans. He is putting 5G technology in our airwaves to destroy our health, and, finally but not the least, to start the coming world wars. Trump is responsible of ushering in all these terrible evil things on behalf of Satan, and thus, any good deed that Trump has done becomes irrelevant if in the end, he is helping Satan to enslave humanity, start the New World Order, pave the way for the antichrist, cause Christians to be persecuted and ridiculed, since he is such a lukewarm and hypocritical Christian and kill and take souls to hell!

**You shall know them by their fruits. Do men gather grapes of thorns, or figs of this- tles? Even so every good tree bringeth forth good fruit; but a corrupt tree bringeth forth evil fruit. A good tree cannot bring forth evil fruit, neither can a corrupt tree bring forth good fruit. Every tree that bringeth not forth good fruit is hewn down and cast into the fire. Wherefore by their fruits ye shall know them. Not everyone that saith unto Me, Lord, Lord, shall enter into the kingdom of heaven; but he that doeth the will of My Father which is in heaven. Many will say to Me in that day, Lord, Lord, have we not prophesied in Thy Name? And in Thy Name have cast out devils? And in Thy Name done many wonderful works? And then I will profess unto them, I never knew you: depart from Me, ye that work iniquity. (MATTHEW 7:16–23)**

This COVID-19 fraud goes much deeper than the elections or any politics. That is just their smoke screen. Trump, being the presi- dent, should not have to rely on Twitter or social media to share the truth. As president, he should have gathered all of these true doctors and let them have their conference about the truth that the elite is hiding from the public on his podium, in front of the press, in front of the world. But instead he just tweets the video because he knows that they will delete it, but he still gets to seem as if he tried! If he really wanted to do the right thing, he could stop this scamdemic, but he is part of them!

I have personally seen many doctors, nurses, and reporters in YouTube, claiming that many people who have died of cancer, heart attacks, car accidents, gunshot wounds, etc. are being falsely classified in their death certificates as if they died from COVID! Many of the doctors and nurses have been forced to lie in the death certificates, and they say they just can't stop them from doing this!

They will use this virus to change our world. To take away our freedoms, to change our DNA with their vaccines and merge us with AI, changing our humanity. They will use this virus and many more to come because they will be releasing Ebola in the US next to kill many of us. This is not about the elections or removing Trump, people! Fox News is part of their news, as is CNN and the rest; it's in the beginning of this book how they own all the news media we see in the mainstream. This is about depopulation of the world and about sending as many people to hell as possible! Do not be distracted by all the circus in the media, focus on Jesus so that you may stay in the truth.

Do your research in regard to the deception in our media. Look up Operation Mockingbird:

> *Operation Mockingbird is an alleged large-scale program of the United States Central Intelligence Agency (CIA) that began in the early years of the Cold War and attempted to manipulate news media for propaganda purposes. It funded student and cultural organizations and magazines as front organizations. (Wikipedia>wiki>Operation Mockingbird)*

Here is a link to show you their mind control protocol: https://clinicaltrials.gov/ct2/show/NCT04460703.

Here they show you how they manipulate the masses through the media to mind controlling them into taking their unnecessary and very harmful COVID-19 Vaccine! Beware! You have been warned!

# CHAPTER 14

❧

# The Scientific Truth About Vaccines

"I have been studying vaccines for the past three years of my life, when it came up in my professional life, and my current opinion about vaccinations is that they have never been safe. Never has there been a safe vaccine. Never will there be a safe vaccine, and it is not possible to have a safe vaccine. The reasoning for that is that the actual process of vaccination defies the natural function of the immune system of living beings. It forts the immune system into a balance that is very unnatural, and that leaves it susceptible to more things than just what you may be vaccinated supposedly for.

"Putting a disease matter into a body and thinking that the manner in which is going in, either usually through a muscle, through a skin, using a very unnatural thing, a needle, combined with all the chemicals and antibiotics and things that the manufacturing companies may not even know about at the time that they are being injected into a muscle, there is no possible way that, that can be safe! Now when you are bypassing the normal immune system by putting this disease matter into a muscle, you are stimulating yet another abnormal response at the sight of the injection. Pulling off all sorts of metals and things that call in the immune cells in this very unnatural way. And the results that these manufactures and designers of vaccines often look for is simply an antibody, which is one small thing in the cascade of immunity that is so incredibly elegant. They probably cannot appreciate—obviously they don't appreciate—if calling a simple antibody, which is highly unpredictable, 'immunity' is insanity! Our body has in-built immune system. If indeed it is such a miraculous product, wouldn't we be noticing how miraculous it is? Are they saying that we are just too stupid to notice that this is killing people and maiming people? That we are too stupid to notice that it's miraculous?

"You know, I think this a lot of the argument, we are just too stupid to notice how miraculous this is, so to protect everybody, we better…they're going to give it to us anyway. Why must such a wonderful product be forced upon people since the beginning of vaccination? If people were really seeing each other dropping dead of smallpox, and they were really seeing each other being saved by a smallpox vaccine, the line would be out of town, you know, to get it. That has never been the case. The history books really show that the people that were vaccinated were among the sickest. That many children were dying after smallpox vaccination. That they were developing terrible ulcerations, beautiful perfect babies forced into this smallpox vaccines, either dying or developing terrible, terrible diseases. And the diseases are often said, oh that would have happened anyways. But parents who watched this happen time and time again know otherwise. So those of us who actually noticed the science is not backing up vaccinations, those of us who noticed that people are being maimed and killed by vaccinations, those of us who have experienced our own vaccine reactions are categorically thought to be mad!"

> Vaccination is a barbarous practice and one of the most fatal of all the delusions current in our time. Conscientious objectors to vaccination should stand alone, if need be, against the whole world, in defense of their conviction. (Mahatma Gandhi)

"Despite the fact that we've actually studied it! You know, none of my colleagues in the past studied vaccines, yet they still would think that the sound bites that they heard over and over, over the years, about vaccines being safe and effective trumped any book knowledge that I may have attained and try to discuss with them. It's baffling! It's like the minds have been sucked into this paradigm so deeply, and it's not just the minds of these doctors, but it's the safety net, and it's the comfort zone, and it's the rewards that they are getting as a result of all their doing."

> *The purpose of vaccines is to make money in the aftermarket. The aftermarket is cancer, leukemia, diabetes, auto immune diseases, infertility, and other cataclysmic diseases. (Dr. Rima Laibow)*

"And the rewards are not watching people get healthy! The rewards are monetary, and the rewards are power; that's it! It is money and it is power. Many of the vaccines enthusiasts' doctors will parrot the phrase that 'babies need to be vaccinated when they are young because the take rates are better for the vaccines.' Parents are being told to bring their two-month, four-month, six-month-old infants in and to have them injected with some twenty-four different disease matter injections."

> *WHAT'S IN A VACCINE? This is what a 2-month-old receives in one Dr. visit: aluminum phosphate, formaldehyde, glutaraldehyde, 2-phenoxyethanol, Stainer-Scholte medium, casamino acids, dimethyl-beta-cyclodextrin, Mueller's growth medium, ammonium sulfate, modified Mueller-Miller casamino acid medium without beef heart infusion, complex fermentation media, amorphous aluminum hydroxy phosphate sulfate, sodium chloride, aluminum hydroxide, yeast protein, sodium chloride, disodium phosphate dihydrate, sodium dihydrogen phosphate dihydrate, Eagle MEM modified medium, calf bovine serum, M-199 without calf bovine serum, vero cells (a continuous line of monkey kidney cells, phenoxyethanol, formaldehyde, neomycin, streptomycin, polymyxin B, sucrose, sodium citrate, sodium phosphate monobasic mono-*

*hydrate, sodium hydroxide, polysorbate 80, cell cul-*
*ture media,* FETAL BOVINE SERUM, *vero cells DNA*
*from porcine circoviruses (PCV) 1 and 2 has been*
*detected in RotaTeq, soy peptone broth, casamino*
*acids and yeast extract-based medium, CRM197*
*carrier protein-polysorbate 80, succinate bufler,*
*aluminum phosphate.)*

"Complete with the polysorbate 80, amounts of aluminum that are absolutely unsafe, with the amount of body weight that they are being injected to which, by the way, is to generate the immune response that is desired. That's why the aluminum is there for. They are being told to bring these children in and the real reason is because they need to get them there at one year, they need to train the parent. So to train the parents, they are injecting these children; how sick is this? If it's only to train the parents, then why not just give them a ceiling injection at two, four, and six months and just keep it to ourselves. Why do we have to inject disease matter that won't be effective and that will be problematic!

"At two, four, and six months, an infant's immune system develops slowly, that's normal. It's part of the design. There are certain inner lookings and TNF which are other kinds of immune-cell-secreted chemicals that fire up our immune system that are specifically, by nature, wanted in a newborn. Vaccine scientists have been working on developing a way to grab those chemicals up because they think nature is flawed. Because they think Mother Nature got it all wrong when designing an immune system of an infant (God designed babies). Mother Nature had no idea how to create a human being that could fight off its own diseases while it was an infant and as it was growing. These immune chemicals that are not secreted at high levels for an infant are done so purposefully so that the immune system can develop slowly, and I will say thoughtfully because the immune system does have a mind of its own. So it has to be able to respond correctly, react correctly, give feedback correctly; this is essentially like a mind in that sense.

"So why aren't these children all dying? Why are they not extremely vulnerable to disease more so than the vaccine enthusiasts actually say they are; it's because of breast milk. It's because of breast milk from healthy mothers who is eating a good diet. This is the design. You know, the design is to have these chemicals at a low level in an immature infant, being supplemented by mother's milk. That's it! It's worked for a really long time. It worked very well, and what that produces is an immune system that is highly competent in later years. And it puts forward an immune system that is still competent even in a world full of bacteria, encapsulated bacteria that would require these responses in us, because the mother is able to essentially protect the baby with antibody through breast milk.

"So the inventors of vaccines have chosen a belief system whereby infants are all born with inadequate immune systems and that the only way they can be safe from hepatitis B, coronavirus, etc. The infant vaccines, that the only way they can be safe from these diseases is getting vaccines into them, as quickly as possible, in multiple injections. So why do we need multiple injections? Well, they need multiple injections basically because these vaccines don't cause the immune response after one injection, that would ultimately be desired by vaccines' designers—or maybe not—because each vaccine actually has its own charge that goes with it, the amount of money that is worth and that is charged for the administration. So the more vaccines given, the more money generated. But also the fact of the matter is that these young babies have a blunted immune response, compared to you or I, and that is one of the reasons why the aluminum is added to the vaccine. It's to stimulate that immune response by pulling aluminum into the muscle and calling forth immune cells to react to it, which is an absolutely unnatural thing.

"So what happens when babies are given a vaccine is that this normal nonreactivity of the immune system is abolished. And the nonreactivity then becomes hyperreactivity, and that is why we are seeing so much asthma, so much reactive airway disease, allergies to peanuts, and so on and so forth, latex. It's because of these injections that these young children are getting. Not only that have the disease matter in them, but that they have provoked the immune system in an unnatural way, shifting the normal balance of nonreactivity into one of hyperreactivity.

"I think the reason that many people don't trust their own immune system is because they have been conditioned to not trust it (mind control). They have never been given the opportunity to actually get sick and recover without an allopathic intervention, and because when they do get sick, they are given acetaminophen, ibuprofen, antibiotics, antivirals, and guess what, when you put those things into somebody who is sick, you will make them sicker. But the person that is sick, they think that the illness that they had just got worse. They are not going to think that the drugs that they took, I can't convince people that the drugs that they took made them sicker and that they would have not gotten sicker had they not taken them.

"Anyway it's very difficult because of the belief system that people have in what is on the shelves and in the stores and what is being advertised on television, helping them with the beautiful pictures of all the healthy people that are used on these ads, and then you have a doctor standing there with a degree who has gone through all this training and education, saying, 'Your own immune system isn't enough to fight this!' That's because the doctor doesn't know how to take care of an immune system because the doctor was what you end up with is a whole society from start to finish that doesn't know how an immune system works, that doesn't know how to take care of it, doesn't know how to replenish the nutrients and minerals that are needed, does not know how to ingest a diet that will support it, and then when it fails, it's God's fault! We need a vaccine! You know, it just wasn't designed properly, or these infections have gotten so much worse that our immune systems just can't fight them. I don't believe that is true, I don't believe that a healthy system that is detoxified and that has attuned the immune system can't handle just about anything that comes along!" (Suzanne Humphries, MD, Nephrologist, International Medical Council on Vaccination)[22]

---

[22] https://youtu.be/4k7jlVEtqrU.

Before I formed thee in the belly I knew thee; and before thou camest forth out of the womb I sanctified thee, and I ordained thee a prophet unto the nations. (JEREMIAH 1:5)

I will praise thee; for I am fearfully and wonderfully made: marvellous are thy works; and that my soul knoweth right well. (PSALM 139:14)

# CHAPTER 15

## The COVID-19 Vaccine

"Good evening, friends, I hope everybody is healthy and in good spirits, considering these challenging times. It seems like every day, our world changes, and it's difficult to know what to believe in the media, so I hope that our group has helped introduced some other bits of information and knowledge and got you to feel a little safer about stating your opinion, and I am really proud to see a lot of the members start posting a lot of the things on their own pages. Thank you very much, because every little bit counts, and I know that it helps quite a bit, so thank you.

"This particular talk is about the COVID-19 vaccine. I really think that this information is very urgent, and I encourage you to really think about the things that I am saying. This is not a new topic for me. I have studied these things for twenty years at least, about vaccines, so I am very familiar with them. I am very passionate about the information. This one will focus on the COVID-19, though. Whatever you find out, please share it with your friends and family and on your social media platforms. I know that Facebook gets really frustrating, many times I have wanted to shut it down myself. However, we need everybody to stay on and to put out news and information and that sort of thing because it does make a difference. You can't just have all the negative things on there, so thanks for helping out on that.

"Before I begin, I am going to say that I do not represent any company or group, I am not getting paid or reimbursed, and the opinion stated are solely mine alone. This information is not intended to diagnose or treat any individual. If you have symptoms, please see your individual health-care practitioner. My name is Dr. Carrie Madej. I am an internal medicine physician on osteopathic training. So I want to start this talk by saying the most important question choice of your life is, what does it mean to be human? This is a very important question. It's going to be very important for this vaccine that is coming up. So let me introduce some basic facts first, and then I will give you some information about what is been going on, since we have been distracted by the media, and I will give you some of the conclusions in the end. And then as far as some of the data that I am going to present, I will give you some references that you look up on your own. Give me a day or two to put those on the group's album page, okay?

"So first of all, some information to digest. Each of us has enough DNA in our bodies that could stretch up to ten billion miles when uncoiled. That is about thirty-five thousand kilobytes of data which is about thirty-five million hours of high-definition video, so what information would this hold? The blueprint for life, how to create it, how your body functions, how it grows, how it reproduces, our thoughts and memories, just to begin with some of those. Also I want you to know that DNA is similar to a computer code or binary code, so if you are familiar with those, you know that it takes a small change in the pattern change or code, and it will have a very grand effect. So you can insert a gene into the geno so that you can put something extra in there, or you can take something out so it's missing one. You can translocate, meaning you take one part of the geno and put it into another area and flip-flop them, or you can take another synthetic or from another organism, a genome, and cut out a part of the genome of the human and insert that other genome in there. When you are doing this, you are rewriting your genetic code. You are writing your software program. And how much change of that code would it take to then be considered not human? And is that ethical and legal? Whether or not we know what is going on, okay.

It's very important things to discuss because they are trying to rule out this technology within this year.

"This is also considered to be an engineering cell line or synthetic cell line or genetically modified cell line. Those are all different words that might be used to have to understand the lingo because it can be confusing, what someone is trying to talk about. An interesting point is that we cannot patent anything natural or from nature. But we can patent something that has been created, modified, or engineered. A good example is Monsanto. It can genetically modify a seed; therefore, it has created something a little different. You may see the corn or the tomato or whatever in the grocery store and it looks the same as a wild type, but it's not. They changed something. So on the outside, it looks the same, but on the inside it is not. So therefore, they control, they own those seeds. Now if it's a wild type, one that grows from nature, they cannot patent that, they cannot own that, okay. So you know, translate that or transpose that onto a human cell line or to a human, that could potentially mean that we could be patented or that human cell lines can get patented. And if it's patented, then it has to have an owner, so I think you might see where I am going with this. And then what if our DNA is modified with genes from another species, are still human? Is this transhumanism? And then what if our DNA, our genome, is modified and thus can be patented and owned, this is not a sci-fi movie or a future event, this is right now, today.

"This is called recombinant DNA and recombinant RNA technology. And this is what is proposed for COVID-19 vaccine. The coronavirus COVID-19 vaccine is designed to make us into genetically modified organisms. That is the same lingo terminology used for Monsanto seeds. Okay. So the frontrunners for this recombinant DNA technology are Enovio, which is back where the Gates Foundation, GlaxoSmithKline, and Sanofi, also Moderna is in there too now, but that is also Gates-backed foundation. I will add that this type of DNA vaccine has never been used on humans before. Let me repeat that, please understand, this is never, ever been used on humans before. Never! They are now proposing to take something we have never used and to inject it into everyone. Vaccine trials are being fast-tracked in a level, in a rate that I have never seen in my life, nor did I ever expect to see this. They are skipping over the animal trials and going directly to human trials. They are not using good scientific methodology at all. They have no randomized placebo-controlled trials for any vaccine which is the gold standard for any therapy to be approved by the FDA. They are not following any sound scientific protocol to make sure this is safe for us, to make sure everything would work for us, and to know everything about it, and they want to inject it into everybody.

"The vaccine manufacturers, in general, are actually exempt from product liability, meaning if it causes significant seizures, paralysis, etc., as a group, they are not liable. They are also exempted from randomized controlled trials. They are doing this with COVID-19 vaccine, but they are also doing this with other vaccines recently where they can just say, well, we've had the MMR vaccine before, we don't need to do that. You might have tweaked it a little bit, it's still the same thing. What kind of mindset is that? I can't believe that because just a little change can make a big difference. Also they are exempt from needing evidence to prove that these things will do what they say they will do. So for instance, they just have to prove that the vaccine is producing antibodies. Okay, just because you have antibodies does not make you immune to something, we don't know that for a fact. We don't know if it really would work out in the population of people. A real and good study would show that it actually works in the population of people. They are not doing that. They said that they don't have time. So it may not work at all! So let's ask ourselves, what is the purpose of this then?

"So another important fact to know about all vaccines is that many of are using the MRC5 *aborted fetal cell lines* from the 1960s. This is an immortalized cell line. *Immortalized* means it does not die. In other words, it is a cell that has lost the ability to go through apoptosis, and a cell that cannot go through that death process is called "*cancer*," that is the definition of cancer. So they are trying to use a lot of words for you to not realize that you are using a cancerous cell. Another term for aborted fetal cells is diploid cells, and they have other terms for them, but I am just giving you the two main ones that they use, if you look at the list of ingredients. Some of the vaccines that are using these cancerous cell lines are MMR, measles, mumps, rubella, chickenpox, shingles, hepatitis A and B, Poliovax, and others. Now I just want to put this point in because people always tell me, what are you saying is fantastical, there is no way this is going on, absolutely not, I trust our governments, I trust our companies, I trust Bill Gates, you are saying false information.

"I just want to tell you that many, many, physicians and researchers have tried to get this information to the public for many years, and they have been silenced one way or the other. Many of my colleagues have tried to do that. I know, I have tried my best, so we have tried to bring this to the public. When there is money behind it, it doesn't work. The media is controlled. So this is why you don't see health-care professionals and other researchers speak up more. You see some still, but you don't see the group of us because we don't feel like we have freedom of speech. I just want to go on an Italian report backed by the government of Italy, and a group of scientists called Corvilla, I will give you a reference to that later. Give its conclusion about some of the vaccines I just mentioned. They are a group of scientists that state that these vaccines have the potential of increased oncogenesis, meaning, increase risk of cancers, increase risk of muta-genesis or mutant genes, what that would exactly mean, I don't know either. Increase risk of transmitting live infections. Well, this is all well known. A lot of times we have a bacteria that is a contaminant, or a mycoplasma pneumonia is a very common bacteria as a con-taminant. This really has nothing to do supposedly with the vaccine itself, but they are in there, so you are getting an infection and on top of the vaccine. So, folks, telling you just this part, this could be con-sidered or, possibly, potentially used as a bioweapon, right? They are injecting cancers into your body, along with very toxic substances, like mercury, derivatives, and aluminum derivatives, and other things like that in addition to the unknown effect of the combination and accumulation of these vaccines together, and the synergistic effect that happens.

"For instance, if you have one vaccine with a known amount of side effects and another one with its known amount of side effects, and you put them together in the human body, within sometime of a time frame, it's not just like a + b = a and b. The two together can have a synergistic effect of a hundred times more detrimental side effects than just what you would imagine, right. So we don't know, there haven't been any studies done on this. The pediatric population is definitely the most susceptible due to their immaturity of their immune systems which should be common sense.

"So let's go back to the topic of why the vaccines are being pushed so heavily on us if the current research and evidence for using them is flawed. So let's follow the money, and that usually will give you some better ideas. In 2011, the German company Curevac was given $33 million for their research and development of RNA vaccines. Then in 2013, Moderna therapeutics was given $25 million for their research and development of RNA vaccines. Then in 2015, Enovio was given $45 million for their DNA vaccines, which they also mention, admitted to using DNA nanotechnology. Nanotechnology is using microscopic, very tiny little robotic organisms. Okay. All of these companies are backed by the Gates Foundation or have been associated by the Gates Foundation in some way. It's important to know that so far, these companies have been unable to get these products licensed for human use due to the fact that these vaccines have failed to provide sufficient immunity in human trials. Sufficient immunity is, again, only stating that you have a certain amount of antibody. This again is not showing that the person is completely immune out in the public to whatever virus or bacteria they are trying to protect you from. It's only looking in vitro, in a test tube, how many antibodies.

"This is not good science here to prove the efficacy of these vaccines. Even if they could get this. In 2010, DARPA, which is the Pentagon's Defense Advance Research Project Military Agency, started focusing on DNA and RNA vaccines, and they had a synthetic DNA vaccine that could be delivered via noninvasive electroporation, which is using kind of a sticker with a microneedle in it, on your skin. You can barely feel it go in there, and in their words, in quotations, is 'to enhance and subvert' humans at a genetic level. This is around the same year Bill Gates heavily started to fund the

DNA and RNA vaccines with the companies mentioned before. In 2012, DARPA acknowledges a brain machine interface. That is AI, artificial intelligence, and the human brain will form a neural network and therefore have the ability to communicate by thought alone or being influenced or controlled remotely.

"Okay, so this is the idea, you go into maybe your smart home, think about turning on the air conditioner or the fan, your favorite program, have the stove start cooking something—who knows what—and it happens because it's Wi-Fi, that sounds cool, right? Think about that, if it's going one way, it's coming back another way. What if the smart home can give you messages too? This all ties in together, so bear with me. So another DARPA program around that time is next-gen nanotechnology N3 program, and it involves non-invasive or minimally invasive brain computer interfaces to read and write directly unto your brain. Do you understand what this means? I am laughing because it's blowing my mind away still, even though I have known about this for a while. Read and write directly…they are rewriting what is happening in your brain, your memories, your thoughts… Now people think this is exciting—it's the Matrix, it's literally the Matrix. I want to learn karate, download it, I know karate. Your body would know how to do it. I want to learn how to be a French cuisine chef, download it, instantly I can do that. I can learn a language, probably within days or one day, I don't know. So that part sounds cool. You think you can control this, something else is controlling it, something else is rewriting your emotions, your experiences, you may have artificial memories of things. You don't know what is reality, you become a computer program, you become a character in a computer program that you do not control. This is not sci-fi, this is today. And this all ties in.

"So also to note that DARPA funded a company that produces soft flexible hydrogels. I have mentioned hydrogels in the past. Injected beneath the skin to perform health monitoring. It's important you hear this. They sync to a smartphone app to give the user immediate health insights. However, hydrogel nanotechnology grows and spreads in the body once implanted. We do not know how this affects our DNA. We know that it can send information

154

directly and continuously to an artificial intelligence. Okay, so all of us on the smartphone, mine included, we have health apps. One way or the other, it's in your phone. Sometimes you have to look under a Google app, whatever, it's there. You can disable it, but you can't erase it. It's impossible! This is the COVID-19 apps you're putting in too has to do with this. They are getting you set up, you have the app, you have the software, now all you need is this little hydrogel that is put there, and now and forever, everything in your body is monitored. For a woman, your ovulation, when you menstruate, how many times you've had sex, and for men, how many times you've had sex, how much alcohol contents in your body, all the vitamins and minerals, if you've fallen down, how many steps you are taking, if you are anxious, your emotions, your sleep, everything, they know everything about you, continuously.

"It's going to an AI program, what is that doing? That is something they are trying to do very fast. They already are getting you set on your smartphone. This is not fantasy. This is real. So in conclusion, we are entering into uncharted territory that can change what it means to be human. THE VACCINES FOR COVID-19 ARE NOT SAFE BY ANY SCIENTIFIC METHODOLOGY! They are introducing cancers and mutagenic in cell lines into our bodies and have been for a long time. They are introducing toxins into our bodies. This has been going on for a long time. They are introducing different animal genomes into our body, and this has been going on for a long time. They do not have proof that what they do, what they say they are going to do will happen. There is absolutely no proof yet, okay. They don't have to have the proof.

"The recombinant RNA, the recombinant DNA technology will cause permanent and unknown genetic changes in a person's body. Permanent! Once their DNA is changed, he or she will live with that change for the rest of their lives and also the ripple effects from that genetic change, who knows what that could be for the rest of their life. There is no going back! It's not like, oh my god, that vaccine did not work, you know, I won't do it again. No! It's do or die with this. I don't know, and I don't think they—whoever is trying to market this—really knows the ultimate outcome. But it doesn't sound good. Essentially this creates a new species and perhaps destroys an old one—us. Us as humans, as we know. It's also introducing nanotechnology and its robotic effects into the body. This is all suggesting the ability to use this vaccine and its ancillary products, things I mentioned just now.

"Some of the names are like ID 2020, etc., to hook us all up to an artificial intelligence interface. This is not a one-way street. It's a two-way street. So I know it's a lot of information to digest, and it scares me, and it has scared me for years. I have been to scientific meetings where they have talked about this, I have been to business meetings where they talk about this. This is real, this is not a fantasy. I studied this since I was in my early twenties, and it's real. And we have to speak up now, for us, for our family, for our future generations, for the human race. It's no joke guys! Please do your own research as much as you can and start talking and talking and don't stop the social media, stay on all of it, and you start flooding the social media with this. We have a chance if we start to recover our people. It's with greatest love and peace I tell you this."[23]

As I heard this message, when she was describing that they will write our thoughts, it brought me back to remember my journey in 1996 with my friend who passed away, Michael. Seems to me that they will have the power to play with people's mind in the same way Satan played with mine during those years. Schizophrenia disorders will be on the rise like never before. That is for sure! AI/ artificial intelligence will be the devil's/antichrist's army. Demons will surely take possession of these robots, and what is most scary about this is that unlike humans, robots have no compassion or empathy whatsoever. They feel no guilt or remorse since they have no conscience. Thus they can be most evil. When they start implementing all these technologies in humans, the first thing that will begin to take place in these people will be the empathy that they feel for others will fade away completely. They will start acting more like machines than humans.

---

[23] https://youtu.be/iRYsN9IL1As.

I also want to point out that I have heard people warn to not even take the coronavirus tests because they say that they are contaminated with the virus. Many people have also reported that they are altering the results and are lying about the truth of the results, but most importantly, they say that whether you do the nasal scrape or the needle, they will inject the hydrogel inside you when they do it. So yes, I have heard many people warn that they are already implanting the hydrogel technology through the COVID testings!

I also want to say that even though this beautiful woman in this video kept on saying to stay in Facebook to spread the truth, I personally was given a dream by God showing me that I needed to get out of Facebook because they were going to start using technology through it to mind control the people. In the dream, I was being accused of doing something very bad by many of my friends who were all part of my FB page, but in the dream, I had no recollection of the memory of me doing what they had accused me of doing. It was just as this doctor was saying in this video. They had put artificial memories on my friends that were in Facebook with me, but I had no memory of what they were accusing me of. It was so scary to me. It reminded me also of when I was ill with schizophrenia in 1996.

I want to mention that in 1996, when I was going through that phase where so many people were giving me weird messages, after almost twenty years, I asked my sister if by any chance she remembered that she and my mother, one day, had said to me that we were the Holy Trinity? To my surprise, she remembered! I then asked her why in the world did she say that to me? She had no idea! Thus this was a confirmation to me that I was not hallucinating nor was I imagining things. These things really took place in my life, and many people were talking to me about weird things just as in the Hollywood film titled *Fallen*, with actor Denzel Washington from 1998. Here is a link to the trailer of this movie: https://youtu.be/JCykURLzSg.

Even though my sister remembered, I am sure, though, that my best friend and other people in my life during those days have no recollection that they were all used to speak to me really crazy and with bizarre messages. I don't understand why it is that my sister was able to remember. But she really does not understand why she did that. She knows that was insane and very harmful to me. I am thankful she does remember because it just shows that I wasn't so crazy after all.

Furthermore, the dream about FB was so real and so scary that right after the dream, I deleted my account permanently. Before that dream, I had seen many people warn me to get out of Facebook because they were going to mind control us through it; they were going to read our thoughts through it, and that they were even going to arrest people for crimes that they only thought about doing through FB. I had not taken very seriously those warnings until God gave me that dream. I also know that Facebook was designed to collect all of our data for the government and the antichrist to be able to use it against us, to be able to enslave us and track our every move. It's in the beginning of this book, what they created social media for. They also admitted having designed our social media, just like casinos and gambling, to keep us distracted, addicted to dopamine and to the praise of others, reducing our attention span to dumb us down that much more, and to mind control us that much more, since we are scrolling down all day and seeing many unnecessary things that clutter our minds, and drain them.

I know that there are people that use Facebook to preach and spread the truth, and they use it responsibly, but that is only a small group of people. The majority of people do waste a lot of precious time in there and are seriously addicted. And as we move on closer and closer to this New World Order, Facebook is not a good place to be in. They already monitor us through our phones, laptops, even some of the appliances in our homes are spying on us, why have one more thing for them to use to spy on us? Edward Snowden let us know just how much our privacy has been compromised, yet so many continue to not care. Here is a link to the trailer of the movie about Edward Snowden: http://youtu.be/QISAil3xMh4.

My advice is to get out of Facebook as soon as possible. Mind control is the scariest thing I have ever experienced. I don't wish it upon my worst enemy! Instead of being in Facebook, read the Word of God, pray and fast, intercede for your loved ones, worship and praise the Lord, these are the weapons of our warfare to fight with, to defeat the demons—talk with the people you love by the phone and share the truth like that. I think it's most powerful if we all did that instead. Here is a link to a news clip in CNBC, titled "Why Elon Musk, Facebook and MIT Are Betting On Mind-Reading Technology," https://youtu.be/R3G5fzz76IQ.

**For though we walk in the flesh, we do not war after the flesh, for the weapons of our warfare are not carnal, but mighty through God to the pulling down of strong holds; casting down imaginations, and every high thing that exalteth itself against the knowledge of God, and bringing into captivity every thought to the obedience of Christ; and having a readiness to revenge all disobedience, when your obedience is fulfilled. (2 Corinthians 10:3–6)**

# CHAPTER 16

## Hydrogel/Quantum Dot Body Snatchers

This is a post from a man in YouTube with a channel called Eyes on the Prize.

> Crucial/critical/highest priority reading as soon you will reach…decision time. No, not about a fake vax. About monthly testing, a.k.a. subservience, i.e., be tested or be a social outcast with zero rights (now rebranded as "privileges"). SHARE! Invasion of the invisible hydrogel/quantum dot body snatchers (Celeste Solum). I received the question often, "I need to take the pathogen test or get the vaccination do to x, y, and z reason? Is it all right in my situation?" According to scientific peer-review journals, the tests—swab, prick, or blood test—they all collects your DNA and goes into the quantum computer for many purposes such as: testing, experimentation, research, rituals, crime and precrime,' as well as many other uses.
> What is a NONO Synbio?

It means that there are nanosize particles in the test and the coming vaccine is a hybrid or fusing of biological life and robots! Yes, my friends, these biological robots entering your bloodstream. Their purpose is to change you from a human to a synthetic entity not redeemable by God. This is an evil plan for the destruction of all humanity and conclusion of Genesis 6, failure to taint all the blood of humanity.

What does hydrogel/quantum dot do to my body?

Upon entry into your blood system, they: Assemble and swarm together, they crawl, travel, and spread throughout your body where they multiply, they change your DNA, adding strands and editing your human DNA. They rewire your body, and it begins to become robotic. They cross the blood-brain barrier. Once in the brain, this nanoglue takes over your brain. You become your own computer AI interface. AI slowly reduces your human brain capacity and elevates AI until the point where AI does all your thinking. You are no longer a human in your mind and body. As will all predators, it finally kills you.

These NONO Synbio particles do several things. According to proclaimed mad scientist Dr. James Giordano, they are a neuroweapon. He is a neurologist and policy-maker with truly terrifying credentials. Combined with doses of chemicals, biologicals, and psychological operations (psyops) to condition your behavior, providing a rich environment for these invaders to take over your body.

What if I already got tested?

The hydrogel is bioaccumulative which means it is not eliminated from your body, but rather it spreads and grows in you, the host. That said, there are many promises in the Bible we can claim. First, repent to the Lord Jesus because of your fear which caused you to worship erroneously. You can only have one master, and you need to clarify to the Lord Jesus that He is your Savior. Cover yourself by the blood of Jesus which is mighty to save. Claim the promise that you are a new creation, each second you are in Jesus. He is constantly regenerating and protecting you. Trust in the Lord Jesus and the Holy Spirit who guides and directs you. Break any curses and witchcraft associated with the test.

That said, sometimes there are consequences for our sins that we must pay. I do not know the final line where a person changes from a human to entity. We may pay a terrible price for playing with the fire of sin. This is all still so new to all of us. We knew it was coming, but we thought it to be in the future. It is in your face, my friends. Whether you consider the hydrogel/quantum dot the mark or not, make your decision on what you are going to do when faced with the ultimatum.

What if I am forced?

God desires that all be saved. I do not know how it will work, but if you resist to the best of your ability, but if you are forced, it is in my opinion—but only my opinion—knowing the character of God, that He will not hold you liable. This also includes underage children, the aged who might not be able to think clearly, and the mentally ill. That said, there must not be any voluntary consent or participation in either the test or vaccine, if in fact this is the Mark, as defined in Holy Scripture, no matter the circumstances.

Isn't Jesus bigger than the hydrogel/quantum dot? He will protect me.

Jesus is all powerful, but He tells us in His Word, which is everlasting, not to take the mark. In Revelation 13, we see that the beast self-heals, which is a signature of the hydrogel/quantum dot. In verse 4, it says, "they worship the dragon." The Word says, "The fear of the Lord is the beginning of wisdom." You must ask yourself the question, do I fear Jesus (a holy fear) or the pathogen and death? Whomever you fear is who you worship. By your compliance, for any reason, you are worshipping. Verse 4 also says, "And who will make war against him?" It is true that President Trump and all world leaders have made public declarations making war against this invisible enemy, but in reality, they have concluded that God's world cannot exist to wage this war. That we knew that a new normal and New World Order. That, my friends, is Satan's kingdom.

Verse 5 and 6 say the beast speaks blasphemies. Blasphemy is being spoken, and God's world is being replaced by the kingdom of Satan, engineered in his image. This is why Jesus says, "If the days were not shortened, no flesh would be left alive." God has turned mankind over to our reprobate mind, resulting in every abomination, wickedness, and lawlessness. The only people who do not worship this evil are the people written in the Lamb's Book of Life. However, war is declared against us, and we are overcome. This is the Word of God, there is no error in it.

Another beast will be coming, with great wonders and miracles. He orders that an image be erected to the first beast who was self-healed. Many of us will be killed because we fail to comply or bow to this image and all it represents, a godless world with no salvation, save the Satanic world order, beasts, dragons, and antichrist.

The survivors chose to worship the image of the beast, which is Satan embodied, and take his mark in their right hand or forehead. I propose to you that the hydrogel/quantum dot, in fact, travels to your brain and marks your brain or forehead. There is evidence that when the precursor to the mark was made globally law, back in 2005, that it was established to place it in the parts of the animals and humans that were holy unto God. Bottom line, Jesus is bigger than the mark, but He says His saints will be overcome for a time, but that there will be a remnant alive to see His return.

But the mark will be announced.

Do you honestly believe that a devil, wearing a red suit with horns and a pitchfork, is going to come out and say, "Hear ye, hear ye, this is the mark of the beast, fall down and worship me"? Satan is clever. Even the governments of the world are engaging in massive deception, yet you believe that Satan will tell the truth on the mark? There is no truth in Satan, and he does not play fair. Jesus says over and over to His disciples, "See that ye not be deceived." He is talking to you. The mark will be obscured and cloaked with deception. It will be sold as necessary and a public good.

Is it worth it, my friends?

You are playing with fire and your eternal salvation when you take hydrogel/quantum dot. Maybe I am wrong. But this substance lines up with Scripture prophecy. Are you going to gamble your eternal life? If you do not know Jesus, now is your chance to choose His sacrifice and embrace Him as your Savior. It is easy. Repent for your sins. Ask Jesus into your life. Believe that He died for your sins. Know that He was born, crucified, and was resurrected and that you will live with Him for all eternity. That is it. You have begun. You do not have to be perfect. You do not have all these rules and regulations you must follow. Just let Him love and care for you.

I will now transcribe a video from an ex-employee from FEMA, Celeste Solum, *The Beast Is Here*.

Hi, this is Celeste, and this is a breaking news report on July 13, 2020, and I just need you to know that the beast is here. I know we've all been anticipating it and waiting, wondering, when is the beast going to animate and be around, and it is here now. And basically, it has come to life through fallen angel technology and witchcraft. It came to be through a common language, just like at the time of the Tower of Babel. And the language that they use is Python. Yes, like the snake, and now they have perfected the Python, and they have Snakemaker coding, and you are going to see that masks are in the coding as well as insidious plots, augur auspice, and even more, and every word is weaponized, and it is dual use for plausible deniability. So you are going to tell people that these are the facts, and they are going to say, "Well, I just see the good part of this, and so there's going to be confusion which, of course, that is the signature of Satan."

There are guidances and glue and that is the geomancer platform and the spellbook, which we've talked about before, but it is no wonder that people are under this obedience spell and kind of in a trancelike state. So this system is going to be required, and you are going to be faced with imminently. Testing, vaccinations, and a sensory to tracing the 24-7 tracing that we've talked about before. I just want you to know that as of last week, I have found that no matter what you do, if you get tested, either the saliva, the prick, or the blood, they are injecting you with the hydrogel/quantum dot, and so you are getting dosed at the time of testing. It is just the way that it is. Of course, you will get maybe a second or a booster during your vaccination or multiple vaccinations, that remains to be seen how many vaccinations we're going to be having, and oh, let me back up for sec. The testing, you are going to have to be tested about every thirty days. And so you are going to constantly be getting this hydrogel/quantum dot injected into your body, and then of course the sensory tracing is the array, and we talked about that in the Scriptures. Array is used in Genesis and Revelation and is God's array. But in the middle, it is a war. And array always means like a weapon and tool of war.

So you can see that throughout the Scriptures and basically, the bottom line, when you do the testing, the vaccination, or let's say it's just a sensory, you agree to a sensory being placed inside your body to let public health know your health condition, it is injecting the DNA of Satan. It's probably the fallen angels, but basically, their father is the father of lies, Satan. So that is what is getting injected into your body, and what that does is it turns you from a human to a something unrecognizable by the Lord Jesus

Christ. And so, I mean, this is even for testing, much less the vaccination and the sensory.

So you need to really be thinking seriously how you are going to stand. We are supposed to stand, we are supposed to oppose this type of a system, and it's more than that. Our eternal destiny is at work here. I did do an article, and it's at Shepardsheartnotlife. It has tons of links for you guys so that you can just follow it and copy and share it with your friends and your family. So we see the beast in Scripture, so I give you an overview of the beast, and of course, there is a beast that comes out of the sea, and then there is a beast that comes out of the earth. I am wondering if this first beast is from the angelic kind that came out of the sea of the sky because in the beginning, the firmament, the Lord God separated the waters, so there was the waters above which became heaven and waters below, and then the earth would be earth and even the abyss. And this is a techno beast, and I first discovered or clued in that this was going to be happening when I tripped on to the PhyloCode, which it was a new classification of life, because they knew that new species were going to be emerging, and it left room for aliens, ETs, demons, the spiritual realm, synthetic life-forms, hybrid life-forms.

So this new code was pretty expensive, it replaced the Linnaeus system that had been in place since Greek's times, and I guess the first time that I really put two and two together was the exercise clay dex. It was a pandemic exercise, and that was code for these new life-forms that we are seeing right now. And they are NONO synthetic bio, or what I call Synbios, so we already have been pretty permeated and saturated by these.

The only way that I believe personally that we can survive in the eternal realm is with the blood of Jesus. This was first proposed in 1975 at the first Asilomar Conference. Now just refreshing your memory, there were three Asilomar conferences: There was the 1975 one that they said that they wanted to genetically modify all biological life on earth. And what is the purpose of that? So they could patent, yet they can't patent God's creation, but they can patent any life-form that has been genetically altered, and that is what we are seeing. And so pretty soon, Satan will own many, many people because of this particular situation. Second Asilomar was the geo-engineering component, and the third component was released in 2018, and it was a framework for the beast system and artificial intelligence.

Now you need to understand that the coronavirus is not a virus like you know it. This is a nanoparticle, a biological synthetic particle that is hollow, and inside it can contain, its payload can contain like a virus, a fungus, a bacteria, a parasite, chemicals, drugs, explosives, demon spirits, and even fallen angel, or giant DNA. Any of those could be in the payload, and they have a mission and that mission can be of precision strike against you personally and your body, or it can be against large numbers of people, like if they just wanted to get a particular ethnic race or people that were noncompliant, let's say to vaccines or something like that, they have the capability to do that. And then this allows plausible deniability because there is a lot of confusion—is it a virus? Is it not a virus? We are saturated with these nanoparticles. I am getting thousands and thousands of peer review articles talking about this technology, and they all confirm one another that this is what is happening. It is why the people did not respond when they got coronavirus, they went to the hospital, they were in intensive care, and their lungs were filling up, the doctors assumed they had pneumonia. I believe now that they did not have pneumonia. What they had were a combination of things.

The nanoparticles swarmed in the lungs, clogging the lungs, causing some hemorrhagic action, and when they swarm, they are multiplying in your body. They really are like aphids in a way, and then the person just dies. This can also shape-shift at the command of the person that is giving the orders for the particular mission, so one week it could be MERS, another week it could be SARS, and another week it could be HIV, and that is one reason that there is no vaccine. No one to man that is going to stop this because, really, it's not a really a virus, and it's not really a bacteria. It is a nanoparticle with a payload inside and whatever is told to deliver, and it can get its orders, and because of like 3D printing, it has that capability inside of it. It can, if it gets told, do a fungus today, do a bacteria tomorrow, do a chemical, explode the body, spontaneous combustion, any of these things are possible. I believe that this technology has been around for a while.

I first experienced it myself in 2002, and I almost died from it. And now it is so much more sophisticated than it was back then. And that's why we are going to see a coronavirus vaccine constructs. They really will not address the issue that you think that you have, but they are there as a behavior-modification mechanism only. So you need to understand that. And this has been going on since 2000 basically.

So the Python language, think of Tower of Babel. Now is Snakemake and in the article, it talks about in this coding, it's got plots, transformations, there's commands, and there's scripts. There's two different parts of this, one is auger, and this is really important that you read this article. I am not going to go into it too much, but auger is an official diviner of ancient Rome. And why is that important? Because of the prophecy in Daniel, and it's so interesting how this makes so much sense now because it was a stone not cut by human hands and a mountain filling the whole world, and then I talk about the mountain in Revelation 8 in the article, so you can read that.

How I watch the pathogen is on a website called nextrain.org, and you can see the different pathogens were released in different parts of the world, like what hit China was different than what hit the US, which is different what hit Europe, which is different what hit Iran, and so forth. And I really go into the auger thing, and I go into the claves, which claves are the new classification of life. That's different. So like instead of having blue birds and robins and hummingbirds, they're all part of the bird family, like humans are now in with birds, dinosaurs, and arthropods. It makes absolutely no sense. And they have specific signature mutations, and those mutations can be caused or can come about through God and His laws of nature. For instance, right now we're at high cosmic rays, the highest that it's been in four hundred years. And that is due to the Lord's cycle that we are going through and also His judgments, but there are also weaponized designer pathogens that man decides to monkey with and engineer. So we got that going on. So the two kind of feed unto each other. Then I go into masks are a part of this coding and kind of interesting about that. Dr. Fauci just said that masks wearing does not really prevent infectious disease, but it is a gesture of showing respect. And so masks are not about preventing infection, but they are about bowing to the god of social justice and respect. Now you think about that the next time someone starts trying to force you to wear a mask, and there's a lot of other reasons not to wear a mask.

Furthermore, there are 3D masks that are being prepared for you that are going to yoke your...they're going to make a 3D image of you, just like an image in Daniel's image, the image of the beast, and it's going to link up with your currency and your health care, and I go into that, and I provide you with links. And then I go into nextrain.com and why it's important and it's designed. It's a little technical, and you can skip over the parts you don't want to go into detail, but it really is important to understand because as Scriptures say, that is line upon line, precept upon precept, and you need to get this under-standing down now because it's every week, every day, every hour, every minute, it is building this. This is real time artificial intelligence, the beast system is an animation and for you to understand and not get way behind in your understanding. And why do you need to understand? Because you need to make some wise decisions. And they are not going to be easy ones. They are going to be decisions about family, where are you going to live, how are you going to live? These types of things.

And then I go into the witchcraft that I first covered it with the Australian wildfires, the United States deployed jet over that had some autonomous and very unique witchcraft geomancer-type technology. This is witchcraft they were using, and so right now over America, in December, seven million drones were deployed over the US. We've got the satellites, we've got jets, and they are using this geomancer technology, which is witchcraft, and they are casting spells over the whole earth. So the whole earth has become this snare or web of spells directed, especially if you are a person of faith. And so I guess, I kind of end my articles, and I want to read this part:

Are you going to lay down and sacrifice your life and lie on the altar of the virtual beast who seeks to devour and destroy you? And so, I am pleading with you, really pleading with you, to lay down your life for the Good Shepherd Jesus, who loves you and values you and cares about you. He shed His blood for you so what more could He do to prove His love for you?[24]

And so that is the breaking news, and we will keep on top of it as the situation arises.[25]

---

[24] celestialreport@protonmail.com https://youtu.be/elnnF21xFiM.
[25] https://medicalkidnap.com/2020/08/06/are-the-covid-tests-a-way-to-surreptitiously-infect-or-implant-people/.

# CHAPTER 17

## Don't Trust the Government

This was posted by Jeff Byerly, HolySpiritWind channel.

This was sent to me by Ken Roberts. This came from a source on FB.

I have not personally verified all the information but is copied from a friend that usually does her homework. The vaccine that is coming...as many of you heard, Moderna is in stage 3 of their vaccine testing. If all goes well, it will become federal law to get the vaccine. Here's something many of you don't know, guess who the first CEO of Moderna was? A Cornell graduate by the name of Anthony Fauci, who was a roommate with none other than Bill Gates. Are you paying attention? It was at Cornell that Bill Gates designed the RFID (radio-frequency identification) and patented it under US2006257852. Are you awake yet? Now let's really go down the rabbit hole. Moderna was a pharmaceutical company that started in Germany under the name IG Farben. IG Farben is infamous for its mass production of Zyklon B, the primary gas used to kill millions during the Holocaust. After Germany fell, IG Farben was dissolved and its assets sold off by a Nazi turned by the name of, you guessed it, George Soros. Soros rebranded the company as Moderna. And who was the primary stockholder of Moderna until his death? Jeffrey Epstein. His role in Moderna is where he made his fortune and established his connections. Let that sink in. Wake up, people! You are being conditioned and controlled.

I will now transcribe a post from a call for an uprising titled *WATCH AND SHARE, YOU WILL NOT BELIEVE WHAT BILL GATES JUST SAID*:

> *Have you ever had this feeling that something was terribly wrong with the world we live in, but you couldn't figure out just what it was? Then you've come to the right place. Secret societies, mystery religions, and the Illuminati have been controlling our reality since the beginning of time, but not anymore, because there is an awakening happening, and you are about to become a part of it. Wake up because this is a call for an uprising!* [This is the introduction to all of his videos]
>
> This is a call for an uprising, welcome to today's show. Bill Gates recently interviewed once again about the upcoming vaccine, which will be forced upon the American people but will be taken willingly by most, just to get back to what they believe or perceive as a normal way of life when things will never be normal again. But you got to hear when they asked the question about the testing results that have gone on, so on far and how such a high percentage of people who have been tested and gone through the volunteered to be tested for the vax, have had massive and major side effects. Now they only men-

tion fevers and chills, which really is pretty much what they claim that you are supposed to feel, and shortness of breath, with this if you catch this virus any way. They don't mention the real dangers and what will really happen when you take it, but he almost laughs it off and dismisses it. And not only that, he says a few things that are important to listen to.

He mentions how in the FDA we trust, which is extremely frightening, and I am going to show you why. Because the FDA is more corrupt than the CIA or any other organizations. They are the ones who allow weed killer to be put in our food, and somehow it gets through inspection and approved, and people get sick and die, no big deal, right! So we'll trust in them, we will trust, in fact, that it might not work, and people might get sick from it. But we should do it anyway. And then he has the nerve to say how everybody needs to get it at least twice, and I guarantee you that this is going to become a yearly thing where you need to get it every year. They are going to start us on early because I guarantee you that 70 percent, at least, of the population in America will say, 'I will get it, I will take it.' The rest of us will be enemies of the state, and that is how this is going to work. Eventually they will say that the numbers don't go down, and they will force us to get it. But listen to the nerve of this guy as he tries to hold back laughter.

The news anchor interviewing Bill Gates starts off by saying, "Well, I want to ask you by saying, you mentioned side effects. The side effects for the Moderna vaccine sound concerning. We looked. After the second dose, at least 80 percent of participants experienced a systemic side effect, ranging from severe chills to fevers. So are these vaccines safe?"

Bill Gates responds, "Well, the FDA, not being pressured, will look hard at that. The FDA is the gold standard of regulators, and their current guidance on this, if they stick with that, is very, very appropriate. The side effects were not super severe, that is, it did not cause permanent health problems for the things (he did not say people, he actually calls them things). Moderna did have to go with a fairly high dose, so you know, to get the antibodies, some of the other vaccines are going to able to go in lower doses to get the responses that are pretty high, including the J & J and the Pfizer, and so there is a lot of characteristics of these vaccines. It's great that we have multiple of them and that are going out there, and I think the US government—"

The news anchor interrupts him, saying, "But, Bill, you know the data better than I do. But, Bill, the data showed that everybody with a high dose had a side effect."

Bill speaks, "Yeah, but some of that is not dramatic where you know, it's just super painful, but yes, there, we need to make sure there is not severe side effects, is the FDA, I think, will do a good job with that, despite the pressure."

The reporter speaks, "How many doses of the vaccine will we need?"

Bill answers, "Well, none of the vaccines, at this point, appear like they will work with the single dose, that was the hope at the very beginning. Maybe one of them, particularly at the second generation, won't surprise us. We hope just two, although in the elderly, sometimes it takes more. So making sure we have lots of elderly people in the trial will give us that data."

The reporter speaks, "You said more than seven billion doses is what we will need."

Bill answers, "Well, if what you are trying to do is block all the transmission, then you need to get, you know, 70 to 80 percent coverage on a global basis. So it's an unbelievably big number."

Reporter says, "I mean, you are talking about a global vaccination program without a vaccine that has not been fully developed yet and a massive scaling up of how to produce one or several vaccines, I mean it's just mind boggling to think about this effort."

Bill replies, "But the private companies have stepped up, and the science has been advanced, the US funds biological research much more than any other country. We have stepped up to fund these vaccine manufacturers, the plants are being worked out now. You know in 2021, there is a good chance that this can get done and because this is about the billions that we need to spend to save trillions and avoid all those deaths."

The reporter speaks, "But who is going to get the vaccine first?"

Bill replies, "That is in discussion. Clearly the US, by funding factories in the US will get priority, but if we can have other factories, and this is where the US government, traditional generosity in global health will be needed, our foundation will be needed, other countries... We want to make sure that other people are not dying just because they can't afford to have access to the vaccine. And so that speaks to the top priority of our foundation. And there is good discussion going underway. The US in this relief bill may put 1 percent of it to make sure we put the pandemic in the entire world, and then that will draw other countries into that effort."

The reporter speaks, "I want to ask you today, the government support taxpayer money that is going towards vaccine development, today we learned Pfizer is going to get nearly $2 billion, Moderna receiving $438 million dollars in taxpayer money, and yet both companies have said they will not sell the vaccine at cost. They are going to make a profit on it. Should pharmaceutical companies profit off this vaccine research that taxpayers have helped fund?"

Bill responds, "Well, the Pfizer case is more of a procurement agreement than an R and D funding agreement. AstraZeneca, Johnson & Johnson have said that they are going to use a nonprofit construct, the exact contracts that were negotiated, I don't have access to, but yes, you'd want to balance the fact of who is taking the risk and who gets the benefit of those things. It's fantastic that the research is being funded, and I hope those agreements, in terms of pricing and access, are very strong."

Now the host of the channel A Call For An Uprising cut the interview short and interjects, saying the following:

Now let me ask you a question, for the people out there who think that we are all crazy nuts, would you put something in your body that was not going to be 100 percent proven to work, even if it was 90 percent proven to work, would you be willing to put that in your body, knowing that there could be extreme side effects? Would you? Because you probably need to be committed somewhere. Why would you put poison in your body if it's proven, and they admit, that is not necessarily going to work. That's exactly what happened with the flu. People were going, you know what, why I'm I getting this shot if doctors are even coming and saying that 50 percent of the time, it doesn't work? But idiots still line up and got the shots, and then they still get the flu, and they still go back the next year to get the shot again. Huh? Now that makes perfect sense.

Some people would be perfectly fine, get the shot, and then get the flu a week later and not even connect the dots. Can you imagine the side effects that are going to come with this, and then they want you to get it twice. Twice, not once—twice. And they talk about how big pharma and how much money they are going to make. Look, that is not what the endgame is not here because they print money. And I know that people on the right will talk about the money and the pharmaceutical game...this is about depopulation. That is what they care about. They don't care about cash, they don't care about cryptocurrency, they don't care about this electronic currency. They know what is coming next. They print it, money shows up in their bank account, they want to destroy the American people, and they want to destroy the people worldwide. Because they want to depopulate it.

They make you think in your mind that we live in an overly populated world. I have said this a trillion times, drive across country and go through Montana and South and North Dakota, Iowa, you will drive for hours and hours and hours, and there is nothing but empty land. But what they do is that they congest people into cities, the cities is always the backdrop in every movie, the cities is always the place where the action is happening, and they pretend these other places don't exist so when somebody goes, 'I would love to move to Montana,' they go, 'Why would you want to move there? There is nothing to do. There is no club scene, there is no bars, there is no partying, there is no celebs, that is not where it's happening, you got to go where the celebrities are and everyone else.' They want to depopulate, even though there is plenty of space.

And the second thing that is just laughable in the words that come out of this demon's mouth is talking about how we have to trust in the FDA. Are you kidding me? The FDA! You want to put the CIA at the top of the most corrupt organizations in the world. That's fine. You want to put the cabal, the CIA, and the Mossad up there, don't forget about the FDA. These are the people who are supposed to watch and protect what goes into our food from these food manufacturers. And they have been caught over and over and over. I don't even need to get into Monsanto. Let's just get into weed killer. You ever go to Home Depot or Lowes, for those young-

179

sters out there, you are not, probably, not picking weeds or into that stuff yet. Well, they have
this product called Roundup, and what it is, is
you spray it on weeds, and it murders weeds, but
don't get it to close into a tree or a bush because
it will probably kill it. Because that chemical will
go down into the roots and rot it. But that is
okay, right, to mix it with your Cheerios or your
alphabet cereal, right... Sprinkle some on, come
on, we are all conspiracy nuts!

So when I do videos on stuff like that, and
it's even in the news because there are such big
lawsuits, they can't even avoid it. Where there are
millions of people in class-action lawsuits, suing
these companies because of the Roundup that is
found in the food that has poisoned their children, not only made their children sick, caused
them lifelong diseases, caused things like, you
know, all types of diseases that they are never
going to recover from without medication but
also caused death. And this is the FDA we are
going to trust to approve the vaccine, despite the
early results that tell us, "Oh, it's making people
sicker!" No one is going to care, no one is going to
listen because they trust in Big Brother. They love
him, Big Brother, and it's what I always say, right.
They think in their heads, why would somebody
want to do this to someone else? Because normal
human beings, with good intentions and good
hearts, have a tough time comprehending the
wicked that exists. And that is why naive people
get walked on, and that is how these criminals get
away with this stuff—because people give them
the benefit of the doubt. And they go, "Well, that
is only in the movies." Oh, Satanic rituals... Oh,
people hating other people to the point where

they would like to see the population destroyed and killed. But that's the truth of the matter. That's what these people want and are trying to do. And the FDA is at the top of the list! Because they will allow anything to go in the food. They'll allow to take a dump and mix it in with the food. They don't care as long as they don't get caught, and when they do get caught, they are just going to go, "Oopsies!" Just like the CIA... Oh, the CIA was running tests on people's brains, creating Manchurian candidates, running MKUltra tests and enslaving people.

Oh, no big deal, the CIA can stay in business and still be an organization that is here to protect us. Huh? It's a joke! But then again, we have the fluoride in the water, the chemicals in the food, we have a passive society that only gets triggered when they are told to be triggered over monuments and things like that. They get triggered, but they don't care that they are getting poisoned from the FDA and Big Brother. Or there is a monument up, we better go tear it down, who cares! How about these guys who are killing us? And poisoning us? Who want this vaccine to be mandatorily put in us is a sick, disgusting, depraved world because of these sick and disgusting people that exist. So Gates, laughing it off for the most part. "Oh, it doesn't matter... you know there is going to be some results that might cause side effects, that's life!" Ah, then no one should not be putting it in their body. How is that? That seems like a simple freaking answer. I can't believe that people are buying into this. I can't believe that people think it's a conspiracy about, you know, depopulation and stuff when

they say it themselves. It's another joke. Thank
you, guys, for listening to today's show.

That is the end of that video. I would like to interject a bit more
about Bill Gates. I have seen a video of him giving a speech where
he says, "So let's look at each one of these and see how we can get
this down to zero, probably one of these numbers is going to have to
get pretty near to zero. Now that is back from high school algebra.
So let's take a look. First, we've got population. The world today has
6.8 billion people, and that is headed up about to 9 billion. Now if
we do a really great job on new vaccines, health care, reproductive
health services (Planned Parenthood/abortions), we can lower that
by perhaps 10 or 15 percent."[26]

Many people are aware that the vaccines that Bill Gates has
administered to people across the world have caused major injuries
and deaths. In Africa, the president warned everyone to reject his
vaccine for the coronavirus and read the Rothschild document which
details their plan to enslave humanity with a pandemic. In America,
many people are demanding to investigate Bill Gates for crimes
against humanity.[27]

Finally here is the sickest thing about this coming vaccine so
far. They are using aborted fetal tissue of babies that were born alive
five to six months; they cut out their hearts while it is still beating
because if it is not beating, then they are not useful. They also do this
to them without any anesthesia. This is satanic, demonic, and a most
horrific wicked ritual to create a vaccine that will be put in humans.
It is a most obvious truth that this is something a Holy God would
not want anyone to take any part in, nevertheless, to put inside their
bodies. These sick fallen angels are trying to destroy our humanity in
every way they can because they are jealous that we can be saved and
go to heaven, unlike them, and thus, they hate us all passionately and

---

[26] https://www.bitchute.com/video/QR347gaRW0uY/.
[27] https://justthenews.com/politics-policy/coronavirus/white-house-petition-
investigates-bill-gates-foundation-gets-over-6000000,
http://toresays.com/2020/04/18/lock-step-the-rockefeller-foundations-2010-
plan-to-enslave-humanity-with-plandemic/.

desire nothing but the same eternal fate that awaits them! Do not let them contaminate your body, soul, and spirit with their satanic rituals! Do not let them inject you with technology that will alter your DNA and turn you into a hybrid and not a human. Be wise! Resist this with all your might, even unto death if you have to. Fight this battle for your soul and wake up from your slumber! Do not trust the government! Do not trust the media or the fake science out there! Do not trust the fake FEMA camp Christians who will be used in the end to convince the people to take this. This is the facts! They live.[28]

This is the link to the movie trailer *They Live*, the movie about what we are living: https://youtu.be/jTK8eff1Zsk.

---

[28] https://humansarefree.com/2020/06/aborted-fetal-tissue-in-vaccines-babies-are-born-alive-at-5-6-months-old-with.

# CHAPTER 18

⌇

# The Seed of the Serpent

I will transcribe a dream from a YouTuber named Gelzel L. The title of her video is *Dream of the Seed of the Serpent/small talk and other dreams.*

This is not an easy topic, I don't know if you guys know much about the wheat and the tare. I know I did a video a few weeks ago about the wheat and the tare, like the harvest is ripe and stuff like that, and I read some Scriptures about it. But this is one was like a dream that I was not expecting. To tell you the truth, I didn't even expect anything like this. Remember the wolf dreams that I had? All these werewolves and stuff like that? Well, this is a little bit extreme.

So in this dream, I saw that I was in this place. It's like I was there, but I wasn't really there. Like I wasn't going through what they were going through. I was just watching there, everything. I was just observing everything that was going on. I am sitting there, and I am watching all of this, and what I saw was a bunch of people, running and screaming. First, this is how it began. It started out with a big boom! Like a big giant boom! You know how back in the day, we were always hearing a big boom? Like it was just a big noise, it went *boom*! So I heard this giant *boom*, and it was so loud, the whole ground was shaking. That is how loud this thing was. So it shook the ground of the earth, and I started seeing a lot of people started running. I saw many people running and running, and then I saw other people that were hurt and stuff like that, and many people died from this big boom. I don't know what caused the boom, I don't know if something had landed and caused a big disaster. All I know, there was a big boom, and the ground was shaking. Maybe it was an earthquake because of the boom. It might have been an earthquake because a lot of people died from this catastrophe, and I saw a lot of fire and smoke from far away, from far, far distance.

And then I am watching a family of two. Just a man and his child. And I see him yelling and screaming—Aah—you know when people are panicking and screaming? So they were screaming, so I see them run into their home and stuff like that, they try to leave, but then I saw these people coming... These people with hazards suits, you know like the disease control people, whatever, and special ops group, like these governments. I am not sure, these special-government-paid people. They were not the military, they were not dressed in military, they were dressed in T-shirts and stuff like that, but they were all in navy-blue type of color. And I saw the CDC and people in complete hazard suits on, and they were going from house to house, knocking on doors, and people had to go—they were taking these people with them.

These people, I don't know who they were, they were like us, they looked like us, they have skin like us, they look like ordinary average people. And they took them, they took a lot of these people, and they were going door-to-door, door-to-door, and finally I see all these people being hauled away in a van or in a bus, and they took them underground. I saw this people being taken underground. And then I noticed this water they splashed on them. The water had this glow to it, a greenish or yellowish color, and it glowed. It was like a chemical type of water, they splashed it on them. And when they splashed it on them, these people started screaming, and they were hysterical, yelling and screaming. So the water was poisoned or with some kind of chemical in it. And they were just screaming and yelling and going all kind of hysterical ways.

The reason why they were doing that, what I saw, was because when they sprayed this water on them, something happened to these people. Their hands, their body, everything started changing. They started changing, all of them started receiving these superpowers. These amazing crazy powers, but not only did they change, and they had powers, their appearance also changed. They were all serpents. They all were snakes, some had snake coming out of their hands, they still had their same bodies, but their hands had like snake heads just pull out, serpents, like sticking their tongue out of their hands. They were screaming because of what they looked like. Some had like a serpent head, some had serpent leg, like they had the tail of a serpent, they still had their full body.

This one person I saw had a bunch of snakes coming out of their body. Huge and like guts of snakes, probably fourteen heads, just coming out of her stomach. One had a whole head of a snake, like Medusa, there were snakes everywhere in their bodies. Even little children. I even saw little kids in the same way. They had snakes coming out of them. They had snakes, and it was part of their body. It was like a mutation of snakes in their bodies or something. And this woman who was wearing a white business suit, it was very tight, a bit short, and she came out, and she looked like she was running this place. She told everyone, "Calm down, calm down, you are now at your true appearance"

And they were screaming and yelling, asking, "What is going on? What is happening, what did you do to us? What is that stuff?"

And she said, "I brought you to your true form. Your real form."

And they were like, "What? No! We don't look like this! We are monsters! We are hideous" And they were like, "No, this is not what we look like."

And she was like, "Do you know who you are?"

And they were like, "What do you mean?"

"Now she had to sit there and talk to them and educate them about who they truly were. She said, "You are the seed of the serpent." That's what she said. She looked at them, and she said, "You are the seed of the serpent."

And they all were like—every single one of them was like, "Oh my gosh, no! No, no, I am not, I will not receive that, no, hell no! Get us out of here."

They were screaming, they were crying, they were shocked! These snakes were all over them and coming out of them. It was just crazy! And I am watching these people like, what the heck? What? There is a seed of the serpents? So this is what I am saying to myself, the whole time in the dream. What? I did not know there was a serpent seed. I knew there were like the Nephilims and stuff like that, but a serpent seed, oh, I was like, *oh*! And they were like crying and screaming, and the woman said to them that, "The reason that we brought you here is to reveal to you who you really are. And this is your DNA. We had to find all of you guys through your DNA." Your DNA was what they were looking for. For some kind of DNA marker of trace of this thing that can bring them. Like whatever they were working, that liquid/water that they were spraying on them, whatever that thing was, it allowed their true appearance to come out. All it was doing was bringing out who they really were. And they showed them the real serpents that they came from. And they couldn't believe it.

And the lady was telling them, "What do you think, I mean you really thought that you were 100 percent human?" That is what she said. She said, "You really thought that you were human. You were made this way. You are a mix breed." That is what she said. She said that they were a mixed breed. And they are serpents. They are the seed of serpents. Then she said, "Now is time for us to train you and get you ready to understand how to use your powers for the time to activate you." She was like, "It is time to activate you guys. It's time for you guys to know who you truly and what side you belong to."

And then one guy, the guy with the little girl that I was talking about, the wife died and stuff like that, but they didn't. The little girl and the guy, he was some Spanish guy, and he was like, "Oh, no! Oh, no! *Hay, Dios mio*! I do not worship Lucifer! I worship Almighty God, there is no way I am worshipping Lucifer! This is not my seed. I do not receive that."

And the lady was like, "I am sorry, but this is who you are, this is who we made you to be. We've been planning you all over the world, for decades now. And you need to accept who you truly are."

And the guy was so mad, he was so upset, he was saying, "God is my Savior, Jesus is my Lord, Jesus is my God."

And it was like, "No, you can't be of this, He will never accept you into His kingdom."

I was like, "What?" I thought everyone can be accepted by God, anyone! And the lady was saying, "Because you are his seed, you don't belong to Him. He didn't make you. They made you. We made you."' And then she was like, "Our brand is everywhere. We are the seed of the serpent. We are everywhere, we are all over the world."

And that's what she was saying. They are running the world is what this woman said. There are people all over the world that are powerful, and they are of the seeds. This is their seed. This world is their inheritance. That is what she said. So this lady was just going on and on, and then they were just crying, and then others were like kind of ecstatic because they were like, "Wow, we got all this power now." So a lot of them were so excited that they received this newfound body and this newfound power. So then I saw them training in areas where they were showing them how to use their power. They were educating them, I guess they were re-educating them, allowing them to understand what war they are fighting and whose side they are supposed to be in.

I am just telling you what I saw in the dream. And it was crazy because these people were first hysterical, and then they were getting all excited about the whole thing. And they were fully and truly submitted to the whole ordeal. They became very powerful, and they trained them to the point where they were so powerful, and a lot of them had supernatural power. One of them spit fire out of his mouth, like a dragon. Like a real dragon serpent. He can spit fire out of his mouth, he can make fire out of his hands. One of them was teleporting, from here to there, and one of them was disguising himself. Like I can see one of them transforming into all kinds of faces. He had many faces and stuff like that. He can be anything and everything he wants to be. There were so many gifts, one can just stop time for a few minutes, not for a long time but a few minutes. One can go backwards into the past for a few minutes or whatever, I don't know, they were so many things, they were able to do so many things. And it was like, wow, these serpent seeds were able to do all of this stuff.

And I am wondering, I can't believe this is happening. And then I saw a lady came, and she was like, "When are we going back home?" Because they were there for a few months, or maybe a year or so. I am not sure how long the time frame was. But I was there observing the whole thing for a long time. I even got to experience how emotional, how heartbreaking this was for many of them. Especially the ones that were truly trying to serve God as their Lord and Savior. I didn't understand that part. How can these people love God and still be part of the seed of the serpent? This blew my mind, like I don't even know how this works. Like how does this work? So I guess you learn something new every day.

I am just reporting what I saw, you guys. This is what I saw in my dream. So after all of this was done, it was time to send them out. Some of them were ready, and some of them were not ready because their power was so great and so hard to control. It was too much, like overwhelming power. Like some of them had multitude powers, and they could not control their powers. They were not ready. Like the lady that I saw all these snakes coming out of her stomach, she was not ready, and the ones that were ready to train their powers, and they were perfect at it, they somehow made their body, all their snakes, and everything disappeared, and they were normal again. They went back to normal form, but all this power was inside of them. They can hide themselves perfectly.

So I saw the lady coming up to those that were ready, and the ones that weren't ready, they had to keep training them, reeducating them, and showing them how to use their power. So I see the guy keeps spraying them, and I saw the guy was like so jealous of what he was seeing. How these people were turning into these things, but at the same time, they had these crazy supernatural powers. So I saw the guy that was one of the workers. He threw some of the stuff on him, he spilled it. Two or three of them did the same thing. One of them was not part of the seed, and when he put that thing on him, he died. He died right away because the regular human body cannot handle these poisons, these things, whatever it is they are using. I don't know, all I know is I saw the guy drop dead. And it didn't do nothing. And the other guy did it, and it actually worked on him, and he started feeling powerful, and he started to have some kind of power, and snakes started coming out of him. So he was part of the seed of the serpents. And it was just crazy. Then the lady was like, "You guys need to stop that, you are working and not participating in what I have in store for these people," and stuff like that. So the lady was getting upset with the workers that were actually spraying the stuff, and I noticed that they had to keep spraying them so the whole thing would fully, completely manifest.

It was not a one-time thing that they did to them. It was like an ongoing thing. So after that was done, I noticed that they were shown a map, and the map that I saw was America. Bold and clear, I saw the map of America. The map looked different, though. It's crazy because the map was looking so different. What I saw was America, I saw Alaska, I saw the top of Canada, and I saw Mexico. So basically my main focus, even though I saw the entire map of America, my main focus was on the west side of America. I noticed the west side, I noticed California. The whole California was under the ocean. And this is a live map we were looking at. California was in the ocean. I don't know what happened. California and part of Mexico—a big chunk of Mexico from that part where California is—a big part of that was also in the ocean. And I was like, "What?" What's going on with that? What happened to the map? What happened to those parts of the world? What went down? And then the lady was like, "I am from California, but I am originally from France, that where my birth home is." And then the lady was like, "I can't send you to California because California is gone."

OMG! I did not even know that, that had happened in the dream. I didn't know until they mentioned it. So yes, this was crazy. So she said, 'I am not going to send you there, I am going to send you to France.' So she sent her to France, she sent the other one to Australia, she sent the other one to Austria, Europe, Italy. I saw people going to Africa, to China, India, South America, I don't remember seeing any islands. What the heck happened to all the islands? It's crazy 'cause I saw America but no islands in the map. So these people were being sent all over the world, and they were already in the world. And it was crazy, they were already there, and these people activated them, educated them, trained them, trained them for this hour or something. I didn't know what they were going to go do, but the lady was saying that they were activating them so that they may be prepared for the big event that was what they were preparing them for. The big event.

And then I woke up from the dream. After they sent them all over the place, I woke up. And when I woke up, I was like, what the heck was I dreaming? What is this? There is a seed of serpents in this world? And I am like talking to God and all confused about this dream and saying, "Lord, what was I seeing? What was that? Is this for real? Are there people out there that are not of

You? That cannot be a part of You, and that You cannot receive them in Your Kingdom, no matter what?" And then something started speaking in my heart, and it was like, "Didn't I say that I was coming back as in the days of Noah?" And I was like, okay, what happened in the days of Noah? It was the Nephilims, the mixed breed of humans and fallen angels, okay. So I was like, but those people were tall, these kids were big, they were tall, the ones that I was seeing looked like us, they were small like us, they were average height. Some of them were a little bit tall here and there, but still they were like us, they looked more like us. I understand the Nephilims looked different. But these people looked like us. How can this be? How is this even possible? And then He brought it back to my memory. "Come on, I told you about the wheat and the tare. You notice how the wheat and the tare grew together because they looked like each other, they looked the same, but when it was time to harvest the wheat and the tare, when is time to harvest the tear, you would notice what they look like, you would notice them." God knows who they are. You don't think God knows who they truly are? And I guess these people are searching for their people. Because I saw them looking through their DNA. What are they using right now, searching through our DNA? You noticed what they are doing with COVID-19? They are running tests over everybody. They want to swap or whatever they are doing… Don't you know they take your DNA like that? Anyways, I am just letting you guys know about this dream.

Then I had another dream. In this dream, I woke up, and it was 8:00 a.m., bright daylight, and I saw the sunlight, and all of the sudden, it got really dark really fast, the sun was completely taken out. Then it got dark, and people started coming out. It got really dark. It was like the darkest dingy gray unpleasant atmosphere, and I noticed like if God had been completely removed out of the atmosphere, and it was a lot of fear, you felt a lot of fear in the presence in the area. You felt a lot of painful fear, like the Holy Spirit has been removed somehow. Like there was no God in this atmosphere. Nothing. There was a lot of hate, anger, fear, and all kinds of stuff. I saw these people coming out of nowhere. A bunch of people started fighting and killing each other for no apparent reason. People were just killing each other, and they loved it! They loved it so much, you can see the love they had from other people's pain and suffering. They were just overjoyed with what they were doing. They were enjoying it, they were in packs, they were in groups and just terrorizing a whole bunch of people all over the streets, all over the area.

I saw some people going into people's homes, taking them out and killing them, stabbing them, enjoying watching the blood, licking and tasting them after they killed. It was just nasty! It felt as if I was watching one of those *Mad Max* type of movies. Oh, it was horrible, it was like a real-life horror movie. I am watching all of this, and it was like no peace anywhere. Everywhere you went, everywhere I walked, everywhere I looked around, everyone was killing each other, everyone was running for their lives. It was like in that Bible verse where you are caught in a lions' den, and right when you got out of there, you are already being devoured by the lion, you go enter into a room full of bears, the farm bears are willing to devour you, and after you are done with the bears, you get caught with the cobra on your hands, and like there is no way out of any of this. It was just complete chaos, everywhere.

And these people, they were just so hateful, so cruel, like, who are these people, where did they come from, how are they acting like this? And then they were like good people that were trying to hide and trying to cry out for help, saying, "Please save us from these people, please hide us from these people, hide us from them." You know who these people were? These people were the people that were waiting for a time like this. Those were the people from my dream, the serpent seed. Those people were heartless, they didn't care who they killed, who they hurt. And one thing I can say about this, thank God I didn't see any children there. I think the rapture had happened or something. And no, I was just there observing everything that I was watching everything for the past few weeks, months, I have been having dreams where I am just observing, just watching everything, and this is what God wants me to do right now. So I am watching all this, and people are just crying. I saw people getting raped, I saw people getting bullied, murdered, there was no police, there was no military around to help nobody. I saw military cars, and these people were in it. They were in the military cars, using them, using the military weapons and all that stuff. I saw bombs being thrown, here and there, it was just, hmmm. America was destroyed! It was ruined. It was ruined by these people. And it was not only here, and I knew to my knowledge it was not only here. It was everywhere, it was some type of riot, chaos, crazy, mayhem, just happening, something caused these people to go crazy. Mad crazy, they started killing everybody. It was just bad everywhere. I saw no government anywhere, nothing to do with government and order, there was no police anywhere or rescue, there was no one there to rescue anybody. I just saw everybody being devoured. It was like a termination of humankind. Mankind was going extinct, and these evil people were the only ones rising up. Anything good that was left in this world was being taken out completely. The restrainer was removed.

Last dream I will share is that I saw a giant hand remove itself out of the planet. When it left, I saw the sky went pitch-black, like lightning, thunder, all kind of bad, the sky was like alive. It looked like things were just moving from the sky, and I saw all these locusts coming down from the sky, a bunch of them. Locusts everywhere, and people were running and screaming, saying, "Help me, help me." People were getting stung by these things, they were everywhere. After that I saw something else behind the locusts. I saw these demonic-looking things behind the locusts, and then they left. And I woke up.

And that was the end of my dream. I love you, guys, take all of this to the Lord, heed these warnings, times of trials is coming upon us. Stay faithful to the Lord, stay true, repent of all your sins daily. Pray that you are counted worthy to escape these things that are coming upon the earth. The beast system is rising. The antichrist is about to be made known who he truly is. A lot of people know who he is. Just know that something big is coming, something uncontrollable.

Things are not going to get better. I know a lot of people are preaching prosperity, good things, things are going to prosper for America, things are going to get better. The president is going to lead us into a better righteous path… I am sorry, guys, as much as I would love for that to happen, it's just not going to happen, you guys. Pray that we all get counted worthy to escape these things. God bless you, loving wonderful brother and sisters in Christ.[29]

Her dream reminded of videos in YouTube of whistleblowers exposing the truth about cloning labs, reptilians, shape-shifting humans, and all the insane things they do. Do your own research while you can so that you may understand the world we live in.

These seed of the serpents are people from all kinds of cultures. They have many things prepared for the rest of us. They will fake a rapture using alien technology, and they will kill many people. Unfortunately many Christians are going to be killed by these technologies because they are going to be fooled into thinking that it's the real rapture, and they are going to come out and want to be abducted by these spacecrafts in the skies. Before the real rapture of the church of Jesus Christ, there will be a fake one. Keep that in mind, please. Also know that the church will experience the impact of a nuclear attack and an asteroid and a huge earthquake before it is lifted off in a rapture. We are going to go through those things because if we would leave before that happens, then who would bring the harvest of souls to Christ during the aftermath of these events? These are the days where millions of souls will surrender to the Lord, and He needs His bride to be here to bring the souls to Him. Also the majority of the church is deceived; thus they are not prepared for the rapture. God will use these events to wake her up and to cleanse her.

The seed of the serpent are the ones behind CERN. They already have used CERN to change our Scriptures. Our Bible have

---

[29] https://youtu.be/rTfMmwx68ig.

been supernaturally changing for some time now. Many verses have been twisted so as to defile the Word of God and also deceive the masses into worshipping the antichrist. Here is a link to one video that shows these supernatural changes through quantum computing and witchcraft: https://youtu.be/utzrYcDsarc. The title to this video is *Alert: The Antichrist is NOW the MESSIAH, JESUS IS NOT! (Jan 2017) Mandela Effect Bible Changes.*

This is one of hundreds of videos that are there that prove that our Bibles are no longer the same. They have the capacity to do this, yet the majority of Christians are completely clueless that this is going on, and they continue to read the Bible, not knowing that they are falling into a strong delusion because of the changes in them. Do your own research concerning the Mandela Effect too if you would like to come out of the Matrix we are in.

The seed of the serpent are the ones behind the deepfake technology that will also disrupt our measure of truth. They now have the technology to get any video out there and alter it in a manner where they can change the content of what was said and use the same exact voice of the person in the video and program it to speak what they would like them to say instead, and they change their mouth movements as they speak to make it seem as if they really said that, even though they did not. Please do your research on the deepfake technology as well.[30]

Please also do your research on Project Blue Beam. With this technology, they will fake the return of the Messiah in the skies. They will fool the whole world.[31]

Study the Book of Enoch, which was removed out of the Bible by the seed of the serpents, because this is the book that explains their existence. But make sure to read the one that is legit because, of course, as they are very slick, there are new-age counterfeit books of Enoch out there as well. I know this is not easy. To know the truth is not easy, this is a common fact, yet I marvel at the amount of people

---

[30] *Deepfakes-Real Consequences,* https://youtu.be/dMF2i3A9Lzw.
[31] *Great Deception Coming! Idolatry/Fake Aliens/Demons/Project Blue-Beam,* https://youtu.be/iGDk9st6yls.

who think they are well informed just because they watch the mainstream media or attend the mainstream best universities and schools or because they attend the mainstream churches. So sorry to inform you that these people own those industries. To know the real truth, one must dig deep in the Scriptures, in prayer and fasting, in obedience to the truth, with integrity and not deceit. If anyone likes to practice a lie, they too will be deceived; if anyone wishes to find the truth, they must pursue it more than silver and gold. It is not going to be easy at all. We are in a spiritual battle!

Please take a look at this documentary about Hollywood called *Hollywood Actors Exposed, Full Length* and see for yourselves how Hitler used Hollywood to prepare his youth to commit horrific crimes and how the devil continues to use Hollywood to form the character of the youth in our world. See for yourselves how Hollywood actors and film producers—many of them—have sold their souls for money and fame and are possessed by demons, and these demons are the ones writing the scripts and doing the acting through these vessels that have given themselves unto them, and so many Christians love to submerge themselves hours and hours in front of the TV or the social platforms or the video games, etc., only to be ministered by these evil entities whose sole purpose is to destroy us and take us down to hell with them.

The seed of the serpent are very advanced in technology, skills of deception, and many other things. It is so sad to me to know just how organized and determined these people are to destroy mankind and how passive and ignorant most of humanity is toward the truth about them and their schemes. If only the majority of Christians would have read their Bibles for real when it wasn't altered by Satanists and now by CERN as well; if only they would have stopped the seed of the serpents from coming into their churches and twist the Scriptures, changing it from what it used to say; if only Christians would have listened to the prophets such as David Wilkerson who, since 1974, warned and warned about the coming events, but they dismissed him as a false prophet. What a tragedy, indeed![32]

---

[32] weweredeceived.com.

# CHAPTER 19

## President Trump

As I previously mentioned in here, the Lord showed me that Trump was a deceiver since he was running for office. I was astonished to see many people of God that I highly admire and respected to be fooled by this man. But what was truly disturbing to me was to watch the discrepancy in their messages and see how many others would not see what I see. Many of the Trump supporter preachers were preaching that America was going to be judged by God before Trump came into office. Then they got Trump in office, and just like that, they changed their message. Now they were preaching that because Trump was in office, America would be great again, the economy will bloom with him as president, and he will be in office for two terms.

Yet here we are, in August 12, 2020, which is the day I am officially writing this chapter, and America is almost unrecognizable and not in a good way. We are most divided than ever. The unemployment rate is historic, and the tensions between foreign nations are at its peak, and the world has never been more set up for the New World Order to begin than it is today. However, these preachers will argue to death that indeed Trump is still the good guy and that everything bad that is happening is because the elite want Trump out of office, and they are the ones creating this chaos to remove him. Indeed, it is created by these people, but Trump is part of their circus. He is one of them. And even if Trump was the holiest person on this planet, if the American people that he leads refuse to repent, refuse to stop aborting the unborn, refuse to normalize homosexuality, sexual perversion, and fornication, if they refuse to stop leaving underage children alone or with psychopaths to go to work, if they refuse to stop living their lives in apostasy and independent from the Holy Spirit, no matter what person is in the White House, the nation only has one fate, and that is destruction and judgment. Because no nation has ever rebelled against the holy ways of our Lord and not be utterly decimated. Honestly we should consider ourselves very lucky that our destruction has not even happened yet. God has certainly wiped out of the map places that have done less evil than America.

I will now transcribe a couple of videos, among many of them, to make you see the truth, and if this doesn't convince you that Trump was never chosen by God to bless America, then nothing will. Trump was never going to bless America, but instead, like all the other Communists and bad leaders in the world in history, God placed Trump in office to judge America and to reveal to all the lukewarm Christians, their own hearts. Because Trump is indeed a reflection of their hearts. If what I am about to write and transcribe now doesn't convince you, then you are under a strong delusion (2 Thessalonians 2:11).

Unfortunately the majority of the American churches have been conditioned to love money, prosperity, and vanity. And that is precisely what Trump represented and promised them, and they took the bait! That Hillary was no good, yes, but that doesn't justify voting for Trump. Voting for the lesser evil is still evil. And in my opinion, I think Trump was more evil than Hillary because he pretends to be Christian. God prefers that we are cold or hot, but the lukewarm he will vomit! Either way, our presidents are not elected, they are selected! Our votes don't matter. They make us think it does, but it's all an illusion.

America was never going to be great again because of Trump, because then that would have made David Wilkerson a liar in his book *The Vision* where he warned the American people in 1974 that it was too late to stop the judgment of God upon this land, and he saw nuclear war, huge earthquakes, tsunamis, asteroids coming upon this land; he saw famine, pestilence, economic collapse, and he saw the division among the people, the rise of the gay community, and immorality becoming the norm, the rise of the perversion on the TV and music industry, the hatred toward the parents from the children, and the love of money in the mainstream pastors. He warned that America needed to repent and that they were headed toward a horrific day of the Lord, yet instead of heeding his warnings and repenting, Christians removed his book out of the bookstores and called him a false prophet. He was mostly persecuted by the Christians themselves. I had never read his book, yet in 2012–2016, God began giving me dreams about tsunamis, asteroids, earthquakes, wars, famine, riots, etc., and this was when I began to study the Scriptures in much more detail and outside of the interpretation of the pastors.

Then this was when I realized that the churches were in apostasy, and thus, I got out of all churches in 2012. I just recently read the book by David Wilkerson, and I was blown away! Everything the Lord had shown me in dreams, and in revelation through prayers, this man spoke in his book. Everything he spoke in this book is also what few of His real watchmen were also saying that was coming. Yet so many fell for the message of "God is going to bless America, and Trump will make everything better," and these people who bought this great lie from the pits of hell were the ones persecuting and mocking the preachers like myself. They were saying that we were speaking from the devil, and that we were not really listening from God. And once Trump got into office, they were all echoing that Kim Clement was right, and everyone who prophesied that Trump was going to be president and fix America was right as well. Did you know that there is a verse in Deuteronomy where God warns His people that if a prophet sees a vision and that vision comes to pass, but that prophet teaches you to go away from His ways, then you are not to follow that prophet?

**If there arise among you a prophet, or a dreamer of dreams, and giveth thee a sign or a wonder, and the sign or the wonder come to pass, whereof he spake unto thee, saying. Let us go after other gods, which thou hast not**

**known, and let us serve them; thou shalt not hearken unto the words of that prophet, or that dreamer of dreams: for the Lord your God proveth you, to know whether ye love the Lord your God with all your heart and with all your soul. Ye shall walk after the Lord your God, and fear Him, and keep His commandments, and obey His voice, and ye shall serve Him, and cleave unto Him. And that prophet, or that dreamer of dreams, shall be put to death; because He hath spoken to turn you away from the Lord your God, which brought you out of the land of Egypt, and redeemed you out of the way which the Lord thy God commanded thee to walk in. So shalt thou put evil away from the midst of thee.**

Thus Kim Clement and all the prosperity preachers that claimed that God chose Trump to bless America have taught the people of God to keep all the pagan holidays, which are an abomination to the Lord. They didn't teach the people to keep the same feasts and holy days that our Lord Jesus kept and gave us His example of how He wished for us to celebrate anything. They taught the people to change the Sabbath for Sunday, they taught the people to give them their tithes and offerings, comparing themselves to the Levites of the Bible and to even the disciples of Jesus, yet they did not live like the Levites or the disciples of Jesus. The Levites were prohibited to have an inheritance with the Israelites because God was their inheritance, and they were ordained to be financially sustained by the tithes and offerings alone because God was their inheritance. They were prohibited to work in secular jobs (Numbers 18).

Moreover, these prosperity preachers also compared themselves to the disciples of Jesus when asking for the tithes and offerings, but they did not teach the people that the disciples of Jesus also abstained themselves from working in secular jobs so they would not ignore their time with the Lord, the study of His Holy Word, fasting, and praying (Acts 6:1–7).

In conclusion, by them receiving the tithes and offerings of the people of God, and at the same time working secular jobs and earning money in many other forms outside of the service of the tabernacle, they were breaking God's holy design, and I learned that part of the reason for this design was to protect God's pastors from getting conceited, since it takes humility to depend on the people they serve and not on their jobs. God showed me that since many of these pastors are given so much revelation, knowledge, supernatural gifts, the whole dependence upon God and His church for their financial livelihood was God's loving way to keep them humble. In this manner, they would know that they were not better or superior to those whom they served. This was also to protect them from greed or the love of money or from putting their eyes on material things. But most importantly, this design was ultimately so that they may have the proper time to be with God, to have time to care for those people that God entrusted them with and whom they will give account to God for their soul, and this design was also so they may have the proper time to be with their families, and, finally but not least, to rest.

Being a pastor is a full-time job. Just like any other full-time job, if they are married, neglecting the spouse or children is not an option, and resting their bodies and exercising is important to win the battles that come against us daily from Satan. No pastor, if they have a spouse and family, should have a second job. That is just too much to do. The first thing that usually gets neglected is praying and fasting and studying. And if they don't neglect that, then they neglect their loved ones, handing them over to the enemy. And if they don't neglect that, then they neglect their mental and physical health, which is also a sin since our bodies are the temple of the Holy Spirit. Thus here is the main reason for the tithes and the offerings, but the prosperity preachers have completely defiled it.

I heard many preachers justify themselves for working and pastoring at the same time by using Paul as an example, but they failed to mention to the people that Paul was single. He did not neglect a family to serve God, and Paul even was the one who advised people to not get married if they can abstain from it so that they may have time to serve God. If pastors are married and have children, their first ministry is their home. If they are out of the home working and then in church, they failed in their most important ministry, which is their family and home. They automatically become disqualified in front of the eyes of the Lord to counsel anyone.

Moreover, the prosperity preachers failed to teach women to be homemakers (Titus 2:1–5) so they may not be leaving underage children home alone or with psychopaths, as research shows that has been going on and why I believe it's the main reason why so many children are hating their parents passionately, just as David Wilkerson prophesied would happen in the last days. This also affected their marriages since it now became very unfair for a woman to have to do all the chores in the home since they also were forced to pay all the bills the same way as the men did. Thus it was not from God that they come home from a hard day of work, just like the men did, and for the man to relax and be taken care of by this exhausted woman. That burden was never the will of God for the women.

The prosperity preachers went along with the seed of the serpent, and they promoted the feminist movement, which is the opposite of the holy design for the family, and many of them went as far as to condemn the homemakers, calling them lazy, incompetent, unholy, leeches, and even accused them of stealing money from the government for not paying taxes. They were accusing them with the verse being preached outside of content, "Whoever doesn't work, doesn't eat." But they would teach that verse without informing the people that when Paul preached that, he lived in a culture where women were homemakers. He was addressing the men. Jesus grew up with a homemaker. He was not sent to day cares and public schools. Wasn't Jesus the example we are to follow? We must start with the way His parents raised Him. His mother was His teacher, and she taught Him the Word of God. This was and still is the design of God for the family, yet the prosperity preachers changed it, and not just changed it, they caused the homemakers to be persecuted and rejected by society.

Furthermore, the prosperity preachers failed to teach men to be the providers for the wives and children (Ephesians 5). They love to preach to the women that they must submit to the man because he is the head, but they failed to teach that what makes someone head of the household is not the gender but whoever is that pays the bills, "He who owns the gold makes the rules." If you study Ephesians 5, you will see that God compares the husband to Christ, who is the head of the church and gave Himself completely to the church/His bride and provided for her everything she needed to be saved. He ordained man in this passage to love his wife as his own body and to nourish it and care for it as if it was his own body. That meant to financially maintain her which, in those days, that was what the men did. They financially maintained their wives, not because their wives were inferior or less intelligent or less strong, or whatever you may want to say. It was because in this way, they had control of their children, what their children learned and saw throughout the day, and what they did or did not do all day. They had control of what they ate and did not eat, and the women also had time to pray more, to be with God more, and attend her husband without it being unfair because working in the home, cooking, cleaning, etc. after she comes from work is called exploitation. That is way too much work, and then she has to neglect important people or things or herself. God showed me that He assigned women to be the Levite of the home, assigned by God to protect her family in prayer and to serve them in love and much humility, while the husband took care of her financially. This way the children would grow up lovingly and loving others in return, and their marriages were strong because they depended on each other.

In addition, the prosperity preachers failed to teach the churches that they were the ones to financially care for the poor and the needy. Not the government. That is also one more reason for the tithes and the offerings. This money was to be used to sustain the preachers but also to care for the widows who had no family.

**If any man that believeth have widows,**
**have widows, let them relieve them, and let not**

**the church be charged; that they may relieve
them that are widows indeed. (1 Timothy 5:16)**

This verse is most revealing as to how far away from the design of God our mainstream churches are today. Here we see that first of all, a widow was a woman without a husband, thus it shows that the husbands were the sole financial providers since they were talking about financially maintaining them now that they were widows. Now that she no longer had a husband, she was in need of financial help. Obviously she didn't have a secular job. Nor did you see anywhere here that they were forcing her to go out to work. They were saying for the family of this woman to take care of her so that they may help the ones that had no family. It's as clear as day. They did not send them to the government or to shelters or left them to be homeless either. They spent their money on helping them instead of buying themselves mansions, luxurious cars and clothes, or spending it on lavish trips, dinners at restaurants, etc. This is the great difference between the original church and what should wake you all up about our fake churches today!

The biblical design from God was for the church leaders to take care of the widows, the orphans, the stranger, the needy, and the poor while the people in the church took care of the leaders of the church, and the men took care of the women, while the women took care of the children (James 1:27).

In this way, they took care of one another and gave no place of authoritative government to control them and harm them in any way. In this way, they kept their freedom from communism and totalitarian authorities.

How is it righteous to own a million-dollar home and a megachurch as a pastor and not even have a shelter for the homeless in the city where that pastor lives? Yet this is the truth about many of these megachurch prosperity gospel preachers who are the ones mentoring our President Donald J. Trump. I don't care if these pastors are donating millions of dollars to different countries, ministries etc. If they are not financially sustaining the poor in their own neighborhood, like the biblical disciples did, then they failed. If they are forcing mothers to abandon their children and their husbands to go to work so they too can pay for their mansions and cars and trips with tithes and offerings, they have failed God and His people!

Now that I have given you a short glimpse of just how many designs of God the prosperity gospel preachers have completely demolished and changed, and just how many wrong things they have taught us, I will transcribe a couple of videos about Donald Trump so you can see for yourself that he is a wolf dressed in sheep's clothing and the leader of the apostasy church in America. God allowed a lying spirit in the mouth of the lukewarm preachers so as to expose all of them! Just as He did in the Old Testament in 2 Chronicles 18.

And God even tricked everyone by making His true messengers preach that the elections would be cancelled, and Obama was going to stay in power because in truth, even though that did not happen the last election and Trump became president, that seems to me that still that is what is about to happen in this coming election. Before the coming elections, they are going to fake an assassination on Trump by nuking Trump Tower in New York City, and they will put Trump in a bunker, the economy will then collapse, and civil war will follow. Then Obama will rise to power, but not in our government because our government will be no more because America will be destroyed! Obama will rise into power and as leader of the whole world because he has been the chosen one. Thus technically God's true messengers were not wrong; they just did not know that God was showing them this coming election 2020.

*I'll give you the "bottom line" to this post, then follow with the research behind it: The global elite, who worship Lucifer, have been "broadcasting" through the Rothschild-owned Thompson-Reuters News on BING, that Obama was chosen as their "anointed one". Furthermore, they have also broadcasted their intended use of Islamic subjugation, to help usher in the New World Order, to utilize CERN to open up the gates of hell and the coming delusion of "aliens" (which Obama having the KEY role in their New World Order plan. OBAMA IS THE ANTICHRIST! The Antichrist is the same entity as the Islamic "THE MAHDI" or "THE 12ᵀᴴ IMAM"*[33]

I will now transcribe a video from the channel Israeli News, with Stephen Benoon.

We are going to be discussing several things in our news broadcast today that clearly are, in some people's opinions, they are conspiracy theories. So in other people's opinions, these things are really real, these things are happening on the earth, but we are also going to be looking at this from a prophetic standpoint, something that I discovered recently written in the Book of Enoch, a book that, in some circles of Christianity and in Judaism, that the Book of Enoch is not part of the Bible, yet it's clearly part of the Ethiopian scriptures. It was even part of the Qumran community, where there has been many fragments, including an incomplete scroll of the Book of Enoch that was discovered. So the Jewish people did accept that the Book of Enoch as an authoritative biblical scripture at one time, and in many Bibles, it's still there, including even the EXIF air that Dr. Stephen pigeon has put out as well, where he put this book back in the Bible. So we are going to be looking at some things from there, and we are going to be looking at some articles that have been considered, well, some might say it's fake news, some might say satire, regardless of the case, there may be some truth to it, and this is what I wanted to talk to you about, these things.

---

[33] https://believeacts2blog.wordpress.com/2020/08/06/8-6-2020-from-1-2-16-the-creepy-photo-on-bing-news/.

Antarctica has really become a major subject in recent, well, in fact in the last year, even more so, there's been every kind of conspiracy theory that it is a place where a mass of alien base, this is where aliens go at, we know of one of the former military officers Byrd, who fought a conflict near Antarctica and lost a lot of men claiming that there were flying disc, flying saucers coming out of the Antarctica, and just all kinds of evidence that is legitimate evidence that clearly seems to show that the Antarctica is certainly a base of some sort. The Germans also, under Adolf Hitler, had a base down in Antarctica. All kinds of things were going on in this region of the world, and this year, actually last year, when the election, John Kerry himself disappeared down to the Antarctica during the very day of election, but what was really strange is that when John Kerry went down there, he goes to New Zealand right afterwards, and there was a massive earthquake inside New Zealand. I am going to share with you, you can see some of the images here in this article, here in the *New York Times*, they will show you images of the earthquake itself—7.8 magnitude earthquake. The earthquake was very, very shallow, and in one article that we saw—that would probably be considered satire—that they have written and stated that the reason the earthquake happened was because John Kerry did a last-ditch effort and went down to Antarctica to try to meet with the, well, as they put it there, he was meeting with the guardians, and the guardians rejected his plea to put Hillary Clinton in the White House. Instead Donald Trump would become president of the United States.

Now I realize that those sound so far-fetched, it sounds so crazy in fact to even think of that, and then of course they said that the earthquake in New Zealand where he went immediately after the Antarctica visit was a warning to him not to come back again. Well, that's what they also said in the article. Those of you that remember, here is a picture here of the patriarch Kirill. Patriarch Kirill is also the head of the Eastern Orthodox Church who went also to Antarctica on a very unexpected trip after he met with Pope Francis in Cuba, and Pope Francis gave him a secret document. It was never revealed exactly what was in the document, but it was the first time the two leaders of the Western Orthodox Churches had met together to try to mend their relationship. He goes to South America afterwards and the unexpected trip to Antarctica. But the question is, why did he go to Antarctica? Well, in one article here, 'The Ark of Gabriel, Antarctica, Russia and the Apocalypse,' speaks about how that the Russian government had actually moved a mysterious article that was discovered at Mecca underneath the ground there and was brought out. Many people died in the process according to the article's claim here and that Russia did a special movement of this ark down to Antarctica. Now again, whether we would say this is just a bunch of garbage or if it's really true or not, I will just leave that up to you. But maybe what I am going to share with you in a few minutes might weigh in your thinking, so I do ask you to just kind of bear with me a little bit here while we discuss these things here.

Anyway, Mecca... if you remember, I believe it was last year, there was a, quote unquote, stampede, and the news reported that some 701 cases, 717 people were killed in this stampede, and this is something that has never happened before Mecca, and actually we found out later that it was 2,000 people were killed there in Mecca and an apparent stampede that killed all these people. Well, not according to some of the articles there. In fact, as you can see this crane that is toppled, that what was actually going on at Mecca was an excavation of this strange art called the Ark of Gabriel that, according to the article here, this was something that Muhammad had said, had prophesied about. And this was buried here beneath this very place, and they were working on trying to bring it out and some type of plasma release was done, and it caused the death of all these people. Again, is this just conspiracy theories or it's just fabricated, who really knows? But one thing that is a fact, though, is that one is a Russian scientific ship headed to Antarctica, and that ship gets stopped at the port there in Saudi Arabia, supposedly to take on supplies.

Well, as you know, Saudi Arabia is not necessarily the greatest friend of Russia, but they did it anyway, right, so then after that, the ship goes to South Africa and then on to Antarctica. So they did stop and pick something up in Saudi Arabia, so maybe the article has got some truth there, after all. And then right after the ship goes to Antarctica, this is when Korea suddenly goes down there and to visit the one and only Eastern Orthodox Church at the Antarctica, so too many strange things are happening, and a lot of people just write it off as conspiracy theories. You know all these things about aliens, and you know all this stuff going on in Antarctica...this is just a bunch of nonsense to begin with. Well, I always kind of looked at these things, and I was, wow, that's pretty interesting. I will tell you, though, this article here, that you are seen now in English, this article did appear in the mainstream Russian media as well. We did a report on this months ago. And I was trying to find the actual report, I could not find it to save my life there, but I wanted to share that with you, and if you look, maybe you can find it yourself. But when we did the report on this, we use Russian mainstream media that does not look at this as being just a fabrication. They actually report it as real news, and that yes, indeed, Russia did do a secret mission down to the Antarctica and had taken a thing called the Ark of Gabriel. So there is a Russian news source out there that does not look at this as some kind of conspiracy. And it went much deeper than what this article goes into. We shared that with you once before, but then something caught my attention the other day.

You can see on your screen now, this is the Book of Enoch, I was reading in the first Book of Enoch, chapter 18, and this is where the angel Uriel was taking Enoch and showing him some very interesting thing, and I am going to share with you, some of the words that I read here in Enoch, and then you will see why it became very interesting to me. We go down to, say, verse 4 and begin there.

It says, "*I saw the winds which turned the sky and caused a disc of the Sun and all the stars to set and I saw the winds of the earth which support the clouds and I saw the path of the angels, I saw the end of the earth, the firmament of heaven above and I went towards the south.*" Okay, so he goes to the end of the earth, and he speaks about going towards the south, and, "*It was burning day and night where there were seven mountains of precious stones and three towards the east and three towards the south.*"

Now I began to think about this. He is talking about seven mountains, but three go to the east and three go to the south, and he is talking about going toward the south, and I am thinking to myself, okay, he is talking about it being that it burns day and night, it was burning day and night. In other words, the sun is not setting. And I am thinking to myself, well, the South Pole, that describes the South Pole, like no other place on earth. The sun just doesn't really ever set, it's always daylight. And so it really caught my attention, but then he made mention about the seven mountains, and of course, he talks about the stones, etc., but then he says east and three go to the south, well, that really got my attention. So I thought to myself, okay, is there a place down at the Antarctica that would kind of match this type of description? Well, oddly enough, there is. It's Mountain Vinson.

Now you have to keep in mind, what you are looking here on your screen, you have Mount Vinson right here, it is called the Seven Summit. There are three going south. Now you would say these are three to the west. It's actually described as southeast and southwest, but keeping in mind when Enoch went here, the earth had not been tilted off its axis. So therefore, north and southeast and west was a bit different, right. If you take and tilt the earth back the way it would have been, this will go just like that, and then you would have the three peaks as it speaks about here, and we have the summit here, three peaks here, those would go down to the south, just as he describes, and here the three would go to the east, just as he describes there. The seven mountains, the Seven Summits, and three to the east and three to the south.

That really began to make sense. But the words here in Enoch get a little strange, though. As I read on, it says, "*Those towards east were of color of stone and was a pearl and one of a healing stone and those towards the south and of a red stone and the middle one reached the heaven like the throne of the Lord and stibium and the top of the throne was a sapphire and I saw a burning fire and what was in all the mountains.*"

Now keeping in mind the middle one was the tall one, and of course at Mount Vinson, that's exactly the way it is. Mount Vinson is the tallest mountain. Now I can't say that this is conclusively correct, I am just putting this here before you as a conjecture, something to think about, just something that I find very fascinating in line with all these anomalies that are happening at Antarctica, all the weird things that are going on. John Kerry, I mean, gosh he did more than one visit to Antarctica here, why? What is going on? Now when I would first look at this, I am thinking Planet X because I can see Planet X is coming, all right, and maybe that has something to do with it as well, but what about some other things? I am going to share with you some very serious things also that are going down there that have been claimed by former military officers, okay. So just hold on a second here.

*So, I saw a place there beyond the great earth there the waters gather together and I saw a deep castle of the earth with pillars of heavenly fire and saw among them, fiery pillars of heaven which were falling as regards, both height and depth, they were immeasurable and beyond this castle, I saw a place and it had neither the sky above it, nor the foundation of the earth below it and there was no water on it and no birds, but it was a desert place.*

Now I am sure now when you read this part here, well, that throws that out. It must have been out in Saudi Arabia somewhere, maybe not. Maybe not. Guys, let's take a look at something else here that is very, very interesting, all right. Let's go actually to the sevensummits.com website, and this is about Antarctica, and it is about Mount Vincent, and it talks about it being the tallest mountain etc. Let me read to you the Antarctica facts, though. Besides the mountain summit, if you down here to, say, about right here, up under the blue right here on your screen, the snowfall in Antarctica is so minimal that the continent has been called the world's coldest desert. In the interior receives less than three centimeters. In other words, less than one inch of precipitation a year, making it the driest continent on the Earth. The Antarctica Dry Valleys in Victoria Land are among the driest places on Earth. Some scientists believe that no rain has fallen there for two million years. Astronauts have visited the Dry Valleys because of their similarity to lunar landscapes. Hmm, isn't that interesting? They call it the coldest desert on Earth. Well, maybe Enoch, he's got something when he said it was a desert all right, as he called it. '*There was no water on it and no birds, but it was a desert place.* There are no birds there, there no penguins when you get that deep in Antarctica. There's just no life at all.

*And a terrible thing I saw there, seven stars like the great burning mountains and like a spirit questioning me, the angel said: "This is the place of at the end of heaven and earth, this is the prison for the stars of heaven and the host of heaven and the stars which roll over the fire, these are the ones which transgress the commandment of the Lord from the beginning of their rising because they did not come out at their proper times and He was angry with them and bound them until a time of consummation of their sin in the year of mystery."*

In IRL, we're going to chapter 19, verse 1 here, *"Said to me, the spirit of the angels who were promiscuous with women will stand here and they assuming many forms made man unclean and will lead men astray so that they sacrifice to demons as gods."*

Now if you notice, that is a continuation, they are not dead, they are still there. And they do what? They will lead men astray so that they sacrifice to demons as gods. Wasn't that interesting? CERN, not long ago, sacrificed a young woman. They claimed it wasn't real, but later according to Russian media, it was real. Russian media was even able to determine which woman it was that had been kidnapped. That was by, not just so much the media, was actually Russian intelligence officers that determined this information, but it was in Russian news, and we shared that in here in Israeli News live. So they sacrifice to demons as gods, they will stand there until the great Day of Judgment on which they will be judged so that the end will be made of them, but they still have very much access to men on this earth, and they are leading them astray and they can transit assuming many forms. That's pretty wild!

I mean, I have never seen anything like this in my life. And the point is that I am make here when we look in chapter 18, it appears to be, and it could be completely somewhere else different on the Earth, all right. I am just saying this as conjecture to you to consider this, but it appears to be that Antarctica is that region that he is speaking of. For one, there has to be a place that is burning day and night. That sun is where they can see day and night. It seems to really match up, and that's what's really, really fascinating in my opinion there. And again, it's like the mountains, if you were taking into consideration the end Olympian destruction that tilted the earth off its axis and put the Earth back right on its axis, and then look at the peaks here on the map in, behind you here, then you would actually have just as it describes it in there in Enoch, three to the south and three to the east, three peaks on the Seven Summit mountain range, and of course, the middle one being the tallest."[34]

I will now transcribe a video by a watchman of God named Jeff Byerly, and his YouTube channel is HolySpiritWind.

The video is titled *100% Hard Truth About Trump.*

> The truth of the matter is that there was no choice and that the results were predetermined by the powers that be, two years in advance, and I have link by Joni Stahl, and you can listen what Joni was told by an insider about the Hillary and Trump elections. Immediately after the election of Donald Trump, I was given the message, "You are now in the beginning of the great deception." In this message the Lord told us, Trump is indeed part of the Babylonian system as are Obama and Clinton and every other politician out there, or else they would not be a politician. They would not even make it that far. He also told us that

[34] https://youtu.be/Bez4DKZ17yU.

the deception is now greater because Trump claimed to be Christian and actually spoke some truth. Back then he did. The Lord also told us that Trump is like the King Saul of Israel because the people demanded a king. The great shaking will commence when the man that I have given is taken away. You can also read more about Trump as being Saul here, *Donald Trump Is Not Who Most People Think He Is* (January 27, 2017).

There are many out there that contend that Trump was God's anointed choice to be the leader of America, but this simply is not true. In the message, I have used Barack Obama, Hillary Clinton, and Donald Trump for my purposes from August of 2016. The Lord states, "I have allowed Hitler, Stalin Mao, Zedong Paul, Pott Kim and Kim Jung Un to rule." There's never been a ruler or a king on the earth that God did not allow to be in power (Romans 13:1). Trump is not Cyrus. The Lord has told me this multiple times. I think this passage from "Repent and come to Me now America, I am returning soon, be ready!" March of 2017, sums it up best. "He, Trump, is a king of Babylon and I did appoint him to be king, just as every king that has ever ruled in any nation on the face of the earth. He is not a Cyrus, David, or Elijah as I have told you before, he is like King Saul because the people wanted him as their king, but he does not have my spirit upon him. Do not be deceived. For how could he be king without the approval of the dark powers and principalities, the rulers of the darkness of this age, and the spiritual host of wickedness in the heavenly places that run the political systems of this world? He was chosen to be king many years ago by Me and then by them.

Because of the outcry of My people, Donald J. Trump was allowed to be appointed, but he is also part of the judgment upon America. He will be taken away as an even more severe judgment will be allowed by Me upon America. This will affect the world financial system, yes, this will happen after the fiery kickoff event, the fiery event that kicks out the entire sequence, like falling dominoes for you, America. After this time, Barack Hussein Obama will rise back to power and become the final antichrist."

In February of 2018, the Lord reveal to us which king of Babylon Trump is like, and it is Belshazzar. And I will read an excerpt from that, 'Donald Trump is also as Belshazzar, for he is the last king of Babylon America. I say to you this day, America, the words that were written on the wall in Daniel 5:25–28:

MENE, MENE, TEKE, UPHARSIN, **this is the interpretation of each word meaning God has numbered your kingdom and finished it,** TEKEL **you have been weighed in the bounces and found wanting,** PERES; **your kingdom has been divided and given to the Medes and the Persians.**

I tell you the Medes and the Persians represent America's end, and many are within your borders and your government offices.'

**That night was Belshazzar the king of the Chaldeans slain (which was the Babylonians).**

Babylon America shall be first taken over and then utterly destroyed after Donald Trump is slain. The one who America really loves will replace him, Trump, and oversee her, America's complete destruction. And we know who America really loves. It's Obama. You'll see. In the message, I wish to speak very clearly to you, so My people are not in confusion when the things that I am about to speak begin to happen.'

In October of 2017, the Lord tells us, "Trump is one of the fall guys, and he will be set up for the fiery kickoff event that will lead to the financial collapse and WW3."

Then in April of 2018, after the bombing of Syria by the American missiles due to the alleged chemical attacks on Syrian civilians, the Lord gave me the message, "One of the fall guys has now done what he has been told to do by his directors." The Lord continues and says, "Trump plays the role that they created for him very well, but when they are done with him, they will discard him, then the beast shall take center stage, he is the star of their show. The one on whom they have been waiting for. He will be controlled by his father, the devil, just as I was filled by the Holy Spirit when I came as the Son of Man. The audience will cheer him on like never before. They will fall down and worship him, they will do anything he asks of them, and they will regret that decision for all eternity."

I remember watching Trump announce the Syrian bombing, and I just knew that there was something different about him. It was not revealed what was different about him until months later, which is what I am to reveal in this message. On July 1, of 2018, I posted a message, "Barack Hussein Obama is the real leader of America." And the Lord went on to say, "Though right now, he, Obama is behind the scenes, he will return but not as president, as I have told you before. Behind the scenes, several wars are being plotted and planned and schemed. He is dividing and will divide America while looking like the good guy, just as he did throughout the Middle East, when he was elected president of America. Donald Trump is the *controlled opposition*. I stress, *controlled opposition*. He is part of the whole plan. He does not know the depths of the evil that Obama does. As I told you before, Trump is one of the fall guys, a scapegoat, someone to lay the blame on."

All right, now I am going to reveal the main truth that the Lord wanted to convey to His people in this message toward the end of January 2019. Many voices in the prophetic watchmen community began to call people to pray for Donald Trump for protection and salvation. There were even intercessory prayer teams formed with different rankings as I understand. I was confused by this, so I took it to the Lord, and I asked Him if He wanted me to pray for Trump, and the answer I got was, "No! I will not hear those prayers. Instead pray for My people who have been deceived by him so that they will awaken." That was the Lord speaking to me.

In March of 2019, I was sent the following message by Ruth Smith who lives in China, and it is called "Gene Enhancement," and I'll leave a link to that in the transcript, and I will read her post. A few months ago, in October of 2018, I saw a recent video with a title *Jack Ma*, and this is very coincidental, you might say. Because I heard a news article by Jack Ma today as I was driving home, and he was talking about artificial intelligence is so great that they are going to be able to make people have a twelve-hour workweek, three days a week, with four hours of peace. Man, that sounds great, doesn't it? I would love it! I work forty hours plus. So that would be great! It's not going to be great. So I will continue.

She saw a recent video with a title of *Jack Ma* and said that the mobile phone will disappear as long as small chips are implanted in the hand. The palm will be the mobile phone of the future. So you'll just be able to look at your hand and speak unto it. After watching this video, I started to pray for Jack Ma's salvation, but immediately I heard this clearly, "Do not pray for him!" I was shocked. A few days later, I prayed for Jack Ma again, and immediately, I heard this very clearly and also very severe, "Do not pray for him, even though you pray for him, I will not listen. But you can pray for his families."

I asked the Lord, "Why is this?"

The Lord said, "He is no longer the human I created. He accepted gene enhancement and his DNA is no longer the human that I created. Now many elites of this world have embraced this gene enhancement technology. Those who have accepted this technology have become a hybrid and have their eternity sealed forever, and they cannot be redeemed."

It is right after I read this message that the Lord spoke to me that Donald Trump has indeed had his genes enhanced in April of 2018, and he is eternally lost. And let me tell you right now, that does not make me happy. People accuse me of hating Donald Trump. I do not hate Donald Trump, but I cannot pray for him. He is lost! Now all I can do is to reveal the truth the Lord has shown me about him to people so that they do not do the same thing and so that they are not deceived by him as well. As we can see, the things that he's been saying lately are not of God at all. He's taken the Lord's name in vain twice. What was said about it by the evangelical community? Not much. And we all know about what he said last week, about him calling himself the chosen one. And somebody from Israel saying that he is like the king of Israel and the Second Coming of God. How ironic that this Jewish man even said this because they don't even believe that Jesus came the first time.

I will continue with this message. I was stunned when He spoke this to me, to tell you all the truth. Although I look back now, and I should not have been because I read it before in a message by Linda Hoshi in October 20, 2018, and that message is called "The Illusion of Trump and Pence with the Warning to the False Prophets." In that vision that she had explains a whole lot. I was shown the following by the Holy Spirit. This is by Linda's vision: "I saw Trump receiving what I knew was DNA enhancement/ manipulation. I saw a surge of power and pride flow through Trump, and while he exclaimed loudly, 'I should have done this sooner!' At that moment Trump's DNA eternally changed. He became a hybrid and is no longer human. I knew he accepted what the Bible warns us about of the mark of the beast (Revelation, chapter 13:16–17). What happened to Trump when he accepted that DNA change is what will happen to all who take the mark of the beast. Don't kid yourself, it won't be called the mark of the beast. It will likely be called something like genetic enhancement, with scientific proof of reversing, changing, and removing genes that cause cancer, disease, aging, and more to appeal to human pride. It will probably make you look better too and lose all kind of weight, and I can keep going on and on. It's going to look really good. Be aware!"

Take note that she had this vision during the month that Trump bombed Syria—April of 2018. Coincidence? No. We all know that doesn't exist, don't we? There's no such thing as coincidence. Now I remember reading this back in October, but I believed it was true, but I still did not get it as I do now. And I will explain that. You can read a revelation that someone else gets from the Lord, but until you get revealed it yourself, you don't understand it in your spirit. But now I do. Because the Lord revealed it to me personally. And if you want that revelation, you have to pray for it. You have to ask Him for it. That is how it works. And I wish that you all would do that.

Moreover, I did not have the revelation from the Holy Spirit back then, but I do now, because the Lord has not only confirmed Linda's vision to me but given me added revelation about it. Revelation from the Lord is indeed progressive, and revelation leads to more revelation. You will notice this, especially when you are reading the Bible. After I received this revelation that Trump is no longer 100 percent human and no longer redeemable, I was scared because I knew that in Christian circles, it is about the least popular thing that you could say. I asked the Lord if I could just keep this to myself and those close to me. He told me I could keep it to myself for a while, until He needed me to reveal it. And that time has come and is come again. This is the word that the Lord wants me to give about this.

"'Many of my own have exalted this man, Donald Trump, beyond measure, he has become an idol in their eyes, and he does no wrong in their eyes. In his own eyes, he does nothing wrong. He is his own god, but he is wrong. He saw no need to repent before Me, and now he never will have another chance. He has led America to become even more hardened and unrepented as well. He never knew Me by the Spirit, but he was my creation, and I loved him, but he is no longer of the race of Adam because his DNA has changed. They called it gene enhancement and promised him that his physical body would benefit greatly from this, and it has, but his spirit has died forever. They lied to him, and he believed it. He was deceived because he had no desire to really know Me. All the prayers of all the people in the entire world make no difference for his spirit now. He has eternally denied Me as his Savior. He is forever lost to me, and he will spend eternity with the one he has chosen. He is now a hybrid. I only died for those that I made by My own hands and My own image.

"Satan and his followers are in total control of Trump now. That is why he is so much different than what he was in the first year of office, and we can see that difference is even more than when I wrote this in May. Most of the kings and the rulers and most of the global elite have had their genes enhanced, and they are under control of Satan as well. Do not follow them. Warn those that you know not to get these gene enhancements procedures done. For they too will be eternally lost to Me if they do. I mark those that are mine, and Satan marks those that are his. He always imitates Me, though cheaply. My son, I told you in February of 2018, that Donald Trump would be slain, and his spirit has been slain, but his body is next. That is when America will see the fiery kickoff event, and Obama will shall return. Financial disaster, civil war, and world war will come suddenly and very close together. This is why Trump was chosen by the hidden powers of darkness. They had been and will continue to use him until they are done with him, and then they will use even his death to cause chaos, violence, hatred, and death among the people. Obama will be welcomed back, and even many of those who hated him before will be relieved, but his false peace will not last long. The complete destruction of America will come under the rule of Obama. He will leave, and then Babylon the Great will be destroyed in one hour."

As this was spoken, I saw a flash vision of Obama seated in a jet plane, looking out the window and waving and smiling with an evil smirk, and then it was over.

"People of America and the whole Earth, I am your only hope, do not look to a man to save you. I am the only Way, Truth, and Life. No man comes to the Father but by Me. I will give you the strength to get through the events that are coming quickly, but you must have faith in only Me. The arm of man will fail you, but My right hand is strong and might to save. Be transformed by My Holy Spirit for this is the only way to eternal life. Renew your mind and your spirit daily by repentance in constant communication with Me. Fill your lamps and fast, full of my pure oil by spending time with Me. I love you all with an everlasting love, and this is why I warn you of things to come." (Yahushua/Jesus)

As always please bring every prophetic word, word of wisdom, word of knowledge, or any other message spoken in the name of Jesus, to Him personally in prayer and tested for yourself to see if it is from the Holy Spirit. I thank you all for listening, I love you all. Amen.

# CHAPTER 20

## The Next False Flag

I will now transcribe a video from a YouTube channel called aminutetomidnite with Tony Koretz. This video is titled *More bombshell information on what's coming this year-Jeremy EX 32degree Freemason.*

Pray about all this to the Lord, since most of the resources bringing this information are serving the enemy, they are currently in the Illuminati, thus although Jeremy is no longer one of them, the other ones are still in there....

Hey, Tony, I wanted to tell you a little more, and there's just a few other things I am going to say, and you can use it if you want to, I just really feel compelled to say this because it's a lot of information. First of all, this is for you, so yesterday I met with my friend, and we talked a great deal, and a lot of things went a little more in detail to me about the situation that's going on, and when that interview started with me and you last year, he told me that they had mentioned trying to hack your account and that they were reporting every video. I mean, I don't know if that means anything, but I do remember one time you said your account, somebody was trying to hack it, but I don't know if that was anytime near the beginning of when we talked or not, or if that's common or any of that. I just felt I need to mention that to you. So I know a lot of things have been really changing lately, more so than ever. My source told me that everything is about to change more than ever, and you cannot prepare for what's coming! That's what he said.

Now, I am not telling you not to prepare, I think that it's a good idea as I've always said, as I prepared, but going through this, God keeps putting in my mind, "Do not fear! Do not fear! Do not fear!" And we know that fear is not from God. I really believe God's going to do miracles in the time that is coming, and other people say it too. I really believe He will, He will feed people. There's a lot of people that can't even buy food or medicine, and I just believe God's going to do it. I believe personally, I am just going to say that, don't fear. The reason he told me that this lockdown occurred was exactly what I thought— so they could take rats away slowly and see how people take it. And they took it lying down, easy, which makes this come even faster, what's coming. But also, he said he wanted all these businesses closed beforehand. All these restaurants and stores that aren't chained so people cannot get food or buy food from other people, is going to have to be industrial, is going to have to be through them or through chains to where, like this COVID pass or whatever else nefarious they have, that they're going to give, you have to have in order to go, so, mom and pop stores, you might have been able to get away with that but in big ones, you will not, and he did. He reiterated that over and over and over that was part of everything they talked about.

It was killing these small businesses for that reason. I never thought about that before. And he said that Biden, obviously, was part of this, which we know they all are, but he was going to remove himself, whatever that means. In some way, maybe health, I don't know...and that is going to cause the issue right there. That's why he said that's why he hasn't chosen a running mate and that Trump is, I am sure he doesn't have all the details, but what he's heard these politicians say is that he is either going to try to delay the election, making it look like, "Well, I don't want to take over here, but let's just delay it until we can get this fixed," whatever the situation is.

And I said before, that I've heard from a sources all that they would stage some kind of removal of him, permanently, and you understand that. I hope that does not happen. But that he will be okay and that it would be fake, and that they will stage an event—a nuclear event—somehow to do with this. They put a prophecy out years ago, I told you in the lodge that there would be a nuclear event in the West, and he said America. He said that they were going to blame it on these leftists protesters, which they still are going to get, you're hearing this, they're going to tag their focus on the black community to get them these vaccines first, and they will, you watch! They will. These are awful people, and they cannot have people questioning this system that comes. They can't have people out there protesting, so people who do that are going to be the first ones gone, and old people that do not...you can't... I mean you're not going to be able to be a slave in their mind, if they have to keep you up or pet you.

So he says that Kushner was disinformation, that was a lie, this source, I am not going
to talk about this source, but I am going to say
that this is one who I know believes in Jesus and
who wants to leave bad but is afraid to and was
there after me, was there the whole time with
me, and he said some of the things they said that
they wanted to do to me after I left. One of them
was setting me up on rape charges when I started
doing these interviews, so that tells you right
there. That's been a while, so now is just to the
point where it doesn't matter anymore. I think
they want you to know, and he agreed because
you can expect it. Your mind is set for it.

I asked him about the monetary system,
and he said that gold and silver would be illegal, it would be illegal to use or barter. He said
they've all invested in online currency, which is
why the cousin that I had a while back knew I
wasn't a Mason anymore. When I said what are
they investing in, that was evidently well known.
And he said they were in Colorado, Montana,
Canada, these places they build and funded,
stocked. I told you I heard they called Babylon
the one in Colorado years ago. I think very well
could be where my family are, which you know,
I don't think you're going to be able to hide from
anything, but I think they're gonna be able to
hide from what they're planning. There will be
another lockdown, it's going to happen, and I
think everybody knows that. And it's going to
be...it's going to be, "the lockdown" is going
to be permanent until the same thing is getting
ready to happen. All these people that are protesting and tearing things up, and it's going be
on steroids.

Like I said before, they said when they go in homes, and they are going to start over this election. The thing that happens, whatever happens, is supposed to happen in September. He gave me the date, September 22. I don't know what is supposed to happen on that day, but he said something major! And he also said, 'November would be the big one.' Now he said that this event with the president was going to make the white right and Christians rise up, which is what I've always heard and that there would be killing in the streets. And this is going to bring in, because of insurrection, a military is what I'm still hearing, and he doesn't even know this. And he did not say anything about participating in it. That may be only for higher level or people…well, he did not say anything about it. But he said that they will go door-to-door, and they will be the ones that make you take the vaccine, and he said they've already started getting rid of police that will not go along with this, and I heard somebody else tell me that. So the ones left will. And I've heard this is the same thing going on in all caliber of that group in society. All law enforcement, fire personnel, medical…that's what I've heard, and we are at a time where nothing they do is going to surprise you.

So whatever it is, so you know, don't be afraid, God is with you, and God is stronger than this and if they…if something…you can imagine how wonderful heaven is, so if we have to go through something bad to get there, then that's fine with me. I think we are going to have to go through some things. I don't personally think we are going to be here in the worse of it, but I think some of us may. So he told me, the first time

I've ever heard this out of the lodge, that Obama would be back. I've always felt that, I've always thought that, but that wasn't a fact. He said he absolutely would be back, but not through election, and he would clamp down, and he said that he's the end because after he comes is a major event where there will be nuclear weapons, and I have heard from the beginning, and I told Tony, I have never said it in any other interview that my politician main source told that a natural event was coming, and I have heard that several times. And I've just never mentioned it because that was all the facts I knew about it. And he confirmed that, and he said that there are events they are looking for that come from space. But he says and indicates that he thinks they are going to do nuclear weapons and blame it on that. I don't know if that is happening with it or if that's it.

You know the book of Revelation says it's going to happen. So it's coming, but before the Revelation, I think, and so does he that they are going to use nuclear weapons and say it's that or maybe with that, when that's coming. Whatever the case, if you can, buy food and prepare at home while you still can do it, and you won't have to leave. And this vaccine, he has told me, absolutely is everything I've heard. It is absolutely not good, which you know. The old and sick is going to… in their life, and he says there is something that he has heard that they have tailored it for different people and different areas. I don't know what that means, he don't know what that means. But if they are wanting to give it to the blacks first, you can use your God-given brain because they are some of the most vulnerable in this country to where they couldn't fight back financially or legally, and a lot of them wouldn't know, and you can see them targeting that group first.

Most people at home are upset with these younger people because of what they're doing, but you know, there's a whole lot of white people out there with those blacks that are tearing the country up, and I think everyone that was out there that can be traced is some of the first ones they are going to get. Because again, they cannot have this type of upset in the new system. But the main thing about all this is, my source told me, in this system, this New World Order, all the young people in the world know it, know it's nefarious, they know the names George Soros, Rothschild, Gates...they know these names, and I've always said, personally, that that system has to fail for a new one to come in, and he says it's a whole New World Order system. It has to be brought down for the Luciferian New World Order to stand, and he says that's the plan.

This, all this, the UN, everything...he said that all this has to fail, and they've built it to do this. They have been planning it, and they have the solution, and I don't think any of this people are going to be hurt. I am sure they'll be taken to some tropical island where they can sip margaritas, but this system, he said, will come down so people think the whole bad system is gone, and everything they went through is for the good. And that's when the Christian right are targeted. Because, he said, they said that we have manifested it, because we've wanted the end-times to come so we could go home, and we have mentally manifested all this bad stuff that happens, that this is what they are going to portray and that we are keeping the world back. We're the only people that hate society, we hate gay people and anybody that's different, and we tell people they sin, and they can't be happy and live the way they want, so we're the negative ones in this world. Prepare for that! That's coming, and our families may be part of that.

And so you know where you are going, and you know do not fear, remember—oh, I forgot his name, the one who was stoned and was looked up and saw Jesus. Think about that, where you're going to be when we're going through this bad stuff. You are never alone, and Jesus Christ is right beside you and with you. And I don't tell any of this to make anybody scared. I tell them so they can expect what's coming because the sources I've had have had a really good track record for predicting, and it's happening. I knew the military would give the vaccine. I said that months back when I was told that. Of course, I did not personally know anything, and I believe also that God has given me the ability to be able to find this information and share it. I really believe that. I've had dreams myself, and I was unnerved for a good part of the year, and I'm not anymore. I'm not afraid at all, and actually I'm ready for this to come so that I could go home. I'm ready for this.

I believe that God truly will make food for people, I believe He will manifest miracles that have never been done before. I almost know it in my heart, and I believe it. So thank you for listening and pray for me and Tony and in these times. I know they are rough…he says this will happen before the end of this year. He's told me this now twice. They want all this done and wrapped up before Christmas. He's made that clear. And he said that people have been coming to these lodge meetings in the city to have these conversations about what is coming. People he don't even know from DC have been coming to these meetings, Scottish rite meetings and discussing the coming events to come and telling people where to go.

He said 80 percent of those Masons are gone, and they out West in Colorado, Montana, and he said that most of them are in Colorado. That was the biggest one because it's a city. He said it's a city, I heard it was a city years ago, but they were building it. They bought something that was the government's and refitted it for their needs, and they called it Babylon. That's what they called it years ago. And I'm talking like in '08, and I've never heard anything else about it, but I know that's where my family went, I know it is. I know it, I mean they would be nowhere else. Nobody has done nothing, and I am still trying to warn people and show them evidence, and they think I'm crazy. "Oh…there is no food shortage coming!" I mean people are actually still saying that. They say to me, "Things are going to get better, Trump is going to make things better when he gets elected again!" If I hear that again.[35]

Before I transcribe the next video, I would like to say that I personally discipled an ex-member of the Illuminati. He was a very high-ranking one. I met him in my megachurch where he had been assigned to go to assassinate my ex-pastor Guillermo Maldonado. The first time he went in there, I was there. In the middle of the service, he walked in, and the lights all went off. The music and everything turned off. The air conditioner too. I had been going to that church for years, and I had never experience that in there. I did not know what happened; we all thought it was just a random prob-

---

[35] https://youtu.be/K3u4_5KEdPA.

lem with the electric grid from the church. But when I met this man, he confessed to me that happened because of him. That was his first time in the church, and he was going to kill the pastor that day, but glory to God, instead of killing the pastor, he had an encounter with the Holy Spirit. He said that when he walked in the place, he felt something he had never felt before, thus he surrendered to the Lord. He spent a few years there, but he got stuck in his spiritual walk with God, as it happened to me. Because unfortunately, that church started out with the fire of God, but now is in apostasy, and they are serving the Illuminati's agenda.

This guy was really frustrated in this church after trying to get with God in it for a few years. I met him in the school that they had. I had him in one of my classes, and the Lord asked me to help him. I explained to him about a deliverance team in Peru where I had traveled to so that they may deliver me properly. I encouraged him to go there and introduced him to them. He went and got much better after that. He and I both ended up having to leave the church. He confessed to me that the same day we met, he had it all planned out; he was planning to kill the pastor once again and all the leaders of the church and other members too because they were really making him angry, and he just said that he no longer felt he could go back to the Illuminati, but he also could not be a Christian. So when I met him, he was planning to kill himself but not before killing a bunch of people from our church. He even had a list of the names he was going to kill.

This guy met a real fallen angel in jail after he was locked up in jail for working for someone very powerful that was in the Mafia. He said he got discipled by this fallen angel through telepathy. He even saw his wings, and he was training him to be like how Pastor Guillermo Maldonado was, meaning he was being trained in doing supernatural healings on people to deceive them with signs and wonders. He was also trained in Rome by the Roman Catholic Church. They were all pure Satanists. Many Catholic monks trained him for months in Rome. He met with a lot of high-ranking Satanists throughout his twenty years of serving the devil. They taught him to hate the Christians and Jews passionately. He told me the Christian universities were led by Satanists. He went to many satanic rituals with many famous people in politics and other people. This is all for real. This is not a conspiracy theory; these people are real, and they are organized.

When I first met him, he said to me, "Desiree, you can tell people the truth until your face turns blue, you can show them all the evidence, and it won't matter because people just don't care, they don't want to know the truth."

I told him he was wrong, but to my horrific surprise, time proved me wrong. It saddens me deeply to see just how aggressive these criminals are at deceiving us and killing us and how passive and lazy most people are in fighting back against them!

I spent years and years showing so many people so much truth and evidence, and it happened just as this guy told me that it would. People just didn't care. Not only did they not care, they mocked and ridiculed me and cut me off their lives. It's so pathetic! Now when all this thing takes place, those same people will be the first ones to raise up their fists at Almighty God and judge Him as an evil God for not stopping these criminals from doing this to us. But they will conveniently forget all the things God tried to do and say to them so as to spare us all from this. The only reason why these people will be able to get this done is because the hand of God of protection upon this nation has been lifted because of years of rejection toward God, His messengers, and His Holy Word. Here we get to now reap the harvest of all of the unheeded warnings and all the mockery and persecution toward the true prophets of God, the ones that did not sell the Gospel for money and who gave up their comfortable lives to preach. I am so sorry to say this, but it's the truth.

Now I will transcribe a video of a prophetic message that matches the video I previously transcribed, and it is titled *Repent And I Will Give You New Wine*, posted on August 11, 2020 by Alan Carrico.[36]

---

[36] http://CANTSTOPGRINNING.BLOGSPOT.COM

Hello, My son, this is Jehovah Elohim speaking with you this day. My children, listen closely, for the enemy has become furious as his time is short. If you are not paying attention to the words and warnings that I am giving My prophets, watchmen, and scribes, then you will suffer greatly in the coming days. The US president will soon go into hiding as he no longer wields any power, for it has been taken from him. I have told many of My prophets and scribes of a "fiery kickoff event" that will happen in New York City, and this is true. There will be a new weapon, the likes the world has never seen, that will be ignited over Trump Tower in an effort to remove the president from power permanently, but he will not be there, though it will be reported that he was.

The deception will become deeper and more overt now, so much that you will hear is suspect to error. Seek Me for clarification, and I will illumine your heart to the truth. Once this happens, the chaos that follows will be a multitude greater than the attack on 9-11-01, and the people will cry out for a former leader who will burst onto the scene. He will speak great things, and many will follow after him. He will then assume control of the nation, and people will rejoice, but this is all from the evil one who seeks to destroy this once-great land. And I allow it, for now is the time that I judge this nation for its gross sin that has become a stench in My nostrils. No longer will America be great again, but her fall will be great. This will send shock waves all over the earth, and every nation will feel its effects. The chaos that follows will be unimaginable, and if you are not in Me, then you will be gripped with great fear. My children, I tell you these things so that you come to trust that I AM in sovereign control of all things, and that in Me you will have peace. I cry out to each of you now to turn from your sin and repent, and I will heal you and cleanse you. I will give you new wine and a new garment that shines as the sun. Come to Me now, My children, for the time of the end has come. I AM.

Read Jeremiah 14.

Now I will transcribe another video that has a prophecy that also matches with the first video. It is titled PROPHECY: *Underneath the Denver Airport Bunker Will Be Destroyed* (Gwendolen Song).

Good evening, friends, this is Sister Gwendolen Song, it is August 8, 2020, and I come to you this evening to share a prophetic dream that the Lord had given to me yesterday morning. This dream is of particular interest to those who live in the state of Colorado. In this dream, I saw a piece of paper, and it was spoken to my spirit, it was a bulletin and the bulletin said in black and red letter, in bold-faced black and red letter, "WARNING TO THE STATE OF COLORADO!" And that was the end of the dream. And it was a very strong dream. It woke me up from my sleep.

Now when I took this dream to the Holy Spirit, this is what was spoken to my heart, this is what was spoken to my heart by the One, the One who testifies to all truth, that this is a warning to the residents to Colorado that the Lord God Almighty is coming in a vengeance to bring down the bunkers of the elite there. All of those underground tunnels that will be used to house the people of lawlessness in the days ahead. He knows where each and every bunker is, and they cannot hide from the Lord. His eyes go to and fro the earth like a mighty war machine, and He will come down and strike them in His vengeance for spilling the blood of the innocents. Again this is the message that the Lord sent me in a dream yesterday morning as an end-time messenger of the Lord. I am bringing forth this message in fullest humility for my King. I am going to read three verses here.

**Proverbs 15:3, "The eyes of the Lord are in every place, beholding the good and the evil."**

**Isaiah 2:19, "And they shall go into the holes of the rocks, and into the caves of the earth, for fear of the Lord and for the Glory of His Majesty, when He arises to shake the terribly the earth."**

**Revelation 6:16, "And said to the mountains and the rocks, fall on us and hide us from the face of Him that sitteth on the throne and from the wrath of God."**

Amen and hallelujah. There are many people who are not aware of these underground bunkers, so at the conclusion of this video, we'll show you some brief video coverage of some of the limited information out there on the Internet. One of the most notorious bunkers is in the state of Colorado, and I will say it's more than a bunker. It is a city of refuge for the elite. And that is under the Denver International Airport, where you are welcomed with a large blue horse named Lucifer when you fly in there. Definitely a mascot of the Illuminati. So that's one of them, and of course

NORAD, and there's other places around the USA.

Friends, the King is coming, that's the bottom line, so let those mockers and scoffers repent and call upon the name of the One true God, of heaven and earth, and if there's anyone out there today who wants the hope of eternity in heaven, a place where the Bible says that there's no more pain, there's no more suffering, no more oppression, you must turn from a lifestyle of sin and live in a manner that pleases a Holy God. Now there's nothing that we can do to earn this gift. The gift of salvation is free, but we must simply believe on the name of the Lord Jesus Christ and what He has done at the cross. He took on the penalty for the sins of all mankind, and we must simply believe in His finished work at the cross and then stride to follow Him all the days of our lives. And again, it's a free gift. So you can say to the Lord Jesus, I don't want your free gift, I would rather go to that other destination. Well, that's up to you, but you cannot serve two masters. You must love one and hate the other, but heaven is waiting for all of those who call by the faith, believing in the name of the Lord Jesus Christ.[37]

---

[37] https://youtu.be/0P1wqfV2g0.

# CHAPTER 21

## My Prophetic Dreams and Revelations

**And it shall come to pass in the last days, saith God, I
will pour out my Spirit upon all flesh: and your sons and
your daughters shall prophesy, and your young men shall
see visions, and your old men shall dream dreams.**

—ACTS 2:17

So I will just summarize some of the many, many prophetic dreams
that the Lord has shown me throughout the years for the coming
future.

I had a dream that I was watching the news in Puerto Rico
where I am from. The news was reporting a tsunami was coming.
When I woke up after that dream, the Lord led me to understand
that there is a coming planet called Nibiru, Planet X, Wormwood,
The Destroyer, that will soon impact the waters near Puerto Rico
and will cause the biggest earthquake around the world. It will cause
many tsunamis, everywhere around the globe, and it will cause three
days of darkness. Millions will die when this rock impacts the Earth.
NASA knows about this, so does FEMA and the governments of the
world; they have known since 1974. But they have kept it a secret
because they do not want to alarm the public. They have been preparing for this event. They even have their telescope in Puerto Rico

where they keep an eye on it. Parts of the debris is what is going to first fall on the Earth, and then the asteroids will gradually increase.

Many prophets of God have been warning about this coming rock. All over the globe, they have been sounding the alarm. They also have been talking about the three days of gross darkness that is to come with it. Many demons will roam the earth during these days and cause great chaos. Unfortunately much of the warnings fell on deaf ears. Much of us got ridiculed and mocked for warning about this; meanwhile, the majority of Christians were lending their ears to the prosperity gospel preachers and putting their hope on Trump to make America great again.

This was one thing I always said to everyone who voted for Trump and really hoped that we were going to fix our nation. I would tell them that no matter what he would do, this rock was coming, and it would cause utter destruction. Thus I knew that Trump was just a distraction. He also knew about this asteroid since he was running for president. All of the leaders know that is coming, and they all have been getting prepared for it. Thus this is one more confirmation that God never put Trump in office to bless this nation but to judge it. The judgment was fixed as David Wilkerson prophesied on his book *The Vision.*

I had another dream where I was standing on the sand of Miami Beach, which is my hometown. I was looking at the ocean water receding, and then I saw how this huge wave was lifting up and coming toward me. I began to run and saw many of the members from my last megachurch in Miami, El Rey Jesus, with Pastor Guillermo Maldonado. I was looking at many of the main leaders from the church standing right in the path of this wave. When I woke up that morning, the Lord asked me to make a YouTube video and let everyone know that there would soon be a tsunami in Miami Beach and to repent. He also warned that the prosperity churches will be judged.

Furthermore, I had a dream that Russia was going to attack the USA.

I also had another dream where I saw a missile coming out of the shore of New York City, and it had a code that had to do with the stock market. When I woke up, the Lord told me that New York

City was going to be nuked, and that would be when the economy would fall for good.

I had a dream where I was walking the streets, and there was devastation everywhere, and I was grabbing people and praying for them.

I had a dream that I was in the White House when Obama was president, and I was looking at a statue of Obama, and suddenly it moved—it came to life. I then ran and found President Obama, and I was frantically telling him, "Obama, the devil is here! The devil is here! Help me!"

And he looked at me with a weird evil smirk and smiled as if he knew that Satan was in the White House, and then he just stayed put, smoking his cigarette, and staring at me with wicked delight and did nothing!

> **And deceiveth them that dwell on the earth by means of those miracles which he had power to do in the sight of the beast; saying to them that dwell on the earth, that they should make an image to the beast, which had the wound by a sword, and did live. And he had power to give life unto the image of the beast, that the image of the beast should both speak, and cause that as many as would not worship the image of the beast should be killed. (REVELATION 13:14–15).**

Moreover, I had a dream where they were forcing the people to take their vaccines. It was horrible. A very terrifying dream this was, indeed!

I have had so many prophetic dreams. I could not write them all down because they are just too many. I also had the Lord give me many prophetic utterances. I will just write a few.

When Trump was voted into office, the Lord spoke to my heart, and He was deeply wounded. He told me that He felt as one who was betrayed by their spouse or lover because His people put their trust in a man and removed their trust from Him. He said the church was so consumed by the material things of this world, they were so consumed by vanity and worldliness, that they failed to see the deception. They were blinded by their pride and greed, and thus Trump was able to deceive them. He was heartbroken as one who finds a lover cheating on them or having an affair. I felt the Lord's heartbreak when He gave me this word.

The Lord also told me that America would come under severe judgment and that it will look like a Third World country when it was all done. He told me that He was going to remove all the idols His people have. They idolized Trump; thus He will remove him. They idolized money, thus He will knock out the economy and the way we are used to doing things to make money. His people idolized their ministries and church leaders; thus He will close many churches for good and expose the false prophets. He was very upset and told me that I was like Jeremiah and that I was to warn the people of the coming disasters and to try my best to persuade them into repentance and to try my best to lead them to see their error. Thus He instructed to me to start preaching in Facebook, then in YouTube, and finally in books. He led me to write my first book, *We Were Deceived*, and now this one. He asked me to bring His people back to Him. Thu, here I am, trying my very best, restlessly, but I must say, people's heart are truly hardened. I never imagined it would be this hard. I thought that after all the evidence and wisdom the Lord gave me, it would be easy, but it's not. Because the majority of the people reject knowledge, and they just simply love lies.

**My people are destroyed for lack of knowledge; because thou hast rejected knowledge, I will also reject thee, that thou shalt be no priest to Me. Seeing thou hast forgotten the law of Thy God, I will also forget thy children. (HOSEA 4:6)**

It was truly heartbreaking to see God's people reject the truth concerning things like where Christmas originated from and what it truly meant. It was heartbreaking to see how they just did not even care to know that Christmas is not even the day that Jesus was really born. Truly heartbreaking for me to see how so many Christians refuse to stop taking part in those pagan holidays, even when ex-Satanists were all over the Internet talking the truth about Halloween and all the insane rituals that are done that day. The majority of Christians turned a blind eye to the truth about Christmas, Halloween, Easter, Sunday mass, St. Valentine's Day, etc. They were just not interested in understanding the pain our Lord feels concerning these deceptions that we have inherited from our ancestors, and we foolishly continue to celebrate and to teach them to our children. Most Christians turned a blind eye to the truth about the feminist movement and the devastating consequences it has had upon society as a whole. They have turned a blind eye to so many truths and persisted in believing the false prophets, putting their trust in men and loving money and vanity. That unfortunately, there is nothing to do now but await the terrible day of the Lord and to reap all of that indifference toward His Holy Spirit and toward the sacrifice His beloved Son did for all of us on the cross.

I must say, after serving the Lord for decades, I am exhausted, but mostly, I feel heartbroken because I can see just how brutal the people of God have been toward our loving heavenly Father. They just have had no mercy on Him, and they have stepped all over His blood, as if it's defiled. Thus I can't judge the Lord for being angry and sending the judgments that are soon to fall upon the earth. Anyone in His place would do the same thing. If He did not judge the world, then wickedness would increase, and most people would not get saved. But most importantly, God will not be mocked.

**Be not deceived, God is not mocked; for whatsoever a man soweth, that shall he also reap. (GALATIANS 6:7)**

In conclusion, America and the world is soon going to start reaping all their sins. The shed of innocent blood, the participation in witchcraft and pagan religions, the indifference toward the most vulnerable and needy people, their greed and pride, etc. And the first ones to be judged will be the ones in His body. The false prophets, the prosperity preachers, the fake Christians and the fake Jews, and all of those who followed them.

**For the time is come that judgment must begin at the house of God and if it first begin at us, what shall the end be of them that obey not the gospel of God?**

# CHAPTER 22

## Their Ultimate Goal Is Hell

I will now transcribe a testimony of a woman named Paulina about hell.

I was born in Colombia, in the capital, in Bogota. I spent my entire childhood and my whole life in Colombia until I was thirty-five years old, which was when I got married. My story began when I was twenty-five years old. I was studying in the university. I was studying tourist administration as my career. I was on my way to the university, and in the moment that I got in the bus, I never imagined that it would be my last day that I would have life. I never imagined I was going to have an accident that day. My routine every day was getting the bus and going to the university and go to class and then to the chats and then back home. And that was what I did. I got on the bus, and I asked the driver to stop in the corner. In Colombia the buses have two doors, one in the front part and another one in the back. I went to the back, and I rang the driver, and he seemed to have heard it, but I thought that he had seen me going down the stairs to get off, and he did not see me and turned the wheel really fast toward the left, and the traffic light was yellow. Thus he was supposed to be stopping, but instead he kept on going, passing the yellow light, and in that moment, the door opened and I fell off from the force of the bus moving.

I fell in the streets, and immediately, when I fell in the street, I did not know anything else about me. The last thing I knew was the voice of a woman who said, "He killed her!"

And I said, "What is happening with me?" I did not know what was happening to me. In that moment, immediately I came out of my body. I saw the multitude of the people on top of me, around me, and I saw a puddle of blood around my head. It was so much blood that was around my head, and indeed, I fractured my head. What happened in that moment? I began to rise up, like floating upwards from my body, and I would see everyone around me, on top of me, I would see the people, I saw the roofs of the houses. I passed the clouds, immediately I passed above the clouds, and then I got out of the Earth.

When I got out of the Earth, I saw the Earth, and I saw the planets. I saw Jupiter, I saw Saturn, I saw Mars and the whole universe. I saw everything. It was an incredible shock for me because I did not know what was happening with me. But I felt a good sensation. I was not feeling a bad feeling, I was feeling good. I felt my spirit was floating, and I was not feeling heaviness. That heaviness of the flesh, it is hard to experience this, but that is how one feels when they are out of the body. Instantly I saw the whole universe, but instantly, it was like in a fraction of seconds, I was transported into a tunnel. And in the tunnel, there was no light. It was totally dark. It was as if you entered into a cave. It was like a pure black cave. I could not see the palm of my hands. I did not see my body. I understood that I was passing another part, that I was not experimenting, that I was not alive because I said, "Am I alive or am I dead?"

I then touched my palm of my hand, and my hand trespassed my other hand. My fingers went right through my hand. It was like it was transparent, and I understood that there was no flesh in me. I thought, perhaps I am dead, or what is happening to me? In that moment, I felt a presence, the voices of presences that were began to mock me, and they were laughing behind me. They were saying very ugly things to me. They were saying, "You are a bad person, you are the worse, you deserve to be here."

And I asked, "Who are you?" And they would not answer me. They would not answer me, they would just laugh and mock me, more and more, and each time they would get closer to me. I was trying to get away from them because they caused me to be very fearful, because they seemed and felt as if they were voices of monsters. And the problem was that when they tried to get close to me, I tried to pass them on the right side. I tripped but then I ran to the front and to the left, but then I ran into a wall, and then that is when I realized I was in a tunnel. In the back of the tunnel behind me, I saw fire, I felt the heat of the flames. I felt and I heard screams that were like someone was being tortured. These people were being tortured. I heard the screams, and I was very afraid. I just didn't know where I was. So I said, "Where am I? Where am I?"

And they said, "Don't you know?"

And I said, "No, I don't know where I am."

And they said to me, "You are at the gates of hell!"

When they said that, I was in complete shock, I didn't know what to say. I didn't know what to do, but I said to them, "I can't be at the gates of hell! I am a good person, I can't die!"

But they said to me, "No, you are dead, you are going to be in here, in this place, forever! You are never going to have any other type of existence! The only future existence for you will be in this place, in this place of torture. You're going to be tortured for all time! We are going to be torturing you all the time!"

And I said, "How are you going to be torturing me? I don't get it!"

And they grabbed me, and they pulled my arm and began to scrape at the flesh of my arms. They had fingernails that were horribly long, so when they grabbed my arms, each arm, it was as if they were skinning me alive. It was terribly painful because when you are dead, you feel things more intensely than when you are alive. The senses become more acute. You feel the physical pain more intensely, and you smell odors more strongly. I smelled the overpowering odor of them because they were pure death. They smelled like dead rats. It was a horrible smell, and I knew I was in an ugly terrible place. And I said to them, "Get away from me, please let me go." But they did not want to let me go. The only thing I could think of...because at that time, I was a Catholic. I went to the Catholic Church, and I figured that was good enough. To be Catholic was, for me, the best. The church that I went to when I grew up as a child, I mean I grew up in a Catholic family. I went to church every week. I went to church on Sundays too. But I did not study the Bible or anything like that. I didn't actually read it. I just listened to the message and read the part that the priest gave us in the message. I didn't study the Bible deeply in any way.

So I was a Catholic who went to church and appeared to be a Christian. I mean, I wasn't really a Christian. It was just an obligation that I was supposed to go to church on Sundays. But that's all there was to it. No more than that. Now my house was full of statues. I had the Virgin Mary, I had St. Theresa, I had St. Martin of the Poor, St. Gregory, and my mom—well, she died when I was very young. She had an illness, and she was always praying to the saints, hoping that they would cure her of her disease which she had in her leg. She had a lot of statues of St. Gregory who was supposedly a doctor or something like that. We idolized the saints. We idolized them a lot. And the most important of all was the Virgin Mary. I grew up adoring, almost to the point of worshipping, the Virgin Mary. I believed that the Virgin Mary was someone very special.

What happened in hell was that when I was there in the tunnel, was that these evil presences told me, "You didn't satisfy the commandments of your God, and that is why you are here."

And I said, "But what are the commandments? I don't know which of the commandments I didn't fulfill? Why do I deserve hell if I haven't killed, I haven't stolen, I haven't been engaged in fornication or anything, you know."

I thought everything was fine in my life. But I had done other things that were not in alignment with the commandments. So then what happened? Right then when they were torturing me and skinning me, the only thing I could think of was the Lord's prayer. You know, the Lord's prayer in the book of Mark in the Bible. So I said to myself, I am going to pray. That's what I need to do. So I began praying the Lord's prayer, "Our Father in heaven, hallowed be Your name..." And each time that I said that, the demons tortured me more and more, and they scratched at me more, and I screamed from the pain, but I said no! I insisted "I am not going to stay here, I know that there is a God that is going to forgive me. I know that there is a God that is going to have mercy on me. He is going to forgive me, and He is going to take me out of this hell. I cannot stay here for all of eternity. I can't stay here forever." And I continued and continued and persisted until I finished the Lord's prayer, and when I finished the Lord's prayer, I remembered that the only name that's above all Earth and even the universe is the name of Jesus. So I said to them, "I know there's a name that's above all the earth and in the universe that is more powerful than you. And I am going to pray to that name that He takes me from here, that He pulls me out of this hell."

And they said to me, "No, no, no, you're going to stay here, you have no hope, you're going to stay here for all eternity."

But I said, "No, I know that if I call on Him, He would hear me, and He would save me." So I began and I said, "Jesus, please save me, please save me." Nothing happened right away. The first time nothing happened.

The second time, they said, "No, no, you are not going to leave here, you will remain here for all time."

But I said, "I am leaving here." And the second time I called out, "Jesus, please help me, I beg You to forgive all my sins, all the bad things that I have done in my life. Forgive me. I repent of all the bad things that I have done. If I treated someone badly, if I forgotten one of Your commandments, if I have not done something from Your commandments, please forgive me and show me what path I should take, what I need to do to make my life holy and to be able to be in Your presence. I don't want to stay here." And then I said again, "Jesus, please save me!" But again, the second time nothing happened.

The whole time I was crying out to God for mercy, they were pulling me back and back, toward the back of the tunnel. They were going to throw me into the fire. The eternal fire. I felt that I was going to burn. I was already beginning to feel the burning from the fire. I felt the flames all over my body, almost. And the only thing that I was able to say was, "Jesus, I promise to follow You for all my life, all my life I will follow Your Word. I will follow You, and I promise to be faithful to You, but please give me one more chance. One more chance to live and to be able to change my life. God, please save me, save me, save me from this place."

And at that moment—*shoo*! The demons just left me, they left me free. And said, "Wow, what is this?" Something had happened, and I wasn't in the tunnel anymore. The tunnel just sort of opened, and there was a spectacular pathway. It was like if you went into a garden, and it was full of flowers, glorious flowers, precious flowers. I mean, never in my life have I seen flowers like that. It seemed as if they were dancing, dancing and, at the same time, singing. They were singing, "Hosanna, hosanna in the highest, blessed be the Savior, blessed be the Lord Jesus Christ. To Him belong all the honor and glory to our Lord Jesus Christ," and I was like, "Wow, this is incredible!" I mean, I felt the love of God towards me and as if God was embracing me and saying, "I love you."

And I felt the presence so large that I drew back, and I began to cry. I cried and I cried because I felt that I did not deserve to be there. I felt that actually did indeed deserve hell. You might say "Why did I deserve hell?" Because I was not clean, my heart was not clean, my feelings were not right. I had done many things that God was going to reveal to me, they were the bad things that I had done. At that moment, I continue walking because the path was spectacular. It was as if I went to a waterfall, and I saw at the source of the waterfall, a very handsome crystalline figure, like the water that fell, and I felt that it was cleaning me. It was cleaning me and washing me of all the dirt from my past life. I felt that all that water was washing me, cleaning my life, my heart, my soul. Then I felt peace, at last I felt an incredible peace. A peace that I had never, never in my life felt. I had never felt a peace like that. Never again would I feel a peace like the one I felt when I was in the presence of God. I felt the love of God towards me, and He said to me, "My daughter..."

At that moment Jesus appeared to me and said, "Stop! Stop for a moment, just wait." So I stopped, and He said to me, "You know where you were going?"

And I replied to Him, "Yes, to hell."

And He said, "Yes, you were going to be condemned to hell."

And I said to Him, "But why?" If I was supposedly a good person. I mean, I went to church, and I took communion, and I confessed and all that.

And He said to me, "Wait, I will show you your life." So you know what happens next. He shows me my life in a movie. Like in a movie that you watch in the theater, and He starts to explain to me, "Do you see this part here, when you were ten years old, you were bad because you lied to your parents and told them that you were going to do one thing, but you did something else. That seemingly little lie is a big lie here, it's a great sin!" I never imagined that telling lies, that thinking bad about someone else, a friend or something, was a big sin in heaven. It's a big sin in heaven, and He said to me, "The worst part is that you idolized my mother, the Virgin Mary."

And I was like, "Yes, well, but is that bad?"

And He said, "Yeah, this is very bad because you should not idolize anyone, no saint, not even My mother because the only one Who deserves the honor and the worship that you want to give is to Me. And the glory is to God, the Father, the Son, and the Holy Spirit. Because we are three in one person." And He said to me, "You only should give honor to God. Not to the virgin, not to the other saints, and not to the other images."

And I said, "Oh, right, Father, you are so right."

And He said, "'Another sin for which you were condemned was the worst sin, for which you were condemned to hell was to not forgive."

And I said, "Who did I not forgive?" I didn't know who I didn't forgive.

And He said, "You know who you didn't forgive."

And I said, "My step mother!"

And He said, "Yes, your stepmother."

And I said to Him, "But it's that she killed my mom! I know she killed my mother!" And I said to Him, "She practiced witchcraft, she put pins in the dolls, that's voodoo!"

And He said to me, "Yes, she is a witch."

And I said, "She killed my mom because I found a doll with the pins in it when my mom died, and then later my dad married her." And I knew that my stepmother had hatched this plan in order to be able to be with my dad. So I had this resentment towards her in my soul. I had resentment towards my stepmother, and I felt that this was the resentment that I had. And I just couldn't forget that about her because she had killed my mother. And for me, that was the worst thing possible. I mean, why would she kill my mother in order to be with my dad. I mean, it wasn't fair because I was an only child at that time, I didn't have any brothers or sisters. The only person in whom I could confide was my mom. My friend and my mom. And then she took my mother away from me. So I was left without a mother, only my dad. And I didn't have any brothers and sisters, so I felt very alone. All through my adolescence, it was a very sad time because I didn't have anyone in whom I could confide my secrets with, whom I could share the things that were important to me because I didn't have a mom. I mean, my mom died when I was fifteen years old. So shortly after I graduated with my high school degree, my mom died, unfortunately, and it happened because of the witchcraft that my stepmother perpetrated against her.

So what happened? At the moment that I died, I felt that resentment eating me up. It's like as if you have something that you just can't get rid of. You can't get it out of your heart. It's a bitterness. A bitterness that hurts you, that saddens your life. And He said to me, "That was your greatest sin, and for that sin, you were condemned to hell."

And I said to myself, "Wow, oh, You are completely right, I deserve hell!" Unfortunately we think that not forgiving is just a small sin, but actually it's an immense sin. And it says in the Bible, brothers and sisters, it says that if you don't forgive your brother, you will not be forgiven, but God will forgive you if you forgive your brothers. It doesn't matter if they had killed your mother, or if they have done something to you or your family. It doesn't matter. You have to love them, and it says that you should love your worst enemy.

That is what is says, and that is what God told me, "You have to love her, you have to love her and forgive her because if you do not forgive her right now, I am going to send you back to hell."

And I was like, "No, no, no, Lord, I promise that I will forgive her, I do not want to go back to hell."

And then He says to me, "Okay, you really need to forgive her from your heart, and in that way you can stay here or you can go back to earth, I am going to let you choose. Either way you can stay here, or you can return.'"

And I thought, "I don't know what I want to do? I mean I want to stay here, I would like to stay here, I mean being in heaven is really satisfying. You feel a love that you have never seen ever in your life. It's a love, is a peace, is a divine tranquility. You are without any preoccupations, with nothing that makes life bitter. It's to feel completely happy. To feel the joy of God. And I said to God, 'I would like to stay here, but send me back to earth so that I can show my dad.' He showed me a vision of my dad. I mean, it's like He gave me an image of my dad and showed me that my dad was suffering. He was crying about me because I had died. And he was suffering so much because of me, so I said to God, 'I want to go back because I want to take care of my dad. I am the only daughter, and I think I need to go back. I have a purpose to fulfill, to go back and take care of my dad.'"

And the Lord said to me, "That is a good reason to go back. But tell me what other reason why I should send you back."

And I said, "Because I want to have a family."

And He says to me, "Yes, that's a good reason, a family."

And I said, "Yes, I want to have some children."

And He says to me, "Okay, that's good, that's a second very good reason. You are going to have a family and a husband, but it won't be until several years after you return earth. You are going to have the opportunity to have a family."

And I did not know why. I said, "Why am I going to have to wait so long to have a family?"

And He said, "Because you have to learn first to read My Word, to learn My Word, to study My Word, and to walk according to My Word, and you have to be born-again."

And I said to Him, "Lord, how can I be born again? I do not know how to do that? I mean Catholics don't know anything about how to be born-again. I mean, I was born, I was baptized, what else do I need?"

And He said, "No, you need to be born-again and baptized again, but this is in order to live a Christian life. To live a life in Christ, with Me, so that I will be by your side."

So I said, "Oh, now I understand. But I don't understand very well, how am I going to do that alone on earth? Who's going to help me?"

And He said to me, "Don't worry, My daughter, I am going to help you, and I am going to guide you. I am going to be with you, right by your side. I am not going to abandon you. I am always going to be by your side."

And I said to Him, "Okay, Lord, that's good, but why do I need to wait to have a husband?"

And He said to me, "Until you turn your life around, and make a 180-degree change, I am not going to give you a husband. You need to completely change the way you live, the way you do things, the way you go about life." Because you see, in my Catholic life, I had gone to the disco, I had gone dancing, I drank, I wasn't an alcoholic, but I had my beer, my wine, you know, the things that don't matter if you are Catholic.

You can go to parties, it's not bad; you can have a boyfriend, it's not bad, right? But if you are a Christian, it's different. If you are a Christian, you have to be very upright in the way you live. You need to be pure like God. Because God does not call us to be perfect, but He does call us to be saints. But I didn't understand that, I didn't understand what that was, I really did not know what that meant.

And I said to Him, "No one has really taught me how to walk in the Word. Nobody has explained to me what that means."

And He said to me, "Don't worry, I am going to direct you to a church where you can learn My Word," and I was like, okay. And He said to me, "If you were to enter heaven here, right now, you'd be arriving by the skin of your teeth."

And I said to Him, "Why?"

And He said, "'You'd only be entering by the skin of your teeth because you haven't won a single soul to Me."

And I said, "'Wait, what do You mean win a single soul for You?"

And He said, "When you win souls, you earn crowns, and the crowns that you earn here in heaven are when you share the Gospel or evangelize and share My Word with someone who has never known Me, never heard of Me, and has no idea what the name of Jesus Christ is. So when you talk to that person about me, and tell them what happened to Me, that I sacrificed Myself for all of you, that I paid the price of sin on the cross, and when you show that person what it is to change their life, that they should give their life over to Me, is when you have won for Me. That is when you have earned a crown in heaven."

I was like, "Wow, that is quite a job!"

And He said, "Yes, it is a big job. This is your new ministry, you have to learn to begin to disciple people, and when you begin to do that on earth, to disciple, is when you begin to earn crowns. And you begin to build your house, your mansion in which you will live in heaven. You begin to build it, while still on earth, when you win souls for Me."

I was like, "'Oh, I never knew that!" I had never been in the presence of God before that moment. If I had not died, I would not have known that this even existed. I would not have known that I had to work to earn crowns in heaven, and that is what I want to tell you, brothers and sisters, that I have many sins, for which I am condemned, but the worst of the sins for which I was being condemned was the idolatry and the unforgiveness. Unforgiveness was the worst sin that He showed me, but also in addition to that, there were the sins of not serving.

And He said, "You were not serving people, you were not humble, and you have to be humble before the Lord, and humble before your brothers and sisters." And He said, "You have to be humble and serve people and begin to love people. Like poor people, actually it doesn't matter if they are poor or rich, but you have to begin to give of yourself to them in order to serve them. That is, you need to give of yourself to serve people. Those are orphans, whether they're widows or widowers, you need to visit the elderly, those who are in their later years, give them love, give them things that they don't have because they don't have a family. And you have to begin to show love to people on earth because the only opportunity that you have to earn crowns is to do what I am telling you. And that is what I want you to do. I want you to begin to show love to people. Things that you have never done in your life as a practitioner of Catholicism."

And I said to Him, "Yeah, you are right, I have never done anything like that as a Catholic. I never had any thoughts of serving people, like in the Christian church, and as a Catholic, I was not particularly concerned with that because as a Catholic, I was just concerned with dressing nicely or being in the best high school or college or being fashionable or watching movies. And all of that, I thought, it was just fine, I mean it was good. But that was all wrong. The sin that I harbored in my life was living a mundane life. It was a great sin."

Later He told me, "Okay, I am going to send you back to earth, but before I send you back to earth, you have to know that you have a purpose, and that purpose is what I am going to explain to you now. Your purpose is to give your testimony to everybody that you come in contact with on earth and tell them that there is a hell, and there is a heaven and that hell is real and that heaven is real and that if you commit even one sin, you are going to go to hell. That is that if your brother doesn't follow the Ten Commandments, he will be condemned to the fires of hell, and it's very sad that there are so many people that will be condemned to hell because there are thousands and thousands of souls in hell.'" I mean, it's a horrible place to go for committing even one single sin. And, brothers and sisters, I need to tell you this is not a place that human beings deserve to go. I mean to say, it's not a place people want to go after they die. And the place we want to go is heaven, not hell. And I beg you right now, brothers and sisters, that if you know that you are committing a sin that you repent today of that sin. Of whatever feeling that you have as a human and that you give your life to Jesus Christ, and that you begin to live your life as Jesus Christ, that you sanctify yourself, that you sanctify your life and give the best of yourself to people. To try to live an upright life, not a life of sin because a life of sin is going to lead you to hell.

And then after that, God told me, "I am going to send you back to earth, but when you return, you are not going to remember much. You are not going to remember certain parts because I am going to erase some things that happened from your mind. Because if you remember the images of those monsters, those demons, you wouldn't be able to live your life and be sane. You'd have nightmares every night. So I am going to erase that part from your memory so that you can survive. But I am going to leave certain parts so one day, you will remember all that happened. In one single dream, in one moment of your life, when you have given your heart to Me, when you have truly been baptized, when you have made the decision to follow Me 100 percent, that day, I will give you a dream so that you can know or remember what happened. So you can give your testimony to all the people."

I returned to earth, and you'll never guess where I was. I was in the morgue. I mean really, in the morgue. I was completely covered with the sheet, and the morgue attendant was taking notes about my condition because I was dead. And then I woke up! The technician, she came when I removed the sheet, and the nurse let out a little yell, like, "Why...what happened?"

And I said to her, "I don't know, I don't know what happened. I am alive!"

And she said to me, "But you were dead, and you've been dead for an hour."

I was dead for a whole hour, and I said, "Well, I know that I was in the presence of God, that it was Him who returned me here, and I know that it was Jesus who gave me the opportunity to return to live here on earth for a purpose."

But I didn't remember anything, brothers and sisters, anything else that had happened, right at that moment. The only thing that I could remember was that I had been in the presence of Jesus, and that is a presence that you never forget. It is superbeautiful, the presence of Jesus, that I felt during the time that I went to heaven. Heaven cannot even compare to earth. There isn't a place more beautiful than to be in heaven, in the presence of God the Father, and above all, to see Jesus. I am telling you, Jesus, you can't even see His face because it's pure light. It was pure light that came right out of His eyes. I saw His eyes, His robe, His white robe that was beautiful and the sash that He has, and it was purple color, and His sandals that were of gold, and His precious feet that had the marks of the crucifixion, both in His hands and in His feet. It's incredible, but one simply melts in the presence of our Lord Jesus Christ. It's something absolutely, incredibly beautiful. And never again could I continue living again the way I had been living before being in the presence of Jesus.

That is, to be a Christian is a promise, is a promise with yourself as a person in order to better your life, to follow the Ten Commandments, to make it better in every way. That is to give the best of yourself to others and to God as well. To give the best of yourself to God because God is in you. Jesus is in you, and through Jesus, we can do all things. And at that moment, it took three months to recuperate, my head was like three times the size of a basketball. The doctors said that they had no idea how it's possible that you are talking, that you have coordination of movement because anyone else that had gone through what you've been through would be in a vegetative stage. They would not be able to talk, they would not be able to walk, they would not be able to do anything.[38]

---

[38] https://youtu.be/2URLk_hwU.

# CHAPTER 23

— ❧ —

# Come to Salvation

I personally met a young woman who had an overdose of drugs and died and also went to heaven, and God gave her a second chance. I also met a young man who also had an overdose from drugs, and he said the demons came and dragged him into hell, but also God gave him a second chance. There are hundreds of testimonies of people from all walks of life that have died and gone to hell, or that the Lord took them to hell in the spirit. Mary Baxter wrote a book called *A Divine Revelation of Hell*, and she also wrote a book called *A Divine Revelation of Heaven*. I highly recommend everyone to read both of them.

I have seen testimony after testimony, of Satanists, atheists, Muslims, Christians, etc. who all went to hell, and all saw the same things. *Hell is real, please do not go there!*

Repent and accept the Lord as your Lord and Savior before it's too late. Before the seed of the serpent kill millions of people with the viruses that they are planning to unleash upon the world or the 5G technology or the wars or the chemtrails, etc. If you would like to accept Jesus as your Lord and Savior, please say this prayer out loud.

Lord Jesus, please forgive me for all of my sins. I recognize that I am a sinner and that my sin separates me from You. I believe that You died for my sins to give me eternal life, please forgive me for all of my sins. I renounce the world, my flesh, and Satan, and I ask You to please redeem me this day and write my name in the book of eternal life. Help me to love the truth and renounce all lies. Help me to walk by faith and not by sight. Help me to walk in obedience to Your guidance and to not go astray anymore. Please help me to resist the devil, the mark of the beast, the vaccines, the RFID chips, the NWO, and everything that is against Your holy ways. Give me wisdom to follow You all the days of my life and help me to not love my life even unto death. Jesus Christ, I accept You as my Lord and Savior, may Your Holy Spirit come inside my heart and change me into your heart's desire. Thank You for Your sacrifice and the gift of salvation, in the name of Jesus, I pray, amen.

I just want everyone to be encouraged and to fight this fight with the armor of God. Put on the whole armor of God daily so that you can withstand in the evil day (Ephesians 6:10–12). Do not be discourage and know that in the same way that the devil has his people, his army, his seed, so does our Lord Jesus Christ has His people, His army, His seed, and we too have supernatural powers given unto us by our Lord for this end-times. We too have been going through brutal training, and we are here and all over the world, ready to fight for the lost souls and ready to undo the works of the devil. Please do not let Satan rob your salvation, do not give up your heritage for a plate of lentils. Do not let his seed convince you of their lies and turn you against God. They are jealous they cannot be in heaven, and they wish the rest of the people to be cast out of heaven, just as they are. Do not let them do this to you. Greater is God who is in us and who fights for us than the one in the world. He already gave us the victory through the crucifixion of Jesus Christ, **but the Kingdom of Heaven suffers violence and only the violent take it by force" (MATTHEW 11:12).**

# ABOUT THE AUTHOR

Desiree Alcantara is a researcher who has been in a quest to find the truth since her teenage years. She was diagnosed with chronic schizophrenia in 1996 and declared incurable by science, but in 1998, she was liberated from a legion of demons in a Christian church. She was completely healed and became totally devoted in finding the truth about everything we have been taught in schools and by the mainstream media and churches. She discovered that we have been deceived and has made it her life mission to expose that deception. She graduated from Miami Dade College in 2010 with a degree in psychology, and she also graduated from the Institute of Leadership King Jesus Ministries as a minister. She published her first book in 2020, titled *We Were Deceived*.

She is married and has one child and is a devoted homemaker. Her main goal is to show the world that Yahushua Hamashiach/Jesus Christ is Lord and the Truth, the Way, and the Life. She wants to tell the world that nothing is impossible for God, and He should be our only hope, not the pharmaceutical industry or the government or the apostate church.

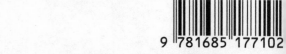